'This second edition is very welcome and timel
more inspiring!'
Dr Emese Hall, *Senior Lecturer in Art Educatio*

'This is the definitive guidebook for those who v
their own knowledge of how to use digital tools
to create digital art works either individually or collaboratively.'
Andrew Csizmadia, *Senior Lecturer in Computing Education,*
Newman University, UK

'This book is full of highly effective practical tasks that support teachers' own
ideas in primary art and contains case studies providing useful examples to
augment the text.'
Richard Hickman, *Emeritus Professor of Aesthetic Development,*
University of Cambridge, UK

Art in the Primary School

Art in the Primary School is an introductory textbook, and a second edition to *Teaching Primary Art*, exploring the underpinning philosophy and pedagogy of teaching and learning art, including how and why digital tools and technologies can be integrated.

This book considers practical aspects of teaching art, focusing on key processes of art making that children might experience in primary schools. It is based around the idea that digital tools and technologies can and should be integrated into the learning and teaching of art, exploring:

- What art is like in the primary school, why it should be taught and what is included in the curriculum
- How learning is planned, assessed, taught and supported in the classroom
- Learning about and from artists and how digital technology can be part of the art curriculum
- Key processes such as drawing, painting, printmaking, collage and textiles, working in three dimensions and making digital art

Uniquely incorporating the use of digital devices, tools and technologies into the subject of art, this book will be essential reading for those training to teach and support learning in art in the primary school.

Jean Edwards is a Senior Lecturer in the Faculty of Health, Education and Science at the University of Northampton, UK. Before teaching in higher education, she taught in primary schools for nineteen years and was a class teacher, art coordinator and head teacher.

Helen Caldwell is an Associate Professor in Education at the University of Northampton, specialising in educational technology and online learning. She is an Apple Distinguished Educator.

Rebecca Heaton is an Assistant Professor in Visual and Performing Arts at the National Institute of Education (NIE), Singapore. She is a distinguished and internationally recognised art educator, who works with children and adults.

Art in the Primary School

Creating Art in the Real and Digital World

SECOND EDITION

Jean Edwards, Helen Caldwell and Rebecca Heaton

Routledge
Taylor & Francis Group

LONDON AND NEW YORK

Second edition published 2021
by Routledge
2 Park Square, Milton Park, Abingdon, Oxon OX14 4RN

and by Routledge
52 Vanderbilt Avenue, New York, NY 10017

Routledge is an imprint of the Taylor & Francis Group, an informa business

First edition published by Pearson Education Limited, 2013

British Library Cataloguing-in-Publication Data
A catalogue record for this book is available from the British Library

Library of Congress Cataloging-in-Publication Data
Names: Edwards, Jean, author. | Caldwell, Helen (Lecturer in Education), author. |
Heaton, Rebecca, author.
Title: Art in the primary school: creating art in the real and digital
world / Jean Edwards, Helen Caldwell, Rebecca Heaton.
Other titles: Teaching primary art
Description: New York, NY: Routledge, 2021. |
First edition published under the title: Teaching primary art. 2013. |
Includes bibliographical references and index.
Identifiers: LCCN 2020046302 (print) | LCCN 2020046303 (ebook) |
ISBN 9780367273361 (paperback) | ISBN 9780367273330 (hardback) |
ISBN 9780429296208 (ebook)
Subjects: LCSH: Art–Study and teaching (Elementary)–Great Britain–Textbooks.
Classification: LCC LB1591.5.G7 E39 2021 (print) |
LCC LB1591.5.G7 (ebook) | DDC 372.5/20941–dc23
LC record available at https://lccn.loc.gov/2020046302
LC ebook record available at https://lccn.loc.gov/2020046303

ISBN: 978-0-367-27333-0 (hbk)
ISBN: 978-0-367-27336-1 (pbk)
ISBN: 978-0-429-29620-8 (ebk)

Typeset in Univers
by Newgen Publishing UK

Access the eResources: http://www.routledge.com/9780367273361

Contents

Preface

We have written this book to support those engaged in learning to teach art or support learning art in primary schools. It is a basic practical handbook to support students on undergraduate and postgraduate teacher training courses. It will be useful for teaching assistants (TAs) who support individuals and groups within art lessons and Higher Level Teaching Assistants (HLTAs) who cover art lessons for teachers' preparation, planning and assessment (PPA) time. Newly qualified teachers just starting out on teaching art to their class and those returning to teaching will also find it helpful.

Over the last few years we have worked together on art and digital technology projects in the UK and in other parts of the world, increasingly valuing the creative potential of incorporating digital technology as part of, or sometimes the main, process. In our work with students, colleagues and children we have used devices, apps and tools to make art; capture the process of making art; collaborate with others near and far; and explore the connection between physical materials and digital devices and tools. This has opened up new ways of working with each other and with children.

We believe that it is vital that everyone who is involved in learning and teaching in art is focused on inspiring children and giving them opportunities to look at and experience a variety of art as well as make their own art that is individual and personal to them. In our own experience as class teachers, subject leaders and university lecturers we have found that children and adults can gain enormous pleasure, excitement and insight from being immersed in physical and digital art. As a teacher you can ensure that your own confident and enthusiastic approach motivates children and allows them to have a positive experience of art that will stay with them into adulthood.

The book is organised into two sections. The first section explores areas that underpin the teaching and learning of art, including why we teach art; the art curriculum; planning and assessment; the work of artists; and teaching and strategies to support learning. We also explore the various ways digital technology can be incorporated as a tool and process along with some consideration of key art movements. The second section explores the practical aspects of art: drawing, painting, making prints, making collage and working with textiles, working in three dimensions and making in the digital and virtual world. Throughout chapters 7 to 11 we consider how digital technology can be used with other art media and in chapter 12 we focus on making art that exists wholly digitally. In these chapters the following areas will be considered: tools and materials; subject knowledge; artists and makers; teaching and learning; connecting to other types of art; and connecting to other subjects.

We hope that in reading and using this book you will be equipped to support and teach art and use digital technology with your pupils with confidence and enthusiasm. You can then go on to devise your own art experiences, activities and events, returning to this book to support your subject knowledge and going beyond it to the many other useful texts that support more experienced and confident teachers.

How to use this book

The features and layout of this book are designed to guide you towards developing your subject knowledge and approach to learning and teaching in the classroom. Some of the features ask you to observe, make or research in order to connect your own learning to experience in school. Others support you by indicating resources and reading that will help you consolidate and develop your approach.

Try for yourself

The practical tasks are designed to support your own investigation and reflection. For students these tasks can be undertaken on placement in school. For those working in schools the tasks can be related directly to finding out more about policy and practice to develop your understanding of art in your workplace. The charts used are provided electronically on the associated website so that they can be printed out and used.

Learning in action

The case studies are stories from practice that provide examples to illustrate the points discussed in the text. Some of them relate to student study and others to classroom experience. These case studies aim to help you build your understanding of subject knowledge and practical art in school. They can guide you to look for more examples when you are on placement or exploring art around your school.

Find out more

The 'find out more' suggestions point you in the direction of further resources to support your own subject knowledge or your teaching in the classroom.

Reflect and extend

The 'reflect and extend' suggestions encourage you to use academic literature to investigate further. These are especially useful for students who may be working on assignments at university. They indicate reports, research and academic journal articles of interest and that underpin subject knowledge and practice in art education.

Next steps and further reading

At the end of each chapter there are some suggested next steps to help you go further with your learning in the chapter, along with some further reading to support your understanding of pedagogical or subject knowledge.

Links to chapter padlets

Throughout the book there are links to material available on the associated chapter padlets. These include the links to resources such as images and websites and examples to support your teaching. It is not necessary to have a Padlet account to view this material. If you do have a Padlet account you can 'remake' the padlets and begin to add your own links and ideas as you personalise and develop what you teach.

01

Chapter One

An introduction to art in the primary school

Introduction

Art makes a unique contribution to our lives and it is vital that when we are preparing to work in schools and educational settings we are ready to give children a wide range of positive and inspiring learning opportunities to engage and enthuse them. These will allow children to explore and connect to contemporary, cultural and personal developments and changes in art and how it is made. This chapter will encourage you to think more deeply about your own experience of art, the role digital technology plays in making and learning about art and the unique contribution art makes to the school curriculum. In this chapter the following areas will be explored:

- The significance of your experience so far

- The contribution art and digital technology make to learning

- Subject knowledge: visual elements

As someone planning to work, or who is already working, in a primary school you must be prepared to teach all the subjects that are part of the curriculum. Whilst it is a challenge to maintain a genuine personal interest in all curriculum subjects it is important that you have the appropriate subject knowledge to support your planning and teaching. You will probably find that your enthusiasm for teaching and seeing children learn will inspire you to enjoy and value some of the subjects you found less exciting as a child yourself. Often when we begin to explore a subject from the perspective of teaching it to a class of children we perceive it differently and understand more fully its potential for learning.

The significance of your experience so far

Your own experiences of viewing and making art using a range of physical media and processes and digital technology will be informed by the experiences you have had as a pupil and as an adult. It is important for you to reflect on these, considering their implications, so that you can support and teach children effectively. As your role in educational settings develops in relation to teaching across the curriculum and teaching specific subjects, your subject knowledge and pedagogical understanding will support you as a teacher of art. You will develop your understanding of the role of the adult in relation to the art curriculum and the teaching. In particular, the rapid development of digital technology means that for many of us what we experienced in our education is different to what can be offered in schools now. Much of the day-to-day technology at home and at school has huge potential to support creativity and making art with our pupils. Being alert to ways of using this potential in learning and teaching can enrich what we can offer to pupils across the curriculum and especially in art.

Your education

Your own education in art and digital technology will vary depending on when and where you went to school and how far you pursued these subjects in school and beyond. It may be that you experienced each of them as separate entities and that digital technology as we understand it now was not part of your educational experience. It is important that you reflect on these experiences so that you understand how they relate to your current understanding. This is particularly important when we exist in a world in which visual and digital media have rapidly evolved and become fundamental to education and so many areas of ours' and our pupils' lives.

Find out more – reflecting on your own education

You will need: the pro forma below, also available online

What to do:

Consider the questions listed below.

Respond to these questions in words and visually by making some notes, some sketches, taking photographs or finding images.

Activity – Exploring the impact your own education has had on you

Questions	Your thoughts	Your images
Your education		
As a child did you like looking at art and playing with digital games and toys?		
Did you make art or craft, or create with digital technology?		
What was your education in art at primary school like?		
What was your education in digital technology at primary school like?		
What was your education in art at secondary school like?		
What was your education in digital technology at secondary school like?		
Did you go on to gain any qualifications in art at secondary school and beyond?		

Questions	Your thoughts	Your images
Did you go on to gain any qualifications in digital technology at secondary school and beyond?		
Were art and digital technology combined or connected in any way during your education?		

Guidance notes

Your interests at home

You may have enjoyed making in art or digital technology at home regardless of what was happening in lessons at school. This may have been related to your family's attitudes and interests, what was available in your home and your own personal enthusiasm and motivation. Children often engage in activities involving making art and playing with or making with digital technology at home without relating it to what they are learning at school – this is something to consider in relation to the children you teach.

Your primary education

Your experience of art and digital technology in the primary years may have influenced your subsequent interest and enthusiasm for these subjects. It may be that in some areas you feel that your own learning has progressed little beyond this stage. Perhaps the teaching you experienced left you at the early stages with no clear idea of how to develop or the experiences you had have quickly become outdated. This may have led you to put your enthusiasm and commitment into other areas of learning in the curriculum until now, when as part of your work in school you are supporting or leading learning in art lessons. If your own experience at primary school was positive and inspiring you will understand how important it is to ensure that the children you work with also have this experience. If your own experience in primary school was indifferent or negative your aspiration will be to make sure that you do not replicate this for the children whose education is now your responsibility.

Your secondary education

At the secondary stage you might have been given opportunities to use unfamiliar media and utilise specialist equipment and new techniques like photography, animation or screen printing. You will have been taught by subject specialists and may have had the opportunity to work on longer and more personal projects to develop your own art. This might be the point at which you gave up the study of art in school. If this is the case it will be vital that you develop your understanding and knowledge of art and digital technology's contribution to it, with a focus on how to teach and support primary aged children.

Your qualifications

If you went further with your education in art or digital technology you may have worked on a GCSE, an A level, an NVQ or even a degree in a related subject. If this is the case your study experience will be a valuable resource to draw upon in your role as an educator. It may later lead you into becoming an art coordinator, or subject specialist, and allow you to support other staff.

In this activity you begin to consider your own education and its implications for your role as an educator. In addition to this, you may have had experience since leaving education that contributes to your understanding and views. Perhaps you now participate in making in areas that could be considered art, design, digital media or craft. It could be an activity you pursue as a break from studying or work, or that has developed from your life. If you are a parent, playing with your own children and supporting them in their own education may have led you to an interest in art, craft, design or using digital media as a user and creator.

Your current awareness

Although your own experience prior to training or being employed is significant, regardless of it you are likely to be planning and teaching art in the primary school. A minority of schools in the United Kingdom have a specialist teacher for art; in some locations internationally, such as in Singapore, it is more common for there to be specialist art teachers in primary settings. Some schools may have informal arrangements between staff to share out the teaching of some subjects in order to use strengths and interests, but in most schools you must be prepared to teach art to your class and the tools of digital technology will be available as part of this.

As an adult you might not be involved in art or craft at all, but you will probably be using digital media and technology to support your work and, even without realising it, have access to tools that allow you to experiment with creative skills and techniques. Or it may be that you have a personal interest or passion in one or a combination of these. Perhaps you belong to a group or class in your chosen art, craft or media-based activity or have attended a class or workshop as a one-off, either by yourself or alongside your own children. Upcycling, an awareness of environmentalism and sustainability and new media developments are increasingly leading people to engage in art, craft and creative technological pursuits – all things central to a contemporary art education. Any enthusiasm that you have in art or art related areas – design, media, technology – will be something you can draw on to support children's learning in your role in schools.

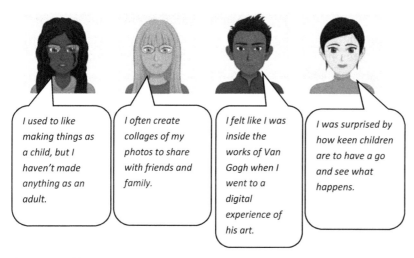

Figure 1.1 Teachers' thoughts about art

Another aspect of our experience of art is looking at the work of artists, craftspeople and designers: some of these will be using technologies as part of their work and creating their outcomes wholly or partly in the digital world. This is also important when learning and teaching in relation to the primary and contemporary art curriculum. Many galleries, museums, makerspaces and other public spaces put on workshops and classes that you can join in order to broaden your knowledge and experience, and these are often free or quite inexpensive.

Find out more – looking at art

Exploring your awareness of art and artists, craftspeople, designers and makers who use digital technology as a viewer

You will need: the pro forma below

What to do: Annotate the headings with artists, craftspeople, designers and technologists or their work that you are familiar with. Add specific names or sketches to remind you if you can.

Activity – Exploring your awareness of art and artists, craftspeople, designers and makers who use digital technology as a viewer

Exhibitions I have chosen to visit	Exhibitions I've come across online	Exhibitions I've been taken to
Art in my home	Art in my workplace	Art in my local environment
Art I or someone I know has made or bought	Art I've seen or heard about	Art I have participated in

Guidance notes

• Exhibitions in galleries on and offline, in public spaces

We are surrounded by examples of art and exhibitions of the work of artists locally, regionally and nationally, on and offline. Many are free to visit, both temporary and permanent, and are sometimes interactive. Even if you don't actively seek these out you may well come across sculptures in the local park or town square or exhibitions online or in your local gallery or museum or on social media. Start making a more conscious effort to look at these when you encounter them.

• In your home or workplace

If you look around your home, garden, class or school you might be able to identify pieces of art, craft, design or technology that you have chosen, been given or used or that hold meaning for you. You might have a painting, print or digital projection on the wall; a woven basket or clay pot on a shelf or table; a particular fabric design on your curtains and cushions. You might be a player of online games, a user of apps or a viewer of animations and films. There may be items and activities that you have not considered to be art but were made or designed by artists, craftspeople, designers, technologists or by your own children.

• TV programmes, blogs, podcasts about art / artists

As well as encountering art in the locality there are many television programmes, blogs, podcasts and radio broadcasts about art or that share art related stories. When a big national exhibition opens there may be news stories, small items on magazine programmes and whole programmes, films or radio interviews with the artist about the exhibition. All of these serve to alert you to exhibitions of significance that could be worth seeking out, to follow your own interest or broaden your knowledge and understanding as well as giving you ideas for teaching and learning. You were probably able to name some artists as you read this because they have a high profile in the media if they have a current exhibition. You might also have been able to list some artists, designers or technologists that you remember learning about at school. If you identified some art that you have in your home you might know who made it and might even seek their work out and collect it. In later chapters, development of this aspect of your subject knowledge will be considered more.

• Participation

Increasingly, we encounter art that we as the audience can take part in. This might be making a small part of the overall completed piece; sharing our participation on social media; being part of an installation or temporary piece of art; or controlling the art itself through the use of mobile devices. This participatory experience can be a powerful one for children, giving them the opportunity to collaborate and be an artist alongside others. You might seek this kind of art out in your locality to share with children or create this kind of art in your school.

In the activity above you were encouraged to consider your awareness of art and artists, designers and technologists around you at the moment. Whilst being able to name or list artists, designers and technologists and their work is no test of your interest or knowledge, your general awareness of the range of artists, designers and technologists has implications for the children that you teach. If your knowledge is fairly narrow this can restrict the choices available to you to use in the classroom and make it more challenging for you to inspire children and introduce them to an interesting and diverse range of experiences.

Reflect and extend

Look up the Google Arts and Culture website.

Link: https://artsandculture.google.com/

Explore this website looking for examples of art that take your interest and expand your knowledge of what people make with traditional and new media.

Explore the section called 'Experiments created by artists and creative coders'.

Link: https://artsandculture.google.com/project/games

Try out some of the activities in this section to see how you can interact with art online.

Art in school: what is it?

From your education and experience so far you might have a view or working definition of what art is. You may also be questioning why digital technology deserves a prominent place within the subject of art. From visiting schools on placement or from working in a school you might have had that view expanded, developed and changed by the children, teachers and art that you encounter. Giving some thought to what art is, what art in school is and what art's relationship with digital technology and society is and identifying when children are learning in and through art will be important for your success and effectiveness as an art teacher. It is possible for children to be engaged in art-like activities that do not truly give them the opportunity to build on their skills, knowledge and understanding in and of art.

If you look the word 'art' up in the dictionary the definition is "the expression of creative skill in a visual form such as painting or sculpture" (Soanes and Hawker, 2008, p.470), whilst 'craft' is defined as "an activity involving skill in making things by hand" (p.227) and 'design' as "a plan or drawing produced to show the appearance and workings of something before it is made" (p.268). More recently, in Hickman's (2018) *An art miscellany for the weary & perplex'd*, a guide for the novice art teacher to define artistic terms, art is referred to as a concept that does not reside in art objects, but in the minds of people – meaning that new concepts, connections and developments in life are shaping how art is viewed, practised and taught. This definition has a robust quality that is able to withstand changes in time, space and technology – an entity central to this book. There are many discussions concerning art's definition and this will change and grow as contemporary artists continue to create art, share it with audiences and experiment with new technologies.

Why do we teach art in schools?

Art has been part of the curriculum in primary schools in the UK for many years. It is only since the late 1980s, with the introduction of a statutory national curriculum, that the content in terms of knowledge, skills and understanding has been specified. In England the most recent document has been in place since 2013, and is criticised by some for omitting explicit references to technology, for compressing content and for being too broad and therefore unsupportive to the non-specialist teacher. But in being broad and non-specific it does offer freedom to teachers and schools to implement art learning in a way most appropriate to their setting and pupils' needs and it allows multiple opportunities for technology to be linked to art if the teacher and school choose to do so. As a subject in UK schools, and in a number of countries internationally, art has a history of being marginalised. However, there is hope emerging that schools are going to be more accountable in the UK for offering a curriculum in which art has a definitive position. The Creative Industries Federation (2019), for example, has published a report calling for creative education to be centrally located in the curriculum – art and technology are central to fostering and developing creativity.

Given the contribution art makes to the education of children and subsequently its significance in the lives of adults (Heaton and Hickman, 2020) it will always be part of the curriculum in primary schools. It is important that schools and all the people working in them have a clear understanding of the contribution art makes to the education of the child. Exploring why art is taught in schools and the contribution it makes to learning will underpin your thinking and planning so that you can ensure that children have the experiences they need in your classroom. Incorporating the opportunities digital technologies offer into the repertoire of tools we use as teachers and in making and viewing art with children can only support and enrich the subject and learning.

In your school

Investigate the school's aims, vision or ethos. These may be displayed in the entrance hall and shared in more detail in a school handbook, website or policy document.

Consider how learning in art will provide a context for meeting these aims.

Look at the school's art policy:

What is the school's vision for the specific contribution art makes to a child's education?

Does using digital technology feature in the school's vision?

If you are a student, look in the information about art in your course:

What does it say about why you are learning to teach art?

What does it say about the place of digital technology in education?

Personal development and lifelong learning

The art curriculum and learning experiences in art allow children to explore their own creativity in practical ways as well as learn about how others have followed their own creative impulses and ideas. There are many opportunities to engage with spiritual, moral, social and cultural (SMSC) development in the art curriculum. Personal qualities that are important in all learning can be applied, developed and strengthened in art. In all of these areas there are implications for children's learning not only in their primary years but for their future as adult citizens and lifelong learners.

Creativity

Giving children opportunities to be creative is something that most, if not all, schools aim for as part of their curriculum and their vision for the children they are educating. NACCCE (1999) defined creativity as "imaginative activity fashioned so as to produce outcomes that are both original and of value" (p.31) and stated that "all people are capable of creative achievement in some areas of activity, providing the conditions are right and they have acquired the relevant skills and knowledge" (p.30). Hickman (2010) goes on to say that whilst it is challenging to define the concept of creativity "we are able to identify two observable phenomena, namely creative behaviour and the objects which arise as a result of creative action" (p.117). The art curriculum can provide many opportunities for children to work creatively using practical materials and digital tools and devices separately and in combination. Although, of course, many other subjects and areas of learning can also do this and there are ways of planning and delivering the art curriculum in a way that does not offer or encourage creative thought and activity.

If we look more closely at the NACCCE (1999, pp.32–34) definition and how it was explained in the report we can consider some implications for the art curriculum and planning and teaching art. 'Imaginative' in this context is taken to mean 'providing an alternative to the expected, the conventional or the routine'. 'Purposeful' is defined as 'actively engaged in making or producing something in a deliberate way'. 'Original' is related to what is original for the individual and their peer group rather than being completely original and unique. Finally, 'of value' encourages us to think about considering the value and being evaluative during and after the creative activity, applying judgement and critical thinking. Art educator Paul Carney (2018) explores Csikszentmihalyi's idea of creative and Creative, where our own personal acts or ideas of making might be called creative and those acts or ideas that gain a wider acceptance might be called Creative.

When you are planning, teaching and supporting learning in art it is important that you build in opportunities for children to respond creatively. If you, as the adult, have a distinct and closed outcome in mind towards which you are guiding and directing children it is unlikely that they will be able to be creative, imaginative or original. Although you will have a learning outcome and some learning objectives for children's skills and the use of media and processes these will need to be balanced with some flexibility and opportunity for choice. Planning time to stop, look, talk and think about the art children are making is important – during as well as after the art is made – along with scaffolding critical thinking so that this is supportive and useful. In addition to this, giving children opportunities to share their art with viewers in school and beyond is also a part of valuing their work and repertoire of twenty-first century creative skills.

LEARNING IN ACTION

A group of teaching assistants are exploring collage using paper, scissors and glue and apps on iPads. They make collages of urban scenes using found imagery from magazines and other collected papers. They are encouraged to include text in their collages as well as images. After these are complete they photograph their collage with an iPad. They use a series of apps to manipulate their image. These include Rollworld, an app that allows them to experiment with rolling up their image; Fragment, an app that allows them to shatter and reassemble their image; and BeFunky, an app that allows them to add filters and effects to change colours and styles. This use of a series of apps is known as 'Appsmashing'. This generates many saved images from which the students have to evaluate and make choices. After their experiments they choose one saved image from each experiment and put together a four-image PicCollage showing their original paper image and examples of how it was changed. These are displayed in a slide sequence on their blog and on screens around the university.

In the case study above students have been given the opportunity to work in both physical and digital ways. Being able to make changes to their original art without destroying it and having the freedom to change it using a variety of tools provokes new ideas for them. A next step would be to move from the digital images back into collage or into another area such as printmaking or painting. They have been allowed to experiment, evaluate their learning and be taught by their lecturer and each other. When working in this way with children they can be encouraged to think and talk about their work, whilst support is available for those not ready to be completely independent. Older children with more experience of the range of media and processes can be expected to make more choices and demonstrate greater independence in their making of art, if they have been taught in a way that supports this.

Using technological tools and processes to support learning in art and making art is now very important to include in art curriculum provision. Technological practices can engage learners in art who feel less confident in their own making skills or who have an interest in this area. Using software onscreen to create art; taking and manipulating digital photos and scanning; making videos and animations; and researching, disseminating and connecting online are all areas that are common in art practice and can be used by primary aged children. It is important to note that contemporary artists use technology as part of their work to help them research, develop ideas, make new and innovative work and market themselves and their work. They are often at the cutting edge of what can be done with new media visually.

As well as ensuring that we plan opportunities for children to be creative we should not underestimate the contribution of art to providing a creative and stimulating environment for children to enjoy and be inspired by. Thinking about the potential for both the inside and outdoor environment to be lively, interesting and diverse and changing places for children to work in is often a strong feature of primary schools. Displays and work sharing, on and offline, synchronously and asynchronously, that promote interaction and response and that value children's work in all areas of the curriculum, and studies of artists' work, all contribute to this. Increasingly, primary schools are including their outdoor space as part of the learning environment with much potential for inspiring art, creativity and the use of technology outdoors. Art experiences can relate to natural and manmade environments, working collaboratively and the production of large-scale works.

Reflect and extend

Find and watch Bob and Roberta Smith's 'message'.

Link: https://vimeo.com/channels/artdesigned/126939749

Think about how your understanding of why art is important relates to what you see here.

Spiritual, moral, social and cultural development

All schools must provide for the spiritual, moral, social and cultural (SMSC) development of their pupils. These aspects of the curriculum are not tied to specific subjects although there are opportunities for children to develop each of them in subject lessons as well as other school experiences. It is important not to overlook these facets of children's learning and use the opportunities that the art curriculum gives you to plan for children to encounter them, talk about them and learn about them. Although they overlap and there are relationships between them it is important not to run them together and treat them as one. Eaude (2008) suggests that spiritual development relates to "meaning"; moral development relates to "action"; social development relates to "interaction"; and cultural development relates to "belonging" (p.9).

Spiritual development, the search for meaning, also encompasses areas such as faith, belief, mystery and the unknown, inspiration, ambiguity and a phrase you might have heard used in school: 'awe and wonder'. It can mistakenly be equated with Religious Education (RE) and sometimes with assembly. This is a narrow interpretation and can lead to missed opportunities for exploration and learning in other subjects and areas of learning. When we consider the possibilities for exploring spiritual development there are many, both when making and viewing art. When children look at work made by artists they will try to infer and speculate to find their own meaning in it and learn about what others have taken from it. They will learn about what has motivated artists to make their art and the inspiration and drive that have led them to devoting their lives and energies to making art. When children are making their own art you might plan starting points that allow children to investigate meaning or take them to places that inspire them and have an atmosphere they can respond to.

LEARNING IN ACTION

As part of a study of places of worship in RE some Year 2 children are taken on visits to a local Hindu temple and a local church. Whilst they are in each location they are encouraged to look for examples of art in each building and they have some time to draw from observation in order to record and respond to what they see.

After visiting each building they discuss what they have noticed, identifying colour as something significant in each place. The Hindu temple is bright and colourful and the church has several striking stained glass windows, including one designed by John Piper that is almost abstract in composition. Some children who are familiar with other places of worship contribute what they have noticed about colour in hangings, clothes and tiles. They begin to consider that a visual element that they have explored in art, colour, can connect to spirituality and faith in its presence and use in places of worship.

Moral development, the values that guide our actions, is an area that we discuss with children in relation to their own behaviour and the behaviour of others in day-to-day school life. When thinking about this area we can also help children to make connections beyond their day-to-day experience to the wider world and the bigger issues of morality. We can introduce children to the work of artists who are or have been concerned with moral issues, those who have drawn attention to injustice in their art or made protests about moral issues of the times. Social media allows artists who work in this way to share their work much more immediately and widely than ever before. In school, moral development and behaviour is sometimes underpinned by a reward system (extrinsic motivation) although our ultimate aim is that children will internalise values that guide their actions (intrinsic motivation). Children can consider why artists made their art and explore the drive, inspiration and determination that can come from oneself compared to that imposed on us. Some children may well experience for themselves that internal drive to work on their art, whether at home or at school.

Find out more

Search online for a piece of art called *La Bouche du Roi*, created by West African artist Romuald Hazoumè to mark two hundred years since the abolition of slavery. This installation uses discarded objects found in contemporary Benin, such as petrol cans, arranged in the layout depicted by the eighteenth-century print of the slave ship *Brookes*, used by Abolitionists in their campaign.

Images, information and videoclips of it can be found on the British Museum website, the Art Fund website and on YouTube. The print of the slave ship *Brookes* can also be found online.

Think about the possibilities for exploring larger moral issues from the past (slavery) and current in today's society (the environment) through this work of art.

Social development, the interaction with others, is an aspect of school life that underpins many of the experiences that we plan for children. Learning to relate to others; working in pairs and groups; sharing and commenting on each other's work are part of many lessons. With the development of technology, collaboration and connectivity beyond the classroom has been made easier. In art lessons the atmosphere is often such that children and adults can talk more freely about themselves and what they are doing as they work practically. Some art projects will give children the opportunity to work in small or large groups to create a finished piece of art, giving them a sense of being part of something bigger than any one person, as well as cooperating purposefully and supporting each other to achieve a common goal. Showing and talking about their own art to viewers, on online and offline platforms, allows children to develop their social skills and confidence purposefully with a wide range of local, national and international audiences.

LEARNING IN ACTION

As part of a wider international project facilitated through Erasmus Plus and eTwinning Year 5 and 6 children, students and teachers from England, Belgium, Denmark and Norway are working together to create mini-sculptures made from the natural and manmade recycled materials they find around them. They are restricted to making a sculpture that will sit on the palm of their hand and they are shown photos of locations from the other countries where the sculptures might be placed, virtually. After their sculptures are complete they photograph them with iPads and use green screen technology to manipulate their scale and place them in new environments. The photos are shared on a joint padlet and tagged to the real locations on a Google map. There is a sense of acting as an artist making a commission, as well as the excitement of seeing their work in other places, created by the use of both physical and digital technology to support collaboration and sharing.

(A more detailed outline of this project, with supporting resources, is available on the chapter padlet.)

In the case study above children have a significant experience that is planned as part of a larger collaborative project between several countries. It supports talking and comparisons between children and their schools beyond the immediate learning in art. Smaller-scale opportunities for developing social skills and self-esteem through taking part in art activities are frequent in the primary classroom and connections can be made locally and regionally through technology.

Cultural development, belonging to a group, can also be explored in art, especially in terms of introducing children to the diversity of art made by other cultures, both now and in the past. This can be an effective and interesting way into finding out more about the cultures themselves through other subjects such as history and geography. Exploring how cultures have explored ideas and meanings visually can give children access to a range of ideas to draw upon when making their own art. It is important when choosing art from other cultures that we draw upon an interesting and diverse range of art, including that made by artists working now in areas such as digital media and technology. It can be useful to first consider the range of cultures present in the school and local community to ensure that you are drawing upon art, craft and design from these as well as introducing children to unfamiliar cultures from the past and present. Think also about cultural experiences that are meaningful and significant in your locality and in the UK so that children know about their own culture as well as those of other people. This might include cultural events that happen locally every year as well as those that are one-offs, such as the cultural Olympiad that will support the postponed 2020 Tokyo Olympics.

Some artists involve many people in the creation of their art: Martin Creed's *All the Bells* in July 2012 and Antony Gormley's *Field for…* are examples of where an artist's work depends on the involvement of communities and very large groups of people working together. This creating together to achieve and enjoy approach is a vital part of schools' ethos and mission. Participation in this kind of project can be a wonderful experience in itself, as well as a chance to come together as a school or community and be a small part of a larger whole.

Personal qualities

Giving children opportunities to develop personal qualities that will equip them to learn, support their well-being and be happy in future life is another important aspect of what schools aim to achieve through their ethos and curriculum. Making choices; using their initiative; taking risks; and experimenting to solve problems can all be part of art lessons. Looking critically, reflecting and making judgements on their own art and that made by others are also integral to art. Following children's curiosity and allowing them to be excited and thrilled by what they see, experience and make as well as gaining personal satisfaction and a sense of accomplishment is all possible in the art curriculum. In addition to these personal qualities, making art and learning about how artists work helps children develop perseverance and determination and appreciate the need to work hard and be committed in order to improve and achieve.

Many art activities, both physical and digital, hold the possibility of exploring and enjoying the sensory experience of making by using tactile materials or using your hands to control actions. Paint, pastels, clay and many other materials have visual and tactile qualities that engage children's interest, quite apart from any task set for them by adults. Digital technology allows children to manipulate and create with colour and light and become makers in an area in which they are usually viewers and consumers. Using both physical and digital tools and materials together and understanding the qualities and contributions of each will come from play and teaching. Whilst it is important to teach children how to develop their skills, so much can be learned by playing with and exploring the tools and materials freely. If children are not given these opportunities to explore, practise and refine their skills they may begin to feel inhibited and less confident in their approach.

Spiritual, moral, social and cultural development and the opportunity to develop positive personal qualities have each been discussed separately in order to ensure that their relationship to the art curriculum is clear. Often there will be opportunities to explore several of these in art activities and projects in school and also in out-of-school learning related to the school or to art galleries.

LEARNING IN ACTION

A group of Foundation Degree students are exploring some resources published by the Institute of International Visual Arts (InIVA) (2010) called 'Who are you? Where are you going?'. This resource is a set of twenty cards each showing an artwork that encourages reflection, speculation, talk about feelings and life experiences. The art is diverse and thought-provoking and most of it is unfamilar to the students.

The students are asked to discuss in pairs the potential for talking about the ideas and feelings generated by the art, beginning with their own reactions and then considering the children they work with. Themes such as homes, moving, families and relationships are identified, along with ideas for exploring these with children of varying ages. Some of them suggest that using pictures can provoke a wide range of responses, perhaps more so than the most open of questions.

They are then asked to consider how this art could be used to talk about artists' work and inspire children's own art. They are encouraged to suggest ideas related to the themes they discussed earlier rather than ideas based on recreations or copies of the art itself. Looking at these examples of artists' work gives students an appreciation for the diverse nature of art available to share with children.

In the case study above students explore the potential of art for inspiring talk as well as broadening the range of art they have encountered, helping them consider the way they use artists' work with children.

Reflect and extend

Find the article 'Art Technology Integration: Digital Storytelling as a Transformative Pedagogy in Primary Education' by Victoria Pavlou, published in *The International Journal of Art and Design Education* in 2019.

Consider how the use of technology has enabled children to bridge the gap between school and their daily lives, how they have been given a voice and a platform for discussing issues – those such as ambiguity and mystery, not knowing and knowing are an important aspect of learning in art.

How can we make sure that children explore this in the classroom?

How has technology assisted interdisciplinarity and transformative practice in the classroom?

Lifelong learners and new possibilities

Although this book is about teaching art to primary aged children there are many aspects of the art curriculum that have a significance that goes beyond learning in the primary school. In school we are preparing our children to become fulfilled individuals and good citizens of the future, a future that is uncertain and changing in its demands and opportunities. It is widely accepted internationally that children will need to be open to new possibilities, as well as be resilient, flexible and determined to meet the challenges ahead of them in adulthood.

Increasingly the world around us is full of visual imagery and technologies that children must interpret, evaluate and respond to – and this can make engagement and filtering visuals challenging. The children we are teaching today in our primary schools are the citizens who will care for, value and progress our cultural heritage in the future. They are the people who will work in education and the creative industries seeking to enlighten, entertain and enrich our lives. It is a moral right for these learners to have opportunities to engage with new and emerging art and technological practices so that they are well equipped for new possibilities in the future.

Reflect and extend

Read 'Section 2: Conversations and reflections – some mini case studies' in Richard Hickman's book *Why We Make Art and Why it is Taught*, published in 2010.

In this section a range of people discuss their art and why they make it. Look for the impact that school and art experiences in school have had. What are the implications for your own thinking about why we teach art in schools?

Digital technology and art

Digital technology is now embedded in our lives and available to varying degrees in our classrooms. As adults working in schools, devices and tools underpin our work in teaching and supporting learning. They give us ready access to others working in our age groups and subjects as well as practitioners in the subjects we teach, a personal learning network of knowledgeable and supportive people and organisations and an audience. In our own lives we may well be using the tools of digital technology to be creative, to network and to record our ideas and thoughts through blogging and using social media. Schools often have websites and social media accounts through which they share what is happening in their schools and network with others. In the recent pandemic the sharing of resources, ideas and support in the world of education was both widespread and inspiring.

For children in the classroom, using digital tools and devices as part of the art curriculum provides many opportunities to enrich learning and work in new ways. This might be when one of a number of tools is used within a sequence of lessons, such as when they research images online when they begin to work or when they record and share outcomes through photography or video. It might be using a digital tool or device as a key part of their making, such as when they manipulate images in an app or use green screen to place and scale objects into new environments. It might be when they use a digital alternative to painting with watercolour or acrylics by painting with an app or tool on a screen. As a new process to add to our existing repertoire of art processes such as drawing, painting, printmaking, collage, textiles and working in three dimensions, it might be when children create an outcome that exists only in the digital world such as an animated GIF, animation, digital projection or film.

Try for yourself – you and digital technology

Evaluating your use of digital technology

You will need: the pro forma below

What to do: Use the questions below to consider your own access to and use of digital technology as a user and maker in school and beyond.

Activity – Evaluating your use of digital technology

Questions	Your responses
What devices do you have and use frequently? (mobile phone, tablet, laptop, PC, etc.)	
Do you have any other devices? (gaming console, VR headset, etc.)	
What devices do you have in your classroom / school to use in teaching? (IWB, laptop and screen, tablets, programmable robots, etc.)	
What social media accounts do you have and use? (Facebook, Twitter, Instagram, etc.)	
Do you have a blog or website of your own?	
Does your school have a website, blog and social media accounts?	
Which digital tools do you use to support your own work in school?	
Which digital tools do you use which aid children in their learning?	
Do you have a virtual classroom environment that you use? (Google Classroom, Microsoft Teams, Seesaw, etc.)	

Guidance notes

Devices

The devices available to you in school or that you own yourself are the ones you will feel most confident in using. School technology set-ups vary enormously in terms of what is available and how accessible they are to use in the classroom. The most important thing for you is that you know about and can use the devices you have to their full potential, both in your own work and with children, and look for opportunities to expand this where you can. This might be connecting with organisations, community groups, charities and local schools and universities.

Social media

Many schools, people working in education and people working in the arts use social media and blogging positively and effectively. As someone working in a school you will need to know and follow your school's policy relating to this area and be a role model to the children you work with. Using social media to connect with other teachers and people working in art education can be of great benefit as can being able to see and join in with artists' work.

Digital tools

The devices we have give us access to a huge range of digital tools, from those that can be used regularly to those that are a special one-off used mainly in a particular unit of work. One of the most important things we can inspire in our learners is that the devices we have at home and at school can be used to create, not just consume. We can use them to make, collaborate and share with others rather than be passive and isolated viewers of what others make and do.

In the activity above you have begun to consider the potential that digital technology, devices and tools have in learning and this will be explored more fully throughout the rest of this book.

What do children think about art?

Young children tend to feel positive about art. They are often willing to have a go, enjoy the process and become absorbed in it. When children of primary age are allowed a free choice of activity, drawing, making activities or using digital tools are usually popular. Anning (2002) identified that even if children later become hesitant about drawing at school they are still engaged in it at home. Giving some consideration to what children think and feel about making art and art in school helps us understand its importance.

In your school: what do pupils think?

Investigating children's views on art

You will need: the pro forma below, a group of children

What to do: Talk with children using some or all of the questions listed below.

Make notes of their responses. Compare them to the discussion in the article (details below).

Activity – What do children think about art?

Question, prompt for discussion	Children's comments, views
1. What is art?	
2. Who makes art?	
3. Do you make art?	
4. Is technology art?	
5. Why do people make art?	
6. Do you have a favourite artwork, or favourite artist?	
7. Do you like doing art at school?	
8. How often does your class do art?	
9. What are some of the art things you do at school? Do you use technology?	
10. How good do you think you are at art?	
11. Do you look at art or talk about art at school?	
12. Do you like doing art things in your own time (when you're not at school)?	
13. Do you want to keep learning about art or technology when you grow up?	
14. Do you think you'll keep doing art when you're a grown-up?	
15. Do you think you may be an artist when you grow up?	

(adapted from Gibson, 2008, p.192)

Guidance notes

Talking about some or all of these questions with children can give you an interesting insight into children's perceptions of art, artists and themselves and their school. In Gibson's small-scale study, conducted with primary aged children in Australia, she found that children had a wide-ranging view of what art is; they could talk about the meaning and value of art with insight and depth and could talk about art in their lives now and in their future as adults. Taking the pupil's voice into consideration is increasingly important in educational research as well as school self-evaluation. You might consider the influence of the school approach to art on children and their perceptions when you analyse your discussions.

In the activity above the opportunity to consider the views and experience of the pupils you work with was explored. More recently Tan and Gibson (2017) have explored children's views and attitudes towards the visual arts through observation and working with them. Their findings relating to processes and products; imagination and creativity; themselves as artists; art as a social experience; and links with the home give us an interesting insight into the value of art in the classroom and the importance of the child's voice in this.

Conclusion

Your role as an adult who is preparing to work, or is already working, in a school or an educational setting is vital to children's learning. Your beliefs and attitudes, subject knowledge and pedagogical understanding will have an impact on the children you teach, imperceptibly and explicitly, throughout your career. Part of your professional role will be to champion learning in all subjects for all the learners you support and teach. For some, art and its integration with technology will be a favourite subject, in which they excel and aim to ultimately pursue in further study and as a career. For many, if not most of them, art will be a pleasurable and engaging subject from which they can learn in a different way even if they do not go on to have anything more than an interest in the arts in later life. In the next chapter the content of the art curriculum in primary schools will be explored in more depth.

Next steps

Develop your awareness of physical and digital art in your locality and in the media.

Look out for examples of spiritual, moral, social and cultural development in art experiences (your own and those of the children you work with).

Consider how technology is integrated into your visual and multisensory world
    and how you use it creatively and as a consumer.
Start collecting and organising useful links to artists and art using Pocket, Padlet
    or another link storage tool.

References

Anning, A. (2002) Conversations Around Young Children's Drawing: The Impact of the Beliefs of Significant Others at Home and at School. *The International Journal of Art and Design Education.* **Vol 21**, No 3, pp.197–208.

Carney, P. (2018) #Creativity. [online] Available from: www.paulcarneyarts.com/single-post/2018/09/19/Creativity-1 [Accessed 10/07/20].

Creative Industries Federation. (2019) *Creative Industries Manifesto.* [online] Available from: www.creativeindustriesfederation.com/publications/creative-industries-manifesto [Accessed 16/07/2020].

Eaude, T. (2008) *Children's spiritual, moral, social and cultural development: primary and early years.* 2nd ed. Exeter: Learning Matters.

Gibson, R. (2008) Primary-age children's attitudes to art, art making and art education. *The International Journal of Education through Art.* **Vol 4**, No 2, pp.177–193.

Heaton, R. and Hickman, R. (2020, 27 October) Purposes of arts education. In: *Oxford Research Encyclopedia of Education.* Oxford: Oxford University Press.

Hickman, R. (2010) *Why We Make Art and Why it is Taught.* 2nd ed. Bristol: Intellect.

Hickman, R. (2018) *An art miscellany for the weary and perplex'd.* [online] Available from: www.educ.cam.ac.uk/people/staff/hickman/An_Art_Miscellany_2018_Richard_Hickman.pdf [Accessed 16/07/2020].

Institute of International Visual Arts (InIVA). (2010) *Who are you? Where are you going?* London: InIVA.

NACCCE. (1999) *All Our Futures. Creativity, Culture and Education.* Sudbury: DFEE Publications.

Soanes, C. and Hawker, S. (eds). (2008) *Compact Oxford English Dictionary.* 3rd ed. Oxford: Oxford University Press.

Tan, M. and Gibson, R. (2017) 'You Feel like You're an Artist. Like Leonardo Da Vinci': Capturing Young Children's Voices and Attitudes towards Visual Arts. *International Journal of Education Through Art.* **Vol 13**, No 3, pp.295–315.

Further resources

Herne, S., Cox, S. and Watts, R. (2009) *Readings in Primary Art Education*. London: Intellect Books.

Ogier, S. (2017) *Teaching Primary Art*. London: Sage.

Pavlou, V. (2019) Art Technology Integration: Digital Storytelling as a Transformative Pedagogy in Primary Education. *The International Journal of Art and Design Education.* **Vol 39**, No 1, pp.195–210.

Watts, R. (2011) Encounters with the Unexpected: From Holbein to Hirst (and Back Again). *The International Journal of Art and Design Education.* **Vol 30**, No 1, pp.52–61.

Chapter Padlet:

https://padlet.com/Jeanne/Chapter1

02

Chapter Two

The art curriculum in primary schools

Introduction

In most primary schools, in the UK and internationally, what we teach in the curriculum is underpinned by the requirements of the statutory curriculum, largely set by the government or Department for Education. Schools interpret these in the context of the resources available locally; the expertise in the school and the interests of the children. This results in common features across schools but variations as well. If you are a student visiting a range of schools on placements these similarities and differences may be more apparent to you than if you are part of the staff working in the same school over a sustained period. The subject of art, as with any subject, may look and feel different in different schools, as will the subject of computing and the connections between the subjects, as digital tools and technologies become used across the curriculum.

In this chapter the following aspects that underpin and affect the content of the art curriculum in a primary school will be explored:

• The curriculum

• Subject knowledge

• School policy and approach

Some of these are applicable to art in primary schools and others are the means by which schools make their art curriculum unique, such as their policy, their choices of artists, connection between art and other subjects and any schemes of work or teaching resources they use to support teachers in planning and teaching the art curriculum.

Reflect and extend

Visit the United Nations Educational, Scientific and Cultural Organisation (UNESCO) website.

Link: www.unesco.org/new/en/culture/themes/creativity/arts-education/about/

Find out more about the organisation's goals and approaches for art education.

This information will help you to understand in a broader context how the contribution you make to art education in your classroom influences a larger platform for the promotion and implementation of art education around the world.

The curriculum

In primary schools in England the current art and design curriculum includes exploration and learning to make art through "drawing, painting, sculpture and other art, craft and design techniques" (DfE, 2013, p.225). The computing curriculum requires "the use of technology to purposefully create… [to use] a range of digital devices to design and create" (DfE, 2013, pp.230, 231). Whilst statutory requirements for subjects in the national curriculum provide a framework for the curriculum in schools there are many decisions that schools can make to ensure that their curriculum is distinctive and meets the needs and interests of their pupils. Internationally, depending on the country of origin, the amount of freedom given to schools to develop their own curriculum fluctuates. Schools may have to align their curriculum with a specific teaching and learning model or philosophy or adhere to or include specific local or colonial content or practices. In the current curriculum in England the subjects of art and computing are both relevant to our discussion in that many digital tools and technologies can be used creatively to make art and some aspects of the computing curriculum can be taught through and in art, providing worthwhile and meaningful opportunities for learning in both subjects.

In addition to exploring and using drawing, painting, sculpture and other art, craft and design techniques to make their own art, children in primary schools also look at the work of artists, craftspeople and designers from the past and the present, sometimes from other places and cultures, and those who work in a variety of media. Older primary-age children begin to consider the reasons why art is made and what motivates and inspires artists, as well as making connections to their own art. There is the opportunity to learn about how artists might seek to provoke the viewer, alert the viewer to injustice or protest about an issue. Often looking at art can help children look at the familiar and see it differently.

In some primary schools around the world art as a subject can be identified on the timetable and in planning as a discrete subject. In others, meaningful links between two or three subjects will be made where this will enhance and enrich learning in these subjects. Some schools embrace the use of technology in other subjects including art whilst others use it more discretely or not at all. This can make it less clear where and when art learning is happening, let alone art learning that involves technological skill and awareness. Combining subjects is sometimes called 'linked learning' or the 'creative curriculum' and art's association with technology or computing regularly takes this position. In some instances, both art and digital technology might be connected within a science, technology, engineering, arts and mathematics (STEAM) approach. It is important when planning in this way that we keep a firm grasp on learning and teaching in art and ensure that it does not become merely a medium for illustrating learning in other subjects. The inclusion of technology needs to be meaningful for children, to enable them to explore and engage with the practices of their technology-rich and media-rich visual culture.

Digital technology and art

When considering the curriculum in schools we also need to consider the changing nature of education as a result of technological advancement. New technologies are constantly emerging, growing and impacting developments and research in education. Art education is no different and so we must envision how future technologies will impact our subject, its pedagogy, its practices and our teaching. We exist in a time, to some the fourth industrial revolution, where open learning spaces – laboratories, studios, experimental spaces, tangible technologies like augmented reality (AR) and intangible technologies like artificial intelligence (AI) – are changing the way education occurs (Leahy *et al.*, 2019). For art education this means it may be timely to re-evaluate and move forward our approaches to teaching and learning. This does not mean disregarding pedagogies and practices that already exist, but considering, for example, if the teaching approach, learning environment or resources observed, used or planned connect with our present time, culture and ways of teaching, learning and working.

In relation to open learning spaces in art education this may mean reconfiguring, adapting or transforming your learning space to take on different identities such as an art studio, graphic centre or fashion house. It may mean taking the art classroom to a new space (the school hall, an outside space, a local gallery or an online location like a virtual classroom or blog space). It could mean being in or facilitating these on and offline spaces in different ways – through experiential learning, inquiry-based learning or by taking on the role of the artist to suggest a few ideas. Fundamentally, the open learning space fosters adaptability, is open to difference and alternative ways of working and provides means to link physical and digital domains through active blended learning, connectivity and inquiry. There are, of course, challenges for the art teacher here with each open learning possibility, a central one being the delivery of meaningful art learning for the children. The art teacher may also have to embrace vulnerabilities and be mindful that some children may find the space difficult to access.

There are also benefits to open spaces. They work towards being future proof, offer greater inclusivity, broad opportunities and chances to share. They also build communities and begin to re-orientate the dynamics of art education. Ogier (2017), in the sixth section of her primary art text, suggests some useful ways in which you, the art teacher, can begin to work 'Beyond the classroom and into the future', which will help you to take initial steps towards using art education as a technological and open space.

Tangible technologies, those someone can interact with, like augmented reality or virtual reality – such as using tablets in the art classroom to bring objects to life (adding voice-overs to sculptures using apps like HP Reveal or EyeJack) or using the app Tilt Brush to virtually paint in 3D spaces – can help learners to understand mobile learning, gamification and contemporary and industry focused skills and applications. Some may feel that these practices are not relevant or appropriate for the primary art classroom, or necessary for the primary art teacher to engage with, but they can offer personalised learning experiences, increased motivation and foster an inquisitiveness to engage and explore the breadth and depth of art as a subject.

Intangible technologies, those with invisible qualities like artificial intelligence, focus on machine learning concepts. In art this could be using tools like Scratch to build codes, understanding how AI artists create their work, using robots or making drawing machines to create artworks for you or using algorithms to make soundscapes. Engagement with AI practices can help learners build empathy with others. Learners could look at ways to create art machines or devices that help those with disabilities to access different art practices or environments, positioning the learner as a change agent. Engagement with AI in art education can also provide an open, creative space where learners can question and explore what machines are capable of, how they work and why we use them. This can be essential to help children make sense of their past, present and future worlds and see how disciplines like art, science and mathematics come together and can embed at an early age the value of art as a deep and valuable emotional and cognitive subject area. Again, there are obviously limitations to tangible and intangible technology use and ways of working in primary art, but even a small and age-appropriate engagement with these concepts and practices will help children access an art education that is positioned for the future.

Reflect and extend

Engage with Sean M. Leahy, Charlotte Holland and Francis Ward's 2019 article, 'The Digital Frontier: Envisioning Future Technologies Impact on the Classroom', *Futures* (Volume 113, 10242).

Make a note of three things that you will do to integrate digital technology more effectively into art teaching and learning opportunities in your primary art class.

Linking art and technology to other subjects

Although art and technology (or sometimes computing) is taught discretely in a lot of schools (in England and Singapore especially), in others connections are made between two or more subjects where these would enhance learning in the linked subjects. This type of approach is sometimes called 'linked learning' or the 'creative / thematic curriculum'. When meaningful links are made these can lead to inspiring and motivating learning experiences for children and give them an opportunity to work creatively. Such experiences can even spread nationally and internationally – such as when schools partner together and engage in learning online. These connections can be made through the identification of an inspiring starting point, a shared interest or build up to an interesting outcome that provides an engaging purpose for the learning. Activities such as visits to local places of interest, visitors to the school, joining in or learning about differences in local and national events or planning a school event are often part of this type of planning.

When working in a connected way it is important for you to have a clear idea of what you are planning for or giving children the opportunity to learn. In the scenario of several connected subjects it is possible for one subject to be the 'poor relation' and be nominally part of the experience, with no real learning focus apparent.

Find out more – is it art?

Identifying when learning in art is taking place

In this activity you will think about the need to be clear when children are developing their skills, knowledge and understanding in art rather than using them to illustrate or serve the needs of another subject.

You will need: the pro forma below or a copy of it

What to do:

Consider the learning experiences listed below and decide whether they will support the learning of knowledge, skills or understanding in art. Indicate using these symbols:

√ – supports the learning of knowledge, skills or understanding in art

? – could support the learning of knowledge, skills or understanding in art depending on the emphasis or approach

X – does not support the learning of knowledge, skills or understanding in art

---

Activity – Identifying when learning in art is taking place.

Activity		√	?	X	If ? or X how could it be changed so it is more focused on learning in art?
1	Children are making a Christmas card exactly following the model demonstrated by their teacher.				
2	Children are looking for different shades of green outdoors, photographing them and combining them in a photo collage.				
3	Children are drawing an accurate picture of a flower and naming each feature with a label.				
4	Children are making a blog post about a favourite sculpture from the local environment, including text and images.				
5	Children are making patterns to demonstrate their understanding of symmetry.				
6	Children are filming each other role playing the relationships between people in one of LS Lowry's paintings.				
7	Children are interviewing each other in the roles of artists and are sound recording their discussion. They discuss what may have inspired artists to make their work.				
8	Children are drawing a diagram of the construction of a Roman road.				
9	Children are making digital animations to highlight caring for the local environment.				
10	Children are collecting, arranging and photographing natural materials, exploring colour and pattern.				

Questions to consider:

Activities that develop knowledge, skills and understanding of art, craft and design.

It is likely that you identified activities 2, 4, 7, 9 and 10 as those firmly focused on learning in art. Exploring a visual element such as colour and learning or using a skill such as making pots from clay and weaving are activities that fall within art. Talking about art and artists are also activities that are based firmly within the art curriculum, although they have links to speaking and listening as they provide the context for the use of speaking and listening skills taught in the English curriculum. Activity 7 may also have links to developing children's spiritual and cultural understanding. All of these activities also use technology as a tool or process to look, record, voice or share the children's art learning experiences.

Activities that may develop knowledge, skills and understanding of art, craft and design depending on the emphasis or approach.

Activity 5 (exploring symmetry) could be based on learning about pattern, a visual element, and how pattern is used in different cultures in art or it could be related to mathematical or computational understanding of how symmetry works and different types of symmetry. The skills, knowledge and understanding related to symmetry could be learned in either mathematics, computing or art and applied in any subject. Activity 6 could be based on learning about an artist and how their life and experiences influenced their art or it could be focused on using imagination, expression and dialogue to develop language and speaking and listening skills in English. It could also be used to teach skills related to film production or extended to consider editing techniques. This activity could contribute to learning in English, art and computing.

Activities that do not develop knowledge, skills and understanding of art, craft and design.

Activity 1, where following the teacher's model is likely to lead to similar or identical outcomes, is unlikely to lead to any new learning in art. It may provide an opportunity to consolidate skills such as cutting or sticking. Activities 3 and 8 are examples of drawing being used within a curriculum area rather than in art. The drawings are being made to illustrate particular features or aspects such as the botanical structure of a flower or the composition of a Roman road and the emphasis is on learning within the respective subjects rather than exploring the quality of line, tone and shape.

In this activity you have begun to think about when learning in art is taking place and when something that looks on the surface like art is more related to learning in another subject. Whilst applying skills, knowledge and understanding from the art curriculum to other learning experiences is a worthwhile idea we must not lose focus on the subject itself within the linked learning unit. It is important to be clear in both thinking and planning about whether the learning experiences will support discrete learning in art; whether they are connected to another subject and support learning in both subjects; whether they provide opportunities to learn in one subject and use and apply the knowledge gained in another or whether they are merely illustrative. In further chapters the possibilities of linking art with other subjects productively will be explored more fully.

If learning in art, and in other subjects involved, is to be effective it is important that a clear grasp of learning objectives and opportunities in each subject is apparent. You can use this kind of judgement and reflection to ensure that if art is connected to other subjects there is learning in art taking place and the connections are not tenuous, forced or superficial. If the art learning is merely drawing or painting a picture related to the content of one of the other key subjects there is less scope for new and creative learning in art or technology.

CASE STUDY

Year 3 and 4 children are working on an international project that connects English and art in two different countries. In English, the children in both countries have been reading magical stories and collecting examples of stories about animals, often with magical or unusual qualities. In art they have been exploring how artists and craftspeople have represented animals in three dimensions. The children in both settings have looked at and recorded the qualities of animals first hand through visits to zoos and bird parks and they have also looked at online collections depicting animals – such as those of the British Museum Collection online – and illustrations of animals in storybooks.

They are going to make a magical animal of their own and write a story in which it is the main character. They will share their stories with each other during an online storytelling experience and some children may even make short animations, using their animal to share.

In art they have been taught how to make a framework with narrow strips of card to create an animal's body and attach other features such as the neck and head, legs and arms. They will cover this with sheet materials such as tissue, plastic or fabric and have been shown how to layer these to create different textured effects appropriate to their animal of choice. Although all of the children will make animals using these techniques there is much scope for individual choices to be made in terms of the size and shape of the form and the colours and textures of the decorative materials used.

In English the children use their animal as the main character in a magical and imaginative story. As they work on their animal sculptures they also talk about, plan and begin to write their stories. There is interaction between the making and the ideas for the story as children choose materials and colours. For some children the time spent making their animal and talking about it allows them to rehearse, refine and develop the story they will write.

The stories are made into small e-books or animations, with a photo of the animal, or an animation of it, on the cover and are shared when the two classes meet online for a shared storytime experience. Later, the books are displayed in the school library with the animals arranged around them.

In the case study above children worked individually to create their three-dimensional animals exploring form, colour and texture in art as well as bringing it to life as the main character in an imaginative story in English. Children were able to draw upon the choices they had made later in their stories, where the tactile and visual experience of making could lead to interesting choices of vocabulary in their writing. This is one example of a meaningful connection between art and another subject – many more can be made.

Making meaningful connections between subjects in the primary curriculum whilst preserving purposeful learning in all subjects involved can be a challenge. When it works well it can bring learning to life in the connected subjects and lead to a more immersive and creative experience for children and teachers. In the case above the children would have the opportunity to learn about the experiences, interests and imaginative and artistic practices of their peers in another country, which could also enhance their global awareness and ability to build empathy and respect.

In chapters 7 to 11 connections between art, technology and other subjects will be explored in practical tasks and case studies.

Subject knowledge: visual elements

For the student, teaching assistant, HLTA, newly qualified teacher or non-specialist primary teacher the phrase 'visual and tactile elements' may be unfamiliar. These words – colour, pattern and texture, line and tone, shape, form and space – allow us to discuss specific concepts in making art and when talking about the work of artists. In this section each of these elements will be defined and in later chapters you will see how they connect to and underpin planning for learning and practical activity in the classroom.

When you teach an art lesson or an art unit of work you will have the opportunity to plan for learning in one or more of the visual and tactile elements using physical and / or digital approaches. It may be that one or two of the elements are the focus of your teaching in one or more of your lessons or activities. It is important that you know which one or two you are focusing on and how they might underpin or connect to the rest of the learning planned in your unit or lesson. In many published schemes of work the visual and tactile elements for the unit are identified in the planning.

Some units of work may involve exploration and learning about one or two (at most three) of the elements. You will find from reading this book that there are strong connections between some elements and these complement each other. Some fit especially well with certain technology, media or processes. It makes sense, for example, that we might explore pattern through printmaking or colour through painting on the screen or paper. This does not mean that we always and only explore colour when painting. Developing your knowledge and understanding of the visual and tactile elements may give you the confidence and freedom to make connections and choices of your own when you plan units of work and art experiences.

Find out more – what are the visual elements?

Exploring your current knowledge and understanding of visual elements

In this practical task you will use your current knowledge and understanding to define each of the visual elements. This will help you refine and develop your subject knowledge as you support and teach art and read this book.

What to do:

- In each box add notes about a definition of the word as you understand it at the moment. Think about the day-to-day definition that relates to the use of the word generally and a specific meaning related to its use in the context of the subject of art.
- Another way of understanding these words is by thinking of examples when making or viewing art, so add notes about these details if you find them helpful.

Activity – What are the visual elements?

line	colour	form
pattern	**visual elements in art**	space
shape	tone	texture

In this practical task you have drawn upon your prior knowledge to consider some significant vocabulary and ideas in art. Consider this a summary of where you are and as you continue to develop as an art teacher this knowledge and understanding will deepen and change as you observe, support and teach art, plan activities, lessons and units of work and gain experience.

Defining each visual element

Each visual element can be defined specifically in an art making and viewing context and it is these definitions that you will seek to understand and explore with pupils. You can explore a basic definition for each element on this ThingLink:

Link: www.thinglink.com/scene/1341718046795890689

A definition for each word in the art context is present at the 'i' symbol.

Reflect and extend

Martin Wenham's book *Understanding Art: A Guide for Teachers*, published in 2003, explains each of the visual and tactile elements in detail and with reference to practical work and the work of artists, craftspeople and designers. This book will support your subject knowledge and can help you develop your confidence with planning and teaching art in the classroom.

Knowledge and understanding

As you explore each visual element you will find that, as in any subject, each one is underpinned by some associated knowledge and understanding.

Colour

When we are exploring colour, for example, perhaps you remember from your own schooldays that colours can be identified as primary (red, blue, yellow) and secondary (violet / purple, orange, green) and that by mixing two primary colours we arrive at a secondary colour (red and blue mixed together make violet / purple). When we mix two primary colours such as red and blue to create violet / purple this colour and the remaining primary colour – yellow – are called complementary colours. When we add white to a colour the colour gets lighter and this is called a tint. When we add black to a colour it gets darker and this is called a shade. Often artists will create darker shades by mixing colours rather than using black pigment. When you were at school you may have explored this knowledge about colour in the context of a formal exercise of mixing colours and painting a colour wheel. There are many other more creative ways of exploring colour mixing that are more appropriate for primary-age children. Some of these involve mixing coloured pigments when painting; collecting and arranging objects of different colours; and using apps and tools to change colours using filters and effects. Colour theory, colour mixing and palettes can be explored online at the links below.

Link: www.canva.com/colors/color-wheel/

Link: https://palettegenerator.com/

Tone

When we use the word tone in art we are referring to how light affects the surfaces we are looking at. Exploring tone in art may be focused on exploring how we represent this and use it in our own art as well as how we identify and talk about it in other artists' work.

Depending on the process or technique we are using we may be able to explore gradual tonal change through mixing paint, blending pastels, chalk and charcoal or light exposure in photography. When drawing with soft drawing pencils we can create gradual tonal changes by varying the pressure with which we press down as we draw and in many art apps we can change tones within a colour through choices we make on a visual menu of colours and shades. If we are using media such as fabric, collage or felt pens we may choose from available colours that keep distinct boundaries and our choice and placement will create contrast or transition between tones. Tone and tones of colours can be used to create a sense of space: making something appear near or further away in the distance. When choosing and using colours in digital drawing or painting the tone of a colour can easily be changed by making simpler or more complex choices from those available within the tool.

Line

In the context of art, lines do not have to be single continuous linear marks but can be as short as points or dashes. We can use lines to create outlines which can then be filled, or we can place lines and marks together to create areas of tone, patterns and textures.

We can explore line using tools that leave marks on surfaces such as pencils, pens, paintbrushes and pastels. We can also use our fingers in paint or sticks in sand. We can guide and place materials that have linear qualities such as wire, thread or string. We can also use needles to sew, creating linear marks with thread on fabric. We can use fingers and a stylus on a screen to make and change marks and lines. Experimenting with simple hand-drawn lines in hand-made animations by making flick books and other early animation devices can serve as a prelude to learning about digital animation.

Pattern

Pattern may be something created in or inspired by nature, identified by our observations or programmed into a device and sometimes it becomes the inspiration for our designs. It may be created by us when we place lines, marks and shapes on surfaces in a design or motif. Sakr (2017) recognises that having opportunities to experiment with pattern is important to child development in art and technology and that opportunities to explore pattern should extend beyond the digital device and focus on interaction with time and space. Wenham (2003) suggests that when we are exploring pattern with children we can think about three types of pattern: linear patterns that are developed along a line, rotating patterns that are developed around a point and surface patterns developed on flat surfaces to cover whole areas.

Children follow and devise linear patterns when they fix multilink cubes together to make repeating patterns using colour, when they create line drawings on an app and when they build with construction toys. They may also make repeating patterns when they thread beads and found items onto a string or when they use digital stamps to recreate their own patterns and pictures. When doing this it is important for the child to be able to identify the beginning and end of the items that make the pattern (the motif) so that they can repeat it. This type of pattern might be used as a border. They will also experience making linear patterns when practising the flowing left to right patterns that underpin joined handwriting in English or when encountering the many structural patterns in Chinese characters.

Rotating patterns begin from a middle point and may be circular like a flower or the cross section of a piece of fruit or expand outwards to fill a regular shape like patterns on tiles. These patterns often have one or more lines of symmetry.

Repeated patterns on a surface can be made from various motifs and extended across large surfaces in any direction, physically and digitally. We often see these types of pattern on fabric, wrapping paper and wallpaper. The surface itself and how the motifs are placed on it are both important to the design and overall impression of the pattern. Sometimes a grid is used to help guide the pattern, or the motifs fit together through a tessellation of shapes, and working digitally here can both save time and give children more scope and control over their work than would be available in the physical world.

Texture

We can think about texture in two ways. Firstly, texture is how materials feel when we touch them. We begin to be able to predict how materials will feel before we touch them or we can touch them without looking at them and be able to name and describe them. Secondly, texture can be represented visually by making various marks. An illusion of texture can be created even though we know we are looking at a flat surface.

Clearly tactile texture is explored through touch. When we explore tactile texture in art and technology we may be encouraging children to take texture into consideration in their choice of materials, perhaps when choosing fabrics and threads in textile work or when designing and creating layers to change electronic temperature measurements or outputs in STEAM and interdisciplinary work.

We may be planning experiences that allow them to explore the tactile qualities of art materials directly, such as when finger painting, manipulating clay, making an object from papier-mâché or sliding a finger around a screen. Some children will dislike the textures involved and be reluctant to use their hands like this, preferring to use tools. When we experience art we may be allowed to experience some works through touch or bodily interaction. The idea of artworks being tangible, tactile, kinaesthetic and multisensory is increasing in popularity, particularly in galleries housing contemporary art.

Visual texture, on the other hand, is explored through looking, talking about and making our own marks in 2D and 3D, physically and digitally – such as in visual and augmented reality. We can see some textures and use them to create impressions by taking rubbings, or we can recreate them in digital space using Tilt Brush. We can experience making marks using textures by pressing items made of different materials into paint and printing with them or pressing items into clay or dough to leave an impression of the texture. Alternatively, we can experiment with making the flat surface of paper or screen look textured by the marks we make with physical or digital pens, pencils, paints, cutting or embossing tools.

Shape

When we use the word shape in the context of art, design and technology it is more concerned with defining areas on a surface or in a space. These areas might not have a precise geometric name as they would in mathematics, but they could be grouped into categories such as geometric, organic or abstract. When we use the word shape in art it refers to two-dimensional shapes on a surface. Three-dimensional shapes will be discussed more fully in the section in form, although of course shapes will be seen and created in two and three dimensions.

In art a shape may be made by identifying an outline with a pen, pencil, paint-brush or thread. It could be made by tearing or cutting paper or other material and placing it on a surface. Shapes can be made physically and digitally by printing or placing marks in a patch so that the marks together are seen as a shape. In addition to this the shapes we draw, cut or print have a background and may be placed near, next to or overlapping other shapes. Shapes interacting together may create a pattern, picture or the appearance of a texture.

Form

In art, and sometimes in technology, form can be defined as something that is three-dimensional in nature. We can experience a large-scale form by moving around an object to look at it from different viewpoints, including being inside, outside, above and below it. If the object is small we can pick it up and move it around to look at it from a range of viewpoints. When we experience form we may think about the form itself and the space within which it sits.

In addition to this the form that we look at and / or touch may be decorated with colour, line, pattern, tone, texture or shapes. In technology this artistic approach to form can still be applied as we can move around and experience objects when engaging with scale, viewpoints, space and perspective – such as when using CAD tools like 3D Slash, SketchUp or BlocksCAD.

Space

In art and technology we can think about space in two ways. Firstly, we might think about space in three dimensions – how forms are made and placed in relation to each other and the environment and how we can move around in space to see, experience or interact with these objects from a variety of view-points. Secondly, we might think about how we can represent space in two dimensions to give an illusion of three-dimensional space on a two-dimensional surface, or with advancing technologies in three or four dimensions. We can also consider how we use space to create patterns and use shapes.

When we think about space in three dimensions we might experience this in relation to placing our own sculptures or looking at sculptures in galleries or in the environment in physical or virtual ways. In this context we need to encourage children to think not only about the form that they are making or looking at but also how it interacts in the environment in which it is placed. They will need to consider its size and scale in relation to where it is placed and the impact it has on people who see it from all angles and distances. This can become complex when you consider virtual and social online spaces.

When we think about creating an illusion of space on a flat surface this can be an area that challenges and demoralises children when they are seeking to draw, paint or make any kind of pictorial representation. Learning how to give an impression of distance using perspective and representing relative size can assume an exaggerated importance for children. Giving children experiences of their own work and the work of artists, craftspeople, designers and technologists, which gives them support in developing the representation of space and the understanding that it is not always the most important aspect of a piece of art, can help address this challenge. It should be remembered that representing the illusion of space in two dimensions is significant in Western art but is not necessarily a key idea in art from many other cultures or in contemporary works, so the range of art children encounter will broaden their knowledge and understanding in this area.

Talking about each visual element

As in any area of the curriculum, understanding and being able to use accurate and precise vocabulary is vital for the teacher and for the learner. In Appendix 1 you can find an extensive list of vocabulary related to each of the visual elements. This can be a useful aide-memoire when identifying any key vocabulary relevant to your planning. Bringing it to life with examples from the children's own making and their viewing of the work of artists will help establish and explore the nuances of meaning.

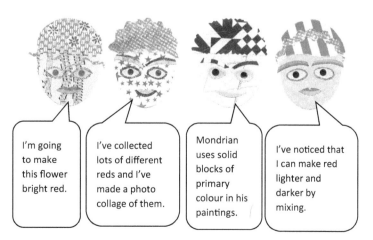

Figure 2.1 Talking about a visual element in context

Find out more

Access the ThingLink at the link below.

Link: www.thinglink.com/scene/1341718046795890689

On this ThingLink for each visual element you can find:

- A definition
- Some examples of art for each element

Explore the examples to consolidate your subject knowledge. If you want to go further you can 'clone' the ThingLink and then edit it to add your own personalised examples, to use as well as or instead of those present.

School policy and approach

In many schools adopting more Western practices the school approach to the curriculum and how it is put into practice will be guided by the school policy. The policy for the subject of art is likely to have been developed by the art coordinator or subject leader along with the staff of the school and a similar procedure is followed for the computing curriculum. In the policy design writers may have been guided by national or international subject associations or the content they produce; associations such as the National Society for Art and Design Education (NSEAD) in the UK or the International Society for Education through Art (InSEA) internationally.

The school may also have a particular commitment to art or the arts more widely – this may be recognised in the UK, for example, by the award of Artsmark or involvement in the Arts Award at Discover and Explore levels. In other countries, like Singapore, schools may be known for offering Learning for Life or Applied Learning Programmes that foster skills and competencies which provide opportunities for learners to gain lifelong skills, competencies and passions for different facets of art. And in Australia, for example, schools may offer Approved Art Specialist Programmes to develop skills, talents and one's individuality in a specific area of art.

If you work in the school, you may have been an active part of writing policies or schemes of work; you may have learnt about them as they were communicated to staff or you may have joined the staff and found out about the scheme or award in a similar way to a student on placement does. If you join a school as a student on placement you will need to assimilate and understand the school's approach quite rapidly and you will have the opportunity throughout various placements to experience and learn from a variety of different approaches, taking the most effective aspects from each to assimilate into your own knowledge, understanding and approach towards art education.

What you will notice from the discussion in this chapter so far is that when thinking about and designing an art curriculum a number of influencers come into play. The school, art coordinator and teacher's role is to connect these influencers and devise policies, curricula and/or lessons that meet:

The school policy

Schools usually have policies, devised by themselves or by governing organisations, to guide learning and teaching. This may be an individual policy for art, a policy for 'the arts' including visual art or a policy for foundation subjects (i.e. not core subjects such as English and mathematics). Although policies in the UK are individual to the school they tend to include the following:

- A rationale and statement of aims for the learning and teaching of art in the school. This may include aims for the inclusion or use of digital technology.

- A description or guide to how the content is organised and taught in the school. This may include a curriculum map or long-term plan and a scheme of work or medium-term plan. It may also include guidance on assessment, perhaps taken from subject associations.

- Pedagogical, conceptual or theoretical models for the subject or ones that the school is aligning to.

- A role description for the art coordinator or subject leader. It is likely that this will include supporting other staff, like digital technicians or teaching assistants, and students in their roles.

- Advice about inclusion, accessibility and equal opportunities – with consideration of values and provision for SEND, EAL and LGBTQ.

- Information about collaboration, partners, interdisciplinary working and community cohesion.

- Guidance about the use of digital technology and e-safety.

- Some policies include guidance about display, exhibition and the presentation and use of children's art work – such as for school publicity.

- A list of resources, where they are kept and guidance about how to use them.

    As Bowden (2013, p.9) suggests, the policy underpins a "coherent and consistent whole-school approach to the subject".

If you are teaching art or supporting in art lessons you should ensure that you have read the policy and familiarised yourself with its provisions, especially in relation to the individual aims and approach of the school. It is important that children receive a consistent experience, with all staff following similar approaches that they have agreed together. As you read this book you will often find suggestions to consult or check with the school policy for this reason.

In your school: school policies

Explore the school policy for art

In this practical task you will explore the school-based guidance and approach explained in the art policy. This will support your planning and teaching.

You will need:

A copy of the art policy and pro forma below

What to do:

Use the art policy to answer the following questions.

Activity – In your school: school policies

Questions	Answers
Who is the art coordinator or subject leader?	
What is the school vision for or approach to art, technology and the combination of the two?	
Is there a long-term plan or outline of what pupils will learn? When? and How?	
Is there a list of resources for art (and how they are organised or should be used)?	
What does the policy say about how art connects to other subjects, institutions or collaborators?	
What does the policy say about assessment in art?	

Questions	Answers
Does it reference any subject associations?	
What does the policy say about including and respecting the values of all pupils?	
If you are supporting pupils in art lessons is there any guidance about how to support pupils with specific needs?	
What does the policy say about the use and display of pupils' work on and offline?	
Does the policy consider technology, internet use and e-safety?	
Has looking at the policy suggested any other questions to follow up?	

Guidance notes

When you have considered these questions and you are left with anything that you need to clarify, try to talk with the art coordinator. As a student you will need to focus on how the answers to these questions affect your placement: finding the planning and resources for the half term or unit or work that you plan to teach, for example. As an NQT / non-specialist teacher you will have a more long-term view, thinking about the art you plan and teach with your class over the year. As a teaching assistant you may be especially interested in the approach to inclusion and accessibility if you will be supporting individuals or groups in art lessons, or have similar interests to teachers if you are covering art lessons as PPA time.

The policies for specific subjects are likely to work in conjunction with other policies that guide staff in more general areas that apply across all subjects, such as learning and teaching, inclusion, assessment, e-learning and health and safety. As you move around the school look around for exemplification of the art policy in classrooms and in the shared and public areas of the school. You should be able to identify some media or processes that children have explored and some artists that children are learning about. Looking at the variety of outcomes might tell you something about how much opportunity for individual response or breadth of media coverage is given to children. There may also be out-of-school co-curricular learning opportunities for children, which allow them to participate in art activities – schools globally often have extra-curricular clubs related to art, technology or specific crafts.

The art coordinator and points of support

As with other subjects or areas of learning in schools an identified teacher (or sometimes a teaching assistant) will be named as subject leader or coordinator. Depending on the size of the school and the organisation of the curriculum this role may vary in name and responsibilities. In small schools staff will have several curriculum areas to coordinate; in some schools subjects may be combined in different ways and in many schools the coordinators of core subjects may well have a much higher profile, reflecting the position of that subject in national or international agenda. As former art and technology coordinators we feel art's nature as a subject and its relationship with display and dissemination meant that we could often make it more visible and high profile than other subjects – but this does take commitment to upkeep. Now, with social media and online platforms, those responsible for other subjects have greater opportunities to profile them, although art and media can have a very powerful voice singularly and in collaboration with these.

One aspect of the role of coordinator (of any subject) is to support staff development and training. This may include leading training in school or encouraging you to seek training beyond the school and sharing back with colleagues. On a day-to-day basis it is more likely to include being a first port of call for your questions. If you are a student in the school, a teacher in the early stages of your career or a teaching assistant the art coordinator can be a great source of support to you. Bear in mind that this member of staff is likely to have class as well as subject responsibilities, so choose your moment.

In addition to the art coordinator there may be other points of support for you, especially if you are trying to unite art and technology in your school or you are teaching in a multidisciplinary way, such as through a STEAM approach. In school you may seek technical support from computing specialists or technicians and you may have a very talented individual or team of teaching assistants, or parents who have specialist skills in a topic area you are trying to implement or pursue. Or you may belong to a group or trust of schools who have staff with specific expertise you could draw upon.

There are a number of sources of support beyond the individual school. The National Society for Education in Art and Design (NSEAD) provides support for teachers of art including resources, publications, courses and advice, along with being the champion of art education in the UK. NSEAD also supports regional support groups, where teachers can meet and work together. Internationally, the International Society for Education through Art (InSEA) connects art educators around the world, providing a community, events, research and publications to support art education. Increasingly, social media provides opportunities for sharing practice and resources through websites, blogs or other platforms, where you can ask questions and seek advice from other professionals in your field – but be careful to do so professionally and consult your school's policy first on social media staff engagement. You need to avoid disclosing sensitive data. Considered connections on social media can be a useful form of continued professional development that can help keep you abreast of the quickly developing educational domain. Developing your personal network of stimulating, supporting and challenging people and institutions can enrich your practice and give you access to inspiration and practical advice.

Art and technology beyond the classroom

In addition to the opportunities offered in school it is likely that there will be out-of-school-hours learning opportunities such as after-school clubs, workshops and activities offered to children. Some of these may be centred on or have ties to art, craft, technology and design – such as code club. You can also encourage children to join in any local activities available at galleries, museums and other local places after school or in holiday periods. Many children draw, pursue crafts, engage with technology and make art at home and it is important that we value this interest and enthusiasm children have for creating and making and draw upon it to support their learning in school. Susan Ogier (2017) has written extensively about opportunities for art that extend beyond the classroom, describing how such experiences develop children's visual literacy, critical thinking and ability to problematise. She speaks about the opportunities galleries and museums provide, offers advice about how to plan, lead and engage in a visit and discusses how to bring artists into the school environment.

With regards to digital technology many companies, museums and universities now offer educational programmes or outreach to schools and some even offer technology trials or loans so that children can have access to industry equipment and software to broaden their knowledge and experience beyond the school's budgetary capabilities. You may even wish to consider how concepts such as 'flipped learning' or the 'flipped classroom' could be utilised in your art classroom – where ideas, tasks and instructions are delivered to learners online or out of the classroom and then explored in deeper, extended or alternative ways when the children come to class face-to-face.

With tools such as Green Screen Technology and Augmented and Virtual Reality, art beyond the classroom can also be experienced in the classroom. This can be useful if your school does not have the budget to take children to a gallery or museum for example. Children can visit the gallery through a virtual experience you have created in the classroom and situate themselves within it. In other subject areas and at different educational levels around the world augmented reality and artificial intelligence practices are filtering into classrooms and learning experiences – whilst this is in its relative infancy in most primary school art classrooms it is a development that we must not lose sight of. Educational practices, through their connection with art and technology, are changing and so we must keep abreast of what is going on beyond the classroom and be willing to trial, experiment and critique new and emerging approaches to art learning.

Use of published materials

Many, if not most, schools will use some published materials to underpin learning and teaching in art and technology, as in other subjects. In our experience, when schools use published material they tend, over time, to change it to meet their needs so that it may become no more than a starting point or underlying structure. Some schools buy in published schemes and some local and national authorities have written schemes of work for their schools. There are various teachers' guides and books that can guide learning and teaching in specific aspects of art such as Meg Fabian's books on drawing (Fabian, 2005) and painting (Fabian, 2009) and Julia Stanton and Eileen Adam's *Art Express* books. Another useful source of ideas and materials are the websites of art galleries and arts organisations such as the National Society for Education in Art and Design (NSEAD), AccessArt and the International Society for Education through Art (InSEA).

Schools make choices from these resources to support their planning and often refer to these in the long-term plan. As a student or teacher planning learning or a teaching assistant supporting learning, it is your role to ensure that when you adapt from these plans the objectives, experiences and outcomes meet the needs of your pupils. As you gain more experience and confidence you will increasingly use these schemes as starting points from which you develop your own ideas that relate to the interests of your pupils, the individuality of your school and the resources of your local community. One factor to bear in mind when using published schemes is that they cannot address the individual needs of your pupils, so thought must always be given to inclusion and differentiation. A significant consideration for students and teachers when working from scheme plans is to be selective, as there tends to be too much content to realistically achieve in the time available. It is more important to choose and use some parts effectively than gallop through all the activities quickly and superficially.

As a student it can be useful to start collecting and storing ideas for teaching art both on paper and electronically, so that you begin to have resources and ideas that you can draw upon to support and enhance your teaching. Taking photos and notes of ideas that you see in school and in galleries, as well as saving links to useful websites, will help you enormously in the future. A good starting point is the primary section of the NSEAD website.

Reflect and extend

In the OFSTED publication *Making a Mark: art, craft and design education* (2012), you can explore further some of the key aspects of the art curriculum and the factors that contribute to its effectiveness. Read the sections focused on the primary art curriculum and consider them in relation to the practice you observe and your own role.

As well as making art and looking at art there are many other contributions that being involved in learning experiences in art can make to children's education. These will be explored more fully in the next section.

Conclusion

There is so much potential for learning in the art curriculum and art is an inspiration for pupils, as well as being an opportunity to motivate and educate them. Including opportunities for pupils to use and create with digital technology enhances this potential, bringing additional opportunities to connect and collaborate in new ways. If you are in a position to take advantage of the opportunities offered to you by the curriculum in its widest sense you will be able to provide meaningful and effective learning experiences for your pupils. In the next chapter, making connections to the work of artists, visiting galleries and working with artists will be explored more fully.

Next steps

- Check that you have a copy of the school's art policy.

- Check that you know who the subject coordinators are and how they can support you.

- Look for people, schools and organisations to support and inspire you.

References

Bowden, J. (2013) *Art and design. Primary Coordinator's Handbook.* London: Harper Collins.

DfE. (2013) *The national curriculum in England: Framework document.* [online] Available from: https://assets.publishing.service.gov.uk/government/uploads/system/uploads/attachment_data/file/381344/Master_final_national_curriculum_28_Nov.pdf [Accessed 20/07/20].

Fabian, M. (2005) *Drawing is a Class Act.* Dunstable: Brilliant Publications.

Fabian, M. (2009) *Painting is a Class Act.* Dunstable: Brilliant Publications.

Leahy, S.M., Holland, C. and Ward, F. (2019) The Digital Frontier: Envisioning Future Technologies Impact on the Classroom. *Futures.* **Vol 113**, pp.1–10.

OFSTED. (2012) *Making a Mark: art, craft and design education.* [online] Available from: www.ofsted.gov.uk/resources/making-mark-art-craft-and-design-education-2008–11 [Accessed: 20/07/20].

Ogier, S. (2017) *Teaching primary art and design.* London: Learning Matters.

Sakr, M. (2017) *Digital Technologies in Early Childhood Art. Enabling Playful Experiences.* London: Bloomsbury.

Wenham, M. (2003) *Understanding art: a guide for teachers.* London: Paul Chapman.

Further resources

Stanton, J. (2009) *Art Express Book 1.* London: Bloomsbury.

Chapter Padlet:

https://padlet.com/Jeanne/Chapter2

03

Chapter Three

Learning about and from artists

Introduction

Looking at and making connections with the work of artists, craftspeople and designers encourages us to go beyond thinking about children as makers of their own art and help them develop as discriminating and critical viewers of the art, craft and design that they see around them. Many of the children we teach will not go on to work in this area or even use art, craft and design in their working lives. However, all of the children we teach will go on to live in an increasingly visual environment, making their own decisions about fashion, interior décor and development of a personal style. As citizens they will encounter art in the public spaces around them, see it in galleries and museums and experience it as consumers of entertainment and advertising. As Charman *et al.* suggest: "For those pupils who do not continue their art practice beyond school, the creative and critical skills of interpretation are equally necessary as a tool to negotiate our world of visual complexity and richness" (2006, p.54).

In this chapter the following areas will be explored:

- Making choices
- Using the work of artists in the classroom
- Visiting art on location
- Working with artists

It is our responsibility to give children a rich and varied experience of the work of artists, craftspeople and designers, which inspires them, builds and evokes memories and feelings and broadens their horizons. These experiences can support learning and teaching by developing children's knowledge and understanding of art, craft and design from around the world, from now and from the past, so that they have a wide view of what art is as well as exploring what inspires and motivates people to create. Children can also learn more about the range of media and processes available to artists, especially how rapidly evolving digital technology can lead to new forms of art. These experiences will stimulate children to look at the world around them with curiosity, so they can appreciate and be critical of the visual environment. Introducing different role models from the world of art can be inspiring for children and open their minds to the range of careers in the creative industries. Children also need to develop a sense of ownership of and care for the art in public spaces and collections that they will inherit as adult citizens. Going beyond the art curriculum the work of artists, craftspeople and designers gives children a context for meaningful speaking and listening as well as enhancing and enriching other areas of the curriculum.

Making choices

If the opportunities available to us are to be used effectively in learning and teaching a basic grasp of subject knowledge on the part of the teacher is necessary; personal interest and enthusiasm is also helpful. Even if you are not a natural artist or viewer of art yourself you can still introduce children to exciting artistic concepts and possibilities. Schools have the freedom to make their own thought-provoking and interesting choices of artists, craftspeople and designers. They have the flexibility to take the individual needs and unique features of their own community and local resources into account. Where a basic knowledge of the subject and local resources is lacking schools can resort to making obvious and safe choices or become too reliant on the choices suggested by schemes of work and published material. Being alert to national art exhibitions and local resources in galleries, museums and public spaces will allow you to make more informed and personal choices to bring your art teaching to life.

Definitions

You will have noticed the phrase 'artists, craftspeople and designers' in this book. These three words are significant and should steer us towards making a range of choices rather than choosing from a narrow group of famous painters.

Artists

A dictionary definition: "a person who paints or draws as a profession or hobby" or "a person who practises or performs any of the creative arts" (Soanes and Hawker, 2008, p.48).

A personal definition: people who create art, especially that which is considered 'fine art' such as drawing, painting, installations, sculpture and photography.

- Artists may include:

Painters, printmakers, sculptors, photographers, virtual reality makers, film makers

Craftspeople

A dictionary definition: "a worker skilled in a particular craft" (Soanes and Hawker, 2008, p.227).

A personal definition: skilled people who make decorative and / or functional objects by hand.

- Craftspeople may include:

Weavers, ceramicists, jewellery makers, felt makers, embroiderers, potters, wood carvers, stonemasons, calligraphers, screen printers, batik artists, glass makers, basket makers, quilters, mosaic makers, mask makers, puppet makers, papier-mâché makers, furniture makers, knitters, animators

Designers

A dictionary definition: "a person who designs things" (Soanes and Hawker, 2008, p.269).

A personal definition: people who create or design objects and the environment, sometimes for others to make.

- Designers may include:

Fashion designers, graphic artists, illustrators, architects, milliners, glove makers, online game designers, product designers, cartoonists, costume designers, landscape designers, interior decorators, etc.

Some of these examples, such as architects, may fit into several categories or may have a visual aspect to their role and yet not fall completely within the categories of art, craft or design. Other examples could include archaeologists and cartographers. Many artists would use media and processes from several fields as part of their work as well as specialising in one. Perhaps you were also able to list some specific examples in the chart. These will be useful later. Throughout the rest of the book the word 'artists' will be used to indicate 'artists, craftspeople and designers'.

As well as definitions based on what artists do we might consider the qualities that many artists demonstrate in their work and how these can relate to our work in the classroom. Qualities such as perseverance, determination, curiosity and problem-solving, which can be also be encouraged in children's making in art by well-planned opportunities in schools. These should include the opportunity to play, experiment and take risks when working with materials and processes. Jarvis (2011, p.316) notes the importance of an approach like this: "an acceptance that children, as well as adult artists, can learn through the accidents of playing and experimenting, and that they must establish a learning context where children can experiment and explore".

Choosing art, craft and design to support learning in art

When you are deciding which artists, craftspeople and designers to choose to support your teaching it is important to consider the bigger picture of the child's experience across one or both key stages. If all the art, craft and design that children encounter is that produced by a distinct group (men, Europeans, people who are no longer alive, painters) this can skew their understanding of who produces art, craft and design entirely. It may also affect their feelings about themselves as makers of art. Having said this, some works of art and significant artists are European male painters from the past and to avoid using their work entirely would deny children access to some important examples. A balance should prevail, so think about the artists and artwork children will encounter over a year, key stage and whole experience at primary school, aiming for a wide range of experiences in the long term.

Male artists	Female artists	Artists who are LGBTQ	Artists who worked in the past
Artists from your locality or region	Artists from the UK	Artists from places all over the world	Artists from different cultures
Art made by individuals	Art made by people working together	Art made for different purposes	Artists using different materials / processes
Artists whose work is temporary	Artists whose work exists only in a digital form	Art made to protest or provoke change	Artists whose work includes participation by the audience

The choices that you make about who and what to look at, talk about and respond to should be varied and inclusive, allowing you to address issues of diversity and reflect changes in society in your curriculum. Including a wide range of people who make art, as well as ensuring that diversity is apparent in the art children look at and talk about, is a powerful way of providing role models and discussing change. Identifying artists who work locally and examples of art, craft and design in your local community, including public spaces, galleries and museums, is important, as is noting online exhibitions. You can also consider encouraging children to have some choice and influence over the artists that are explored. Following children's interests may allow you to include some children who may be uninterested in traditional fine art and help you refresh your own knowledge. Animation, graphic design, comics and graphic novels, computer games, installations and the use of digital technology such as augmented and virtual reality can be motivating for all, but especially for older Key Stage 2 children.

In looking more closely at the artists you refer to you may have identified some gaps. It could be that it is beyond the scope of your role to address these gaps currently. This will depend on how decisions are made about the art curriculum in the school and how much flexibility there is in making changes. Your awareness of the impact of the choices that are made and your overview of how the lesson and unit of work fits into the year, key stage and whole-school experience can help you to make interesting and worthwhile connections or suggest changes in the future and make the most of the material indicated to you in existing plans.

Beyond the choices of people whose work is explored you should also consider where there are specific pieces of artwork named. It is important to remember that it is seldom that one piece of art, craft or design can represent the entirety of that person's lifetime of work. Children should not take away an impression that the only painting Van Gogh ever painted was *Sunflowers*, for example. Where specific pieces of work are named, especially in published schemes, you should be clear about what the children are expected to learn about or from this and how it fits with their own making of art work, so that you go beyond copying the work or using it in a superficial way.

LEARNING IN ACTION

A town centre school has audited the art, craft and design available to them as a basis for making choices about what children will look at and use in art and across the curriculum. This includes:

- A survey of the art in indoor and outdoor public spaces within easy walking distance of the school
- Consideration of the school site as an environment for art
- A visit to and contact made with the art education officer at the local art gallery and museum, exploring the permanent collection and changing exhibitions
- A survey of the skills and interests of staff, parents and friends of the school
- Buying into the local authority loan scheme for original works of art
- Investigation of sources of funding for bringing artists into the school to work and for making visits further afield to regional and national art galleries
- Investigation of local, regional and national projects and awards that schools can take part in
- Investigation of digital technology that will support learning and teaching in art

This audit is led by the art coordinator and supported by staff and governors of the school. It results in consideration of the resources, talents and expertise of the local community and how these can be used to support learning and teaching in art.

As a student, NQT or teaching assistant this is likely to be too big a project for you to undertake unless you have a strong personal interest in the subject or you are aspiring to be an art coordinator. You can, however, think about these areas in relation to the class you are teaching and plan to use what is around you effectively to support learning and teaching.

The quality and availability of resources is a significant factor in the choices you can make. If certain works of art are named in the long-term plan or scheme of work, supporting resources such as original works of art, good quality reproductions, digital resources and associated information should be available in school. The reproductions you choose should be considered in terms of scale – it may be helpful to be able to show children the actual size and proportions of a work of art by using a similarly-sized piece of paper, so that they understand that all works of art are not A4, laptop screen or IWB screen size. If you are unfamiliar with these then finding out more about them before you begin planning, teaching and supporting is essential.

Find out more

Explore online to find the following resources and save them to your favourites:

Google Arts and Culture – images of art from many galleries and museums and galleries around the world.

Link: https://artsandculture.google.com/

Art UK – a searchable database of paintings available to see in the UK and resources to use in education.

Link: https://artuk.org/

National Art and Craft Directory – an illustrated directory of artists and makers working now that can be searched by name, media and various other terms.

Link: https://nationalartandcraft.com/

Engage – the national association for gallery art and education professionals, promoting access to and understanding of the visual arts through gallery education.

Link: https://engage.org/

These are all useful websites for exploring works of art to use in the classroom and finding places to visit.

As you increasingly look around for examples of artists' work to use in your teaching it can be useful to devise a way of organising them so that you can readily access them when the time is right. Saving links to favourites, copying links to an ongoing Word document and keeping a folder with images you have collected or cut out can all be useful. A useful tool is the virtual bulletin board 'Padlet'. This online tool and app will allow you to collect, display and share images and links with text or audio commentary. Boards can be made public, secret or private and be password protected for use in school. The social media tool 'Pinterest' is another way of collecting and organising visual material online. Here you can label 'boards' by theme, pin images to them and search the boards and images of other users for images that you want to add to your collection. Other link collectors such as Pocket or Google Keep can also be useful.

Exploring the work of artists in the classroom

There are many ways in which the work of artists can be used to support and stimulate learning in art and across the curriculum. I have found that looking and talking about works of art is a way for children to explore and respond to what they see or sometimes feel. Making connections to art they are making themselves is another way of responding to art, as long as this is planned sensitively and avoids copying. Choices can be made that support learning not only in art but in other areas of the curriculum, leading to purposeful connections being made between art and another subject.

Talking about the work of artists, craftspeople and designers

When you are planning for children to talk about the work of artists it is important to consider how you can scaffold talk about art effectively. Charman *et al.* (2006) suggest that whilst we can encourage children to talk about the visual elements and processes we must also equip children to interpret, explore and express ideas in relation to the art they see and experience.

When talking about art with children, especially younger children or children who are inexperienced in talking about art, having a structure to support looking and talking can help them develop and extend the vocabulary and thinking skills required. This may include a clear identification of the vocabulary and sentence structures that will be useful, some key questions and an order in which to begin questioning, moving from the known to the unknown and the more speculative. The level and development of the children's vocabulary should be considered, as well as the needs of children learning English as an Additional Language or those who have a special educational need that has an impact on their communication and language.

Try for yourself – talking about art

Considering the vocabulary and questions that you could use to talk about a work of art, craft or design

In this practical activity you will have the opportunity to identify the words, sentence structures, prompts and questions that you could use to talk with children about a work of art. Planning this out before you begin can help you ensure that all children are included and learn from the experience. Use what you know about speaking and listening and devising open and closed questions to help you in this task.

You will need: this pro forma or a copy of it

What to do:

- Choose a work of art, craft or design.
- Identify vocabulary and key questions in relation to it using the headings in the boxes below as a guide.

You may wish to use Seurat's *La Grande Jatte*. This painting can be used on an IWB and there is an opportunity to zoom in on different parts of it, focusing on detail. It was completed in 1886 and shows us activity on an island in the River Seine in Paris. There is another painting by the same artist, executed at around the same time in the same location, called *Bathers at Asnières* that you could also look at to compare.

Link: https://artsandculture.google.com/asset/a-sunday-on-la-grande-jatte/twGyqq52R-IYpA?hl=en

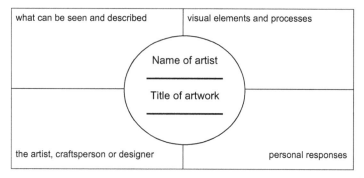

Figure 3.1 Activity – Talking about art

Questions to consider:

- what can be seen and described

Asking children to describe what they see is a basic way into looking at any work of art. It allows them to identify and name. This can be developed by asking them to find named items; asking them what is next to, behind, furthest away; asking them to choose a part and describe it so others can find it or other homing in type questions. Another approach is to provide children with real items, pictures or words to find in the work of art or use the spotlight tool on the IWB to take them on a tour of the painting before revealing it as a whole.

- vocabulary, visual elements and processes

Questions and prompts in this section are likely to be underpinned by the choice of work of art that you have made. Perhaps your choice relates to a visual element, media or process that the children are or will be using and this will guide your questions. You might encourage children to look for how an artist has represented space or used colour in their work. You might aim for children to look for particular ways of using natural materials or combining threads in a weaving. With older children a comparison may be drawn between this work and other works of art the children know, or their own work. Specific vocabulary that children need in order to discuss the work should be introduced or revised.

- about the artist, craftsperson or designer

Questions in this section may develop as children look at the work of art. You may want to be able to share some knowledge about the artist or prompt children to devise questions so that they can do some research of their own. Children could devise their own questions that they would ask the artist if they could. Some of these questions may be more speculative and open. Some could encourage older pupils to consider the function of art, who it was made for, why it was made and how the artist prepared to make it. These questions may provide opportunities to make connections to where the art was made (geographical context), when the art was made and what else was happening at that time (historical context).

- encouraging personal responses and speculation

Questions in this section could be entirely open and allow children to respond individually. This will vary depending on their age and experience and could include the feelings and memories evoked by the work and any questions children would like to ask about it. Making connections to their own work could be useful here – Is there anything we can learn to help us with our own art work? for example.

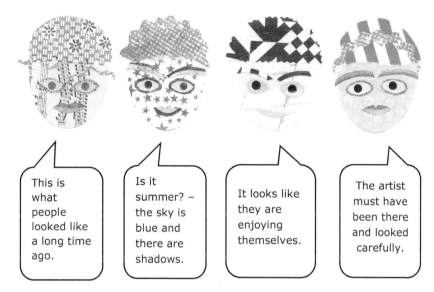

Figure 3.2 Talking about a work of art

In this practical task you had a closer look at planning for a talk about a piece of art. You might take elements from this approach to use at different times, depending on your plan for learning. It is important to avoid being overly prescriptive. I have found that when we allow children to think about what they see without any preconceptions they can speculate and imagine more freely and creatively. As Charman *et al.* (2006) state: "Teaching pupils a method of looking at art does not need to place a stranglehold on what is essentially the creative act of making meaning. Rather, it offers a way of scaffolding what can otherwise seem a confusing process with no clear way in" (p.57).

Reflect and extend

Charman *et al.* (2006) in their book *The Art Gallery Handbook* suggest an alternative scaffold for talking about art based around:

- a personal approach
- ways into the object
- ways into the subject
- ways into the context

You could find it useful to explore how this approach could support and develop looking at art, craft and design with children.

When introducing a work of art to children, finding imaginative ways to attract children's attention is important in provoking and sustaining interest. Planning different ways into the work of art rather than immediately looking at the entire piece encourages children to look in a more focused way. Showing children small details can be an interesting way to start looking – either by covering a reproduction with a large sheet of paper and cutting windows in it to open one by one or, if the work is available online, using the highlight or zoom in tool on the IWB. Taking children on a narrative tour of the work of art by visiting different parts can be another way, especially if you are looking at a representative piece of art. These strategies can help children look at different parts of the work rather than becoming overwhelmed, not knowing quite where to look or superficially skimming over the artwork. Older children should be challenged to go on to make comparisons between works of art. Your choices of the work that children will compare should be planned to allow children to make meaningful comments that they may then go on to relate to their own work.

LEARNING IN ACTION

At a recent local exhibition of artists' responses to visits to Venice over the last one hundred years a group of PGCE students identified the following comparisons that could be made:

- Two works of art by the same artist
- A work of art by a contemporary artist and one by an artist who lived a hundred years ago
- Two works in the same medium by different artists
- Two works of art with contrasting approaches – e.g. a detailed line drawing vs a loose, free painting
- A work of art by a female and by a male artist
- Two works of art with different viewpoints of the same place
- Two works of art with different compositions

In this case study a relatively small exhibition was explored but it gave rise to many ideas that could be used to inspire comparisons and discussion. With a class of children perhaps only one or a limited number of these would be chosen to explore in depth. Along with exhibitions, many galleries and museums have educational resources available to support and guide planning and teaching. During 2020 many galleries and museums provided additional access to their online collections and developed digital exhibitions and tours. Whilst these are no substitute for seeing original works of art they are useful resources to support learning and introduce children to collections, themes and artists.

Another approach that is made possible by digital tools is the opportunity for teachers and children to curate their own online exhibitions. Choosing a group of works of art to express personal views, follow a theme or explore an artist or medium can involve individuals and groups in purposeful research and thinking. Tools such as Google Slides, prepared with frames in a gallery-like setting or ArtSteps, a site and app that allows images and video to be displayed in an augmented and virtual reality exhibitions space, could be useful here.

Using the work of artists to inspire making

Some of the units of work that you teach may be inspired by or include reference to an artist's work or a specific piece of work. It is essential that this work is used thoughtfully and most especially that children are not expected to routinely copy works of art. This practice leads to similar or even identical responses rather than individual and personal outcomes. There are many other ways of using works of art in the classroom that are more effective and inspiring to children. In the examples below, exploring the human figure in motion is the underlying starting point for choices of art / artists to look at and explore.

Approach	Examples
Using the work of two artists so that children can make choices in the features and ideas they take and use	Paula Rego – drawings for *The Dance* 1988 Kenneth Armitage – drawing, *Scurrying Figures* 1984
Using the work of an artist working in one media or process to inspire work in another	Look at images of painted figures on Greek vases (simplified profile figures in movement, two colours) and make collages using these qualities
Using the work of an artist working in two dimensions as a starting point for working in three dimensions (and vice versa)	Look at images of Giacometti's depiction of figures (linear qualities) as preparation to make string prints
Using a visual element as a starting point and looking for work that exemplifies different approaches	Form – Giacometti (elongated / simplified forms), sculptures from the classical world (realism), Peter Jansen (kinetic figures)
Using the work of an artist / several artists to help solve a problem or make suggestions about how to overcome a challenge	Explore how artists have conveyed movement – catching figure mid-action (runners on Greek vases), time lapse photography (Muybridge)

Approach	Examples
Using the work of an artist to introduce a material, tool, technique or process that the children will then apply to ideas / subject matter of their own	Peter Blake's collages using images of people – apply this to sport, dance or other physical activity
Using the subject matter as a starting point and then asking the children themselves to find artists who have represented it in different ways before they go on to have a go themselves	Ask pairs to choose a sport or activity that involves movement and look for two examples of this in art to share with the class
Using abstract art to help children think about alternatives to 'making a picture of…'	Richard Long – recordings of walks in landscapes
Using the work of an artist who works in an original or unorthodox way to get children thinking differently	'Transmission drawing' by Morgan O'Hara, responding directly to the movements of people in drawing

Other approaches you might investigate are using several examples from the same artist to help children consider how they changed and developed over time and using two examples of where one artist has responded to the work of another artist. The approaches discussed above avoid planning for children to copy the work of artists but rather inspire, teach or suggest ways forward for the art children will be making. Deciding which approach to take in any half term or unit of work would depend on the overall learning objectives you were planning to meet.

Using the work of artists to make connections with other subjects

Your choices of the work of artists can also support meaningful links to other areas of the curriculum and enrich the overall learning experience for children. As discussed earlier, it is important that when you identify and plan for these links they are not tenuous or forced. The learning objectives relating to art and to the other subjects must be kept in mind so that you are clear about the learning which is to take place in each. This will vary from subject to subject and in relation to the chosen areas of each subject that are connected by planning.

English

There are many skills that children develop in English that require the context of another subject to make the use and application of skills meaningful. Aspects of speaking and listening including description, speculation, narration, making presentations, participating in role play and drama can be set in the context of talking about works of art or artists' lives. Research skills such as finding information in books and on the internet, scanning and skimming, summarising and presenting can be connected to finding out more about art and artists. Many works of art and images can inspire poetry and stories as well as talk. When working digitally the app ChatterPix can be used to add a moving mouth and speech to art. This is especially effective when working with art that contains people in portraits, scenes with human figures and statues of people. Imagining oneself into the mind of the sitter or subject can allow children to explore artists' motivations and feelings. Green screen technology can be used to place the child into a work of art and give them a guided tour of it or enable them to become part of it in a creative way.

In all or some examples the main focus of learning is English and art is providing a context for the use and application of skills. When art is the main focus of learning in the discussion and exploration of a work of art the focus is more likely to be on visual elements, how the artist solved problems and used tools and processes in their making, why the art was made and how it affects the viewer. Children will be using and developing their subject-specific vocabulary and making notes and can also devise and write labels / catalogue entries for their work.

History

When considering connections between art and history we might identify how pictures and objects can show us what the past was like – what people wore, where and how they lived, what some people looked like and a depiction of significant events. This can enrich children's understanding of the past and what life was like for people. Older children will also explore how and why art was made in the past, as well as considering how far we can rely on what artists show us, how art might be used to persuade and inform and whether we can get a complete picture of the past by looking at the art that has survived. Portraits and sculptures of key figures can open up a conversation about the ways in which attitudes and thinking have changed in terms of how the significant figures we commemorate are chosen, for example. A further link to consider is identifying how the past, and works of art and artists from the past, inspires artists working now. Children can also consider how the development of materials, equipment and technology has affected what artists can make and how their work can be shared with audiences.

Geography

Similar considerations can be made in relation to geography. Art from other places can show children what those places look like, sometimes conveying aspects difficult to appreciate in any other way, such as the atmosphere, the weather and the colour and quality of light perhaps. These places might be real, imagined, contemporary or from the past. Comparing how artists from different eras have represented a place and what that place is like now can help children consider how places and the environment change for better or for worse. Artists from the past and those working now are often inspired by places and the feeling and atmosphere of places, as well as the land itself or a wish to protect the environment.

RE and spiritual development

There are opportunities to explore the way faith and belief have inspired art by looking at the art made for places of worship and made by people inspired by faith. Looking at art in churches, temples, mosques and other places where people worship or contemplate can help children consider the way art can have a spiritual and symbolic meaning. In this way, connections between art and Religious Education can be made, as well as considering art in relation to spirituality outside organised worship and religions.

Science

Connections can also be made between art and science. Curiosity, careful observation and exploring materials are important in both subjects. Children can apply some of their learning in art, especially drawing, in their recording in science, learning about how a skill can be applied in different ways to meet the different requirements of a task. Scientists have used drawing and painting to record their observations (botanical illustration, for example) and artists have been inspired by discoveries in science as well as what they can see with the tools scientists use in their work.

When making connections between the work of artists and learning in other subjects, it is important to be clear about what is being learned in art and what in the other subject. Although physical education, design technology, mathematics, music and PSHE have not been discussed in depth here, the same principles for making choices and clarity of planning apply. Connections between the art curriculum and computing will be explored in more depth in the next chapter.

Visiting art on location

One aspect of using the work of artists is the unique contribution seeing original works of art, craft and design can make to the learning experience. You will probably have experienced for yourself the feelings of seeing the original version of a work of art that you know only from reproductions. Reproductions tend to be misleading in terms of scale and appearance. When we encounter the original we can appreciate the size, colour, form and overall impact anew and this can be breathtaking. It is important that we help children understand the difference and appreciate that the original work of art in its setting can inspire feelings and an understanding that it may not be possible to get from a reproduction.

Opportunities for using original works of art must be planned in at the long-term stage so that the organisation required for making visits can be undertaken in plenty of time. The school policy, guidance from the local authority and statutory requirements should be followed, ensuring that any visits are safe for adults and children.

Works of art, craft and design can be found both locally and nationally, as well as online. Knowing what is available in your locality and region can allow you to make choices of art that reflect or are important in and to your community. Making contact with the education officer or curator responsible for school visits at your nearest gallery or museum can help you in planning for a productive visit. You should also look for works of art in public spaces like town centres and parks as well as art at stately homes and in theatres. As well as art, craft and design that is permanently displayed it is likely that there will be temporary exhibitions in your locality that you can use as a focus. This requires more flexibility, but liaison with gallery / museum curators or education officers can support you in planning ahead. Galleries tend to know what their exhibitions will be well in advance, giving you time to plan them in where appropriate. This can give you access to the work of contemporary artists and often there will be associated activities, including the chance to meet or even work with the artist.

Preparing for the visit

Before any visit to a gallery it is important that you prepare in a number of ways. Making contact with the curator or education officer to talk through any input or activities that will take place is an important first step. The curator or education officer is more likely to be able to meet the needs of your children if he or she knows about their prior experience and individual needs before the visit. Along with this, visiting the gallery or exhibition yourself before you go with the children will also help you plan. Many galleries and other places of interest allow people who are planning to bring a school visit to make a pre-visit free of charge. If a visit is impossible, research and find out as much as you can from the gallery's website and from talking with the staff.

Planning for the visit in terms of how it might inspire and support learning both during and after it takes place ensures that you use the visit to its full potential as a learning experience. The children will need to be prepared for their visit in terms of expected behaviour and conventions of behaviour, which may be different than other places they have visited. Also, making sure that children have the background knowledge and vocabulary to use and respond to on the visit is vital. You can do this in collaboration with the curator or education officer, so that the group get the best out of the visit. This is especially important for children learning English as an Additional Language or with a special educational need related to language.

Immediately before the visit the adults who will accompany the class on the visit must be prepared in terms of health and safety, risk assessment, behavioural expectations and their own role in supporting the class. This might involve focusing on one or a named group of children or being more general. It is also important to ensure that they can support children's learning. This could involve focusing on children who will need support with behaviour, listening to and responding to language or working practically.

LEARNING IN ACTION

A class of Year 1 and 2 children are getting ready to visit their local art gallery as part of a unit of work based on sculpture. Before they go their teacher reviews some of the vocabulary that the curator will use. These words include:

- Basic vocabulary – sculpture, sculptor, three dimensions, solid
- Words to describe position and viewpoints – behind, at the side, in front, around, above, below
- Words for the materials sculptures are made from – marble, stone, wood, clay, metal, bronze
- Words for how sculptures can be made – carved, cast, moulded, assembled

Their teacher also reviews expected conventions of behaviour in the art gallery especially:

- Walking around the gallery
- Talking quietly to each other and to adults
- Looking but not touching unless the curator gives permission

The adults who will be accompanying the class on the visit are all present for this session so that they too are fully briefed and can support effectively. One of the adults can speak the first language of some of the children and she will support two newly arrived pupils in accessing the session.

At the gallery, the curator talks with the children about two sculptures that show different ways of representing the human figure. One is Jacob

Epstein's *Head of Vaughan Williams* and the other is Barbara Hepworth's *Four Figures Waiting* – both of these are cast in bronze. The children are able to use some of the vocabulary reviewed before their visit in their discussion of the sculptures.

Much of the preparation for the visit flows from the content of the visit as planned with the education officer, from the overall planning and from the teacher's knowledge of the children's learning in art. Whether the visit is a one-off or part of an ongoing sequence, I have found that the time spent in preparation is always worthwhile.

At the gallery

At the gallery, your visit or session could be led by a curator or education officer or you might lead the visit yourself. There are a number of ways you can help children get the best from the visit. If the session is led by a curator this is a great opportunity for you to observe and learn from their practice as a specialist in their field. In the future you will be able to use some of the teaching ideas and subject knowledge in your own work where appropriate. If you lead the visit yourself it can be useful to consider some initial starter activities and a more focused activity after this.

Starter activities

When you go into the gallery it can be useful to settle the children with an introductory activity, to allow them to have a look around in a purposeful way and get a sense of where they are. This could include:

Learning focus	Activity
Comparison of reproduction to original	Giving pairs of children a postcard and asking them to find the work of art represented on it
Looking carefully	Giving children a picture of an item / name of an item that appears in some art and asking them to identify examples of it in the art
Inferring / looking at visual clues	Making quiz cards that ask children to look for clues in specific works of art, perhaps with a main and a supplementary clue
Reading / finding contextual information	Giving children details from the label or title to the art and asking them to seek out the matching piece

Learning focus	Activity
Visual elements	Ask children to look for examples of artists who have used a specific visual element – find a picture where the artist has used bright colours, find a sculpture where the artist has used curves, etc.
Time, historical context, chronology	Ask children to look at pairs of work made at different dates and find out which was made first
Place, geographical context, location	Ask children to look at pairs of works showing different places / landscape features / link to map as appropriate
Media and processes	Ask children to look for examples of a medium or process or different examples within one area such as painting or textiles

Your choice of starter activity could be based on what the children will later go on to explore more fully and your own knowledge of the class. It could also reflect the age of the pupils and their prior experience of visiting galleries or other offsite locations. It might also relate to the busyness of the gallery. At some local galleries your visit might take place before the building is open to the general public, giving you more freedom to move around and use the space. At larger, national, galleries this is unlikely to be the case and you will have to work around the other visitors.

Looking more closely

When you consider what your main focus for learning in the gallery will be you should be guided by your objectives, what is available to look at and talk about and the outcomes you have in mind for when you return to the classroom. You may have experienced yourself how easy it is to become overwhelmed by all there is to look at in a gallery or museum and the tendency to flit from work to work not looking and responding in any depth.

Choosing one, or at most a few, pieces to look at more closely is an effective approach. Alternatively, looking in depth at one key work altogether and then giving children a choice about what else to look at can allow some freedom for personal exploration. If you regularly talk about works of art with children in the classroom they are more likely to be able to talk productively and express themselves when in an art gallery looking at original work. If you have already visited the gallery and identified some prior knowledge children may need, conversation will be more informed. As well as talking about works of art there is often potential for using drama techniques to develop a response to a work of art: freeze framing, hot seating and dialogue improvisation can be used to place children inside a work of art and explore it from a different perspective.

As teachers or teaching assistants, observing can be a great opportunity to record children's ideas and vocabulary as there are likely to be adults observing you or the curator working with the children. In terms of support and inclusion, if you have pupils with particular needs in relation to speaking and listening the support you offer in the classroom should also be available in the gallery situation; and if a curator is leading the session they should be fully briefed about how to include all of the children effectively. If most of the visit will be spent looking and talking it can be useful for you to take notes and create reminders so that when you are back at school you can prompt and help children recall what they have learned.

As well as talking about works of art children could work practically to record what they see, experience, feel and think in the gallery. This could be in their sketchbooks or separately on paper or in mini-sketchbooks made for the purpose. Worksheets, although tempting, should be avoided as filling them in can lead children to focus on the worksheet rather than the experience itself. Perhaps, if absolutely necessary, prompts to guide children in looking and help them gather relevant information could be provided.

After the visit

When you return to school from visiting a gallery or viewing works of art in another setting there are a number of ways of using the experience in supporting learning in art and in other subjects. Given the time and the challenge involved in planning and carrying out a trip it is very important that the experience does support learning effectively. You will have identified a connection between the gallery experience and work back in the classroom at the planning stage. Perhaps you are going to explore and respond to a similar subject or inspiration such as the human figure, landscape or poetry. You may be planning for the children to work in the same media, such as watercolours, plaster and wood or textiles. You could be teaching them about the same visual element such as pattern, line or space. You could also be making a connection to another subject, such as researching paintings of your locality from the past, to both explore painting from observation and identify changes that have happened over time.

Use the sketches and notes, or your own notes, of what children said and any other materials brought back from the visit that will provide a strong connection back to the experience. There may be items that you can bring back such as guidebooks, postcards and posters and there may be information available online. It is unlikely that you would have been able to take photos in the gallery. Keeping in touch with the gallery and sharing the children's work produced after the visit should also be considered. Curators and education staff are often interested to see what children have been inspired to do after their visit.

Reflect and extend

Read Angela Eckhoff's article 'The Importance of Art Viewing Experiences in Early Childhood Visual Arts: The Exploration of a Master Art Teacher's Strategies for Meaningful Early Arts Experiences', published in 2008 in the *Early Childhood Education Journal* (Volume 35, Issue 5, pp.463–472). Focus on the four strategies (game play, questioning, storytelling and technical talk) explained with examples on pages 4 to 7 and consider how these might support your teaching.

Working with artists, designers and craftspeople

There are opportunities for children to meet and learn from people working as artists, designers and craftspeople. These opportunities could come about in a variety of ways including:

- Through personal contact with artists who have connections with the school, e.g. parents, governors, members of staff and their families and people living local to the school.

- Through outreach activities arranged via your local art gallery. Often when exhibitions take place activities involving the artist are planned for local schools and the community.

- Through having an artist to work in school as part of a one-off project or ongoing initiative. Some charities and organisations fund artists to work in schools. For a list see the further resources section at the end of this chapter.

There may be other opportunities available to you depending on where your school is situated – if you are close to a college or university with art students this may be a great source of people willing and enthusiastic to share their work. If your local area has an arts festival or open studios you might find artists willing to include children as a way of reaching a wider audience for their work. You might be able to hold a local art exhibition yourself in a community room or school hall, supporting the arts and artists in your community and making contact with people who might help you with the art curriculum.

When considering this aspect of the art curriculum you could use contacts with artists living now in the local community to develop the children's understanding of art as an opportunity for employment and personal fulfilment. Inviting artists into school to share and talk about their work allows children to learn more about what motivates people to make art and how it shapes their lives. Having an artist in residence work for a sustained period in the school with a class or year group is another way of connecting to people who make art. This is a wonderful opportunity to work with someone who has developed specialist skills in an area of art, craft or design and it is often a chance for children to use different materials and learn a new process or an alternative way of using a familiar process.

If you are going to work with someone whose job it is to make or design art it will be important that you make sure that they and the children have a positive experience. Working with children in a school setting can be very different to talking to members of the general public, so you should consider how best to brief and prepare your visitor. It may be that the artist you work with has experience of working with a range of people, but you have the knowledge of your class from the inside that can be vital.

Conclusion

Making choices that inspire learning in art and identifying opportunities to collect ideas contribute enormously to the enthusiasm and motivation that you can create in art. There are so many ways in which you can do this – the most important thing for you to bear in mind is that you do have the opportunity to choose from a very wide range of resources, starting points and learning outcomes. Units of work can be personal to your school and the children in your class if you want them to be. Changing what has always been done can feel like a daunting step but it is well worth the time and effort for the children and for you. In the next chapter, planning for learning in art will be explored in more detail.

Encouraging children to visit galleries and museums can widen their horizons and influence their learning and lives beyond school. When I began taking classes to my local art gallery each half term I found that over time this led children to talk about the experiences at home and ask their parents to take them back in the holidays and ultimately join in with holiday activities – many families had not engaged in this before.

Next steps

- Identify the different ways in which learning in art will be inspired in the class / year in which you work.

- Begin to broaden your knowledge of artists, craftspeople and designers so that you have more choices available to you.

- Investigate makers of art in your locality, including people who work in school and parents.

- Investigate the original works of art available in your immediate vicinity (within walking distance perhaps).

References

Charman, H., Rose, K. and Wilson, G. (2006) *The Art Gallery Handbook. A Resource for Teachers*. London: Tate Publishing.

Jarvis, M. (2011) What Teachers Can Learn from the Practice of Artists. *The International Journal of Art & Design Education*. **Vol 30**, No 2, pp.307–317.

Soanes, C. and Hawker, S. (eds). (2008) *Compact Oxford English Dictionary*. 3rd ed. Oxford: Oxford University Press.

Further resources

Baverstock, A. (2011) *13 British Artists Children Should Know*. London: Prestel.

Finger, B. (2010) *13 Modern Artists Children Should Know*. London: Prestel.

Herbert, K. (2019) *We are Artists*. London: Thames and Hudson.

Orfali, A. (2004) *Artists working in partnership with schools. Quality indicators and advice for planning, commissioning and delivery*. Newcastle: Arts Council England.

Schumann, B. (2009) *13 Women Artists Children Should Know*. Munich: Prestel Verlag.

Chapter Padlet:

https://padlet.com/Jeanne/Chapter3

04

Chapter Four

Digital technology and art

Introduction

This chapter considers more closely the place of digital technologies in the curriculum and in art lessons as tools for creativity and learning, and considers how these relate to the wider field of digital art. A key idea is that digital technologies can be used as a way of extending the available repertoire of art tools and the range of artistic outputs available to teachers and children in schools. Incorporating the creative use of a range of digital tools gives children the opportunity to be an active maker rather than a passive consumer in the digital world. Seen in this way, digital tools and technologies offer new avenues to explore, complementing physical art making rather than replacing it. Indeed, the introduction of digital methods can often result in a creative interplay between digital and physical forms of expression.

In this chapter the following areas will be explored:

- Digital technology and the art curriculum
- Digital technology in the art classroom

Ever since the information age began to develop in the 1950s, 60s and 70s, artists saw potential in the rapidly changing landscape of digital innovations. Significant milestones were the advent of personal computers, notably the introduction of colour graphics on the Apple II computer in the 1970s, the introduction of Photoshop in the 1980s and the widespread adoption of the internet in the 1990s, which gave artists a platform for sharing their art and collaborating with each other. As the field continued to evolve, new software appeared for manipulating sound, light, video, animation and images, including computer-generated graphics and projected images. This greatly expanded the range of choices at artists' disposal. A key feature of this field is that often devices and tools that appear as expensive and specialist quite rapidly become part of day-to-day life and as such have made their way into the classroom and the home, a trend which continues today. Ensuring that we as teachers can use them purposefully, safely and creatively is an important part of our practice.

Digital technology and the art curriculum

When we think about how digital technology connects with the art curriculum it is useful to consider a definition of digital art as a new media process to go along with drawing, painting, printmaking, collage, textiles and working in three dimensions. The genre 'new media art' emerged to describe the various artworks that have been created alongside the development of media technologies. As Tate defines it: "A term new media is used to describe the sophisticated new technologies that have become available to artists since the late 1980s that can enable the digital production and distribution of art" (Tate, 2020a) and in our contemporary society the term 'digital art' sits within the umbrella of new media art: "Digital art is a term used to describe art that is made or presented using digital technology" (Tate, 2020b). It is sufficiently well-established in the world of art to be an area that can be seen as part of the art curriculum in schools and some of the tools artists use are as available to us in schools as are any other tools and materials used by artists.

Although it is not recognised as a distinct movement of art, according to the definitions above digital art describes a broad field of activities and there are many subtypes involving different forms and combinations of media and methods. The growth of digital art has opened up new tools and combinations of media, resulting in new artforms. To name a few, digital art includes video installations, immersive environments, virtual reality, digital painting, generative computer art, sound visualisation, digital installation art and photo manipulation. Digital artists can paint with media such as light or sound or pixels on a screen. Their collages might incorporate found digital imagery. They can work in new dimensions through augmented, mixed and virtual reality. There is even a term, 'tradigital art', to describe art that combines traditional and computer-based techniques, such as the digital manipulation of images for printmaking (Gollifer, 2000).

Digital art has also given us novel ways of interacting with art rather than simply viewing it and of incorporating audience responses into the artwork. A key concept of much digital art is that it creates sensory or interactive experiences that invite participation from the audience. Such interaction can alter the relationship between the artwork and the audience from passive to active as the art itself changes in response to the audience. In this way, the digital sphere not only offers additional creative potential, but it also opens up new ways for pupils to collaborate with each other and with the artworks and artists themselves. Engagement with art becomes less passive and all the more engaging.

We can draw an example from a recent exhibition at Tate Modern of the work of Olafur Eliasson.

The work *Your uncertain shadow* uses coloured lamps to project shadows of the viewers onto a wall and constantly changes in response to their movements.

Figure 4.1 Art is made through a collaboration of artist and audience interaction

This artwork comes to life through the active participation of the viewer. Chris Milk's work *The Treachery of Sanctuary* works in a similar way, where the viewer becomes part of the art through the projection of shadow wings, until it appears they are taking flight.

Link: https://olafureliasson.net/archive/artwork/WEK100100/
your-uncertain-shadow-colour

Link: http://milk.co/treachery.html

In addition to this, the internet has revolutionised ways in which art can be made, distributed and viewed. Artists can now crowdsource their work and tap into social networks. These networking opportunities promote the collaboration and exchange of ideas between artists across the world. As a result, their work may have more accessibility and relatability, and wider cultural reach.

It can be argued that digital art and design techniques are an integral aspect of art in our cultural era and therefore should be important skills for children to master. Digital ideas and techniques are finding their way into degree courses. For example, the UCLA Design Media Arts degree emphasises innovative creation with digital media. Alongside a foundation in form, colour, space, motion, typography and interactivity, they offer courses in video, visual communication, network media, game design, 3D modelling, animation and interactivity. Undoubtedly, the addition of digital technology to the arts has expanded the available creative opportunities and we can also think about translating some of these approaches into the primary classroom. In this context, too, digital technology offers new forms of collaboration for pupils creating art together and for interaction between themselves and their audiences. Infusing the art curriculum with digital technologies offers expressive possibilities and children's imaginations can be stimulated in different ways.

Digital forms of expression

When digital devices, tools and technologies become part of the repertoire of media and processes used to make art, there are many opportunities to work entirely digitally or with a combination of digital and physical approaches. We can think in terms of a continuum that begins with art wholly made and existing in the real world, through art made or experienced using a mix of digital and physical materials to art that is made wholly using digital tools and exists only in the digital world. This could be using new technology or providing digital alternatives to existing media and processes.

Digital alternatives

Some apps and tools offer us alternative ways of working, such as drawing with a stylus on a screen instead of with a pencil on paper or using a painting app on a tablet to paint digitally instead of using a brush, paint and paper or canvas. These alternatives are not replacements, as they have some inherent advantages and disadvantages as well as elements in common with their physical counterparts.

When we make decisions about what to use in the classroom it is important to bear this in mind.

The term digital painting applies to art that is created on a digital device in a similar fashion to physical painting and may be viewed on a device digitally or outputted as a piece of art on canvas or paper to view. David Hockney's well-documented exploration of digital and analogue modes of representation showed how the two media can complement each other, as he experimented with the Brushes app on the iPad to explore texture, colour and pattern in the landscape. Children can be similarly inspired to rethink how the world is represented by exploring digital lines, colours and textures. As with Hockney, drawing and painting apps can prompt children to rethink how to achieve techniques such as blending colours, changing stroke thickness and varying transparency and colour hues when using a finger or a stylus on a screen. Exploring familiar physical techniques in a digital medium can encourage children to talk about elements of art such as tone, hue and colour intensity. Apps also enable these values to be manipulated, allowing children to reflect on the effect of altering the properties of colour and tone much more rapidly than they might be able to when using paint.

There are some advantages to painting digitally. The fact that the digital medium allows the artist to undo and redo their work encourages experimentation and risk. As Hockney says: "The iPhone makes you bold" (cited in Gayford, 2011). Many apps also capture the process of creating the art so that it can be played back at speed as an animation, opening up the possibility of demonstrating and discussing techniques and decisions. On a digital device, children can quickly try out a range of effects without fear of losing what they have done so far and avoiding the mess and effort of working with water and paints. For some children this is an advantage.

Link: https://medium.com/digital-art-weekly/how-artists-connect-with-digital-ver-sus-physical-painting-the-case-of-david-hockney-a85b23f1c9a1

There are, of course, disadvantages to replacing real paint and brushes with a digital version. The sensory pleasure of mixing and applying paint of different thicknesses, the unpredictability of what the paint will do and the challenge of learning to control this are wonderful experiences for children. Giving them opportunities to experience both types of painting regularly and comparing them would be the most appropriate approach at the primary school stage, helping them make considered choices from the range of digital and physical tools avail-able as they become ready to take control of their own work.

Another example of digital art is the work of the French artist Thomas Lamadieu, who created a playful series of works entitled *Sky Art*, which drew inspiration from the geometric shapes of sky between clusters of buildings. To make these works he identified the space left when we look up between buildings and filled these spaces with people and animals, creating an imaginary scenario of a recognisable but changed world.

Link: https://tlamadieu.wixsite.com/roots-art

Link: www.thisiscolossal.com/2013/04/
sky-art-thomas-lamadieu-illustrates-in-the-sky-between-buildings/

The combination of digital drawing and found photographs is an approach that could be applied in the classroom. In responding to Lamadieu's work, children can be encouraged to think about how looking at the spaces around and between objects makes us look at the world differently. A tour of the school environment with digital cameras looking for gaps and spaces should yield some good examples. A Google image search of 'sky between buildings' also generates sources of inspiration for *Sky Art*, and Lamadieu's idea could be adapted in the classroom to combine pen and ink drawings with the digital images, perhaps inspired by the idea of imaginary characters who live in the clouds. Lamadieu himself suggests that his drawing of the bearded man stands for 'the big man in the sky'.

Link: www.independent.co.uk/arts-entertainment/art/news/this-artist-draws-on-the-sky-between-buildings-10195695.html

In exploring Lamadieu's work and creating their own images, children might focus on line, pattern, shape and perspective, drawing inspiration from geometric tile patterns. With careful scaling, resizing and scanning, their finished images might be entirely digital, lending themselves to being combined into a collaborative online book using Book Creator, perhaps accompanied by poems read aloud or sound effects. An extension could be to apply the technique to create abstract designs based on aerial photos of lakes or the spaces between the branches of trees. An artist who works in a similar way is Ben Rubin, whose subway drawings of creatures interacting with unknowing passengers have potential for imaginative exploration with children.

Link: https://mymodernmet.com/ben-rubin-subway-doodle/

Digital art

Including digital tools and technologies in the art curriculum also offers us the opportunity to work with entirely new media and processes that exist only in the digital world. These experiences allow children to be at the forefront of new art and technology with artists and makers. Creating art that is wholly digital provides them with a new area in art making and viewing to explore. As both viewers and makers of art we are at the relatively early stages and as such we might lack confidence in choosing which artists to explore and what to do in the classroom in terms of using apps, tools and devices effectively in art. We can view this positively as an opportunity to find our own inspiration and try out ideas for ourselves. Digital art can be more multisensory in nature, drawing in visual representation along with sound, light and interactive features. Its forms might be more immersive and collaborative than other forms of art. Inherent to digital art is computer-generated art, a clear link to the computing curriculum.

Creating with light and space

The Light and Space Movement, which began in California in the 1960s, aimed to explore a new artistic medium of art and space. The work of artists such as Robert Irwin, Doug Wheeler and James Turrell consists of immersive light installations and focuses on the viewer's perceptions of light and sensory phenomena. As a branch of West Coast minimalism these artists worked with only two materials, space and light. This movement has influenced many contemporary artists who also work with space and light such as Olafur Eliasson, Brigitte Kowanz and Ann Janssens.

LEARNING IN ACTION

A group of primary school teachers, students and lecturers explore the possibilities of creating art using light and apps on iPads. They learn to use an app which keeps the camera shutter open for longer to capture light (Slow Shutter or Light Trails), along with torches, fairy lights, glow sticks and LEDs in a darkened space. Working in pairs and small groups is vital here, with a camera operator and artist using the lights. Once they have learned how to use the app they experiment freely with the lights; switching them on and off, moving them, making marks, lines and shapes and writing with them. The outcomes are captured as photographs saved in the camera roll. After an initial period of play there is discussion of how to recreate specific effects so that they can then work more purposefully.

There is a great sense of fun and excitement in the room as they experiment and create. At the end of the session they have many photos to choose outcomes from.

They look up the work of light artist Andy Neal for more ideas.

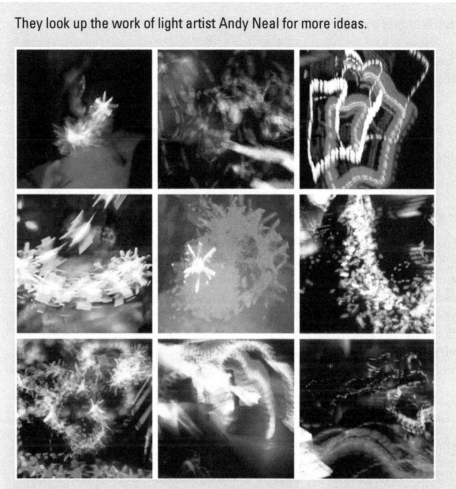

Figure 4.2 - Creating art using lights and a slow shutter app

In the example above light and apps are used to make art that exists only digitally, captured in photos in this instance. After the session teachers and students discussed how this approach could be extended by fastening lights to sticks and clothing and videoing movement in a darkened space. The connection to PE and dance was explored, as was taking the photos and manipulating them further using other apps, including adding music, sound and text.

Reflect and extend

Explore these links to find out more about how the Light and Space Movement has had a formative influence on the digital art of today:

Links:

www.artspace.com/magazine/art_101/art_market/light-and-space-52248

https://conasur.com/immerse-art-the-light-and-space-movement/

Displaying digital art

As digital art has developed it has become clear that it needs sharing and displaying in different ways than art we have collected and viewed in the past. Existing galleries have developed in response to this, for example the additions to Tate Modern in London. Digital art is often displayed in places other than galleries, being projected onto the side of buildings or onto screens around us as well as shared on social media or as augmented and virtual reality experiences. Gradually, galleries specifically featuring digital art are appearing, such as the world's first wholly digital art museum in Japan which offers an intense sensory experience. The playful nature of the digital artworks on show here makes them an accessible introduction to digital art for children and highlights the experiential possibilities that can be achieved through the interactive, immersive use of technologies.

The Mori Building Digital Art Museum in Tokyo, created in 2018 by teamLab Borderless, is the first wholly digital art museum in the world. It offers a digital art journey consisting of over fifty dynamic intermingled light and sound installations, using 530 computers and 470 projectors, which flow into one another and surround the viewer as they wander through a series of doorways into zones across the 10,000-square-metre space that constantly changes. The interactions between the visitors and the artworks are key as the exhibits evolve through the movement of people, so that the spectacular displays of light and colour are ever-fluctuating. For example, in the *Flower Forest: Lost, Immersed and Reborn*, 2017, projected flowers' growth depends on visitors' movements, and in the *Forest of Resonating Lamps*, 2016, lights change colour as they are approached.

Link: https://creativecommons.org/licenses/by-nd/2.0/

Link: www.flickr.com/photos/ginomempin/31113750598

Figure 4.3 Experiencing digital art at The Digital Art Museum in Tokyo

There is a dedicated art playground floor for children called the Athletics Forest, where they can explore and create in a 3D kaleidoscopic world filled with animated graphics, colours and lights. Within this space, children's drawings are scanned and instantly become part of an animated river of images; they can build an imaginary city by placing real objects on a digitally responsive wall; and giant balloons change colour in response to touch. Children can try bouldering in a light forest, slide down a fruity slide or jump on a bouncy floor to create planets in a space-themed area.

In describing their intentions teamLab Borderless say:

> "We want visitors to understand how digital technology can expand the conception of art. The art we create is made up of both the art and the viewer, and the existence and behaviour of the viewer can influence the art" (British Council, 2020).
>   Link: www.britishcouncil.org/anyone-anywhere/explore/digital-creativity/first-digital-art-museum

Through these interactions between people and artworks and amongst the artworks themselves, borders are dissolved between audience and art and between individual and collective responses to art. These works can never be seen in exactly the same way twice.

Find out more

Although video cannot really capture the magic of a visit to the museum, one way to offer children in England a taste of the Japanese gallery is through YouTube or 360VR videos:

Link: https://youtu.be/9jOFlhMk2K0

Link: https://youtu.be/dc_5gw1XWwY

In the classroom we can use the technology we have available to create multi-sensory environments or installations using digital technology, drawing from both the art and computing curricula. Creating a curated collection of artworks that use light and sound makes a good entry point for exploring these media in the classroom, as illustrated in the Learning in Action example below.

LEARNING IN ACTION

A group of student teachers created immersive sensory spaces combining light, sound and tactile elements for pupils to explore and add to as environments for storytelling. They used cheap and cheerful sets of lights and speakers in dark dens to create the environments. iPads with small portable projectors created interesting effects within the spaces. Pupils were creative within the spaces in several ways. They photographed the lights and manipulated them with apps such as Rollworld, BeFunky and Fragment to create abstract designs. They painted and drew with fluorescent paints and highlighter pens, sculpted with glow in the dark putty and then shone UV torches on their creations in the dark dens. They used glow drawing apps on the iPads to create their own designs in the dark. Sensory drawing apps such as Mega Photo allow for the digitisation of physical artwork or photos into animated kaleidoscopic effects, which can then be projected onto walls or onto white 3D objects, white tents or walls using a miniprojector. The ease with which different effects can be achieved with these apps helps refine children's artistic judgement as they test multiple options before selecting an effect to save as the finished piece. As children interact with the immersive spaces and exert their own influence upon them, they can draw upon the elements and principles of art to reflect upon the synergy between art, spaces and audiences. Sensory activities and experiences such as these lend a new dimension to children's perceptions of the imaginary worlds that inspired them.

The art experienced in the example above can be captured using photos and video and displayed in an online exhibition, using a tool such as ArtSteps.

Computer-generated art

Computer-generated art, also known as algorithmic art, is another key area of digital art to view and create with children. These terms apply to visual art that is generated by an algorithm – in other words, a specific set of instructions for carrying out a task. This gives rise to the art term 'algorists' to describe computer artists who use algorithms creatively (King, 2002; Bryant, 2011; Edmonds, 2018). An algorithmic procedure is a precise sequence of instructions that can be applied to mathematical operations in a computer environment. However, the term algorithm can also describe any other well-defined procedure such as a recipe, and algorithmic recipes are embedded in various strands of the arts, such as within musical scores, dance notations and even architectural plans. This strand of digital art thus has the potential to make links with the computing curriculum in schools, both through 'plugged' activities involving computer programming and 'unplugged' activities exploring the algorithms or repeated patterns and notations that occur in dance and music.

One of the pioneers of computer art in Britain was the artist Harold Cohen, who invented a computer program known as AARON in the 1960s that used an artificial intelligence system to make large drawings on paper autonomously using a small robot. Cohen then went on to colour many of these by hand. Writing about the role of the computer in art in 1974, Cohen predicted that the computer would become a fundamental tool for almost every profession, including artists (Cohen, 1974). Cohen's legacy is to influence the ways in which contemporary artists use coding as a creative language, transforming computer programming into a means of creative expression. Cohen's relationship with AARON evolved alongside the medium of computing for over forty years, with exhibitions in many of the world's major art spaces, and in 2011 he created an exhibition entitled 'Collaborations with my other self'.

Find out more

Explore these links to find out more about Cohen's work:

Link: https://computerhistory.org/blog/
harold-cohen-and-aaron-a-40-year-collaboration/

Link: www.studiointernational.com/index.php/
delving-into-coding-the-art-of-harold-cohen-aaron-computer-generated

Link: www.youtube.com/watch?v=MwHQx9BrHQc

The intersection of artificial intelligence and art has led to other forms of computer-generated art such as fractals, which generate infinite geometric patterns resembling those found in nature, or algorithmic art in which designs are automatically generated by an algorithm.

Another recognised UK artist, Ernest Edmonds, currently Professor of Computational Art at De Montfort University, has been using computational algorithms in art since the 1970s, when he began to experiment with punched cards and paper tape. Over the last fifty years, Edmonds has exhibited throughout the world and was awarded the 2017 SIGGRAPH Distinguished Artist Award for Lifetime Achievement in Digital Art. In his article, 'The Creative Process Where the Artist is Amplified or Superseded by the Computer' (Cornock and Edmonds, 1973) he outlines that the experience of interacting with computers via devices, lights, switches and objects might be a creative process for people. He imagines a future where time and interaction is central to art practice and where the artist is more concerned with setting up situations than with finishing them. In other words, the work is not complete until the audience engages with it. As the technology moved on, Edmonds was able to write software that produced colourful generative work and he began to explore the relationship between transmitted colour on a screen and reflected colour in paintings. Today we can interact directly with the computer by sound and gesture, transforming the process of generating this kind of art.

Find out more

Other early digital artists worth exploring include Frieder Nake, who programmed a plotter in the 1960s to add random elements into a drawing so that it generated chance results, and Allan Kaprow, whose work *Hello* in 1969, produced in collaboration with a television station, anticipated the connections and interactions which might take place through digital networks.

In primary schools we have access to the tools and devices we need to make algorithmic art and indeed it is a requirement of the computing curriculum in English schools that children use technology to code in this way.

Try for yourself – generating art through computing

Trying a simple computing app or tool to create art

You will need: the app or online tool Scratch

Link: https://scratch.mit.edu/

What to do:

Use repeat loops and turns to create patterns: simple algorithms for drawing polygons can be modified by adding a turn to create patterns.

A range of flower patterns can be achieved quite easily by manipulating the type of polygon, the pen colours, the degrees of turn and the numbers of repeats.

For examples to follow have a look at the chapter padlet.

To follow on from this, you might explore the four interactive art projects in the Scratch Starter Projects on the Ideas page, again making small changes and manipulating the variables to see what effects you can generate.

Link: https://scratch.mit.edu/starter-projects

A search for 'generative art' within Scratch brings up many beautiful examples of this visual art genre that are made through the use of an autonomous system. Many rely on complex code but some are simple enough for children to under-stand and modify, such as this program for generating Fibonacci flowers which produces a different design each time it is run.

Link: https://scratch.mit.edu/projects/2277214

A range of effects can be created simply by changing the shape of the sprite in this program. This is known as remixing, and it is common for people to share their remixes on the Scratch project pages so there are plenty of examples available. You can create your own collection of art designs and add your pupils' remixes within your own project space, a Scratch Studio. It is also worth noting that if you log into Scratch you get the option to save snippets of code to a 'backpack' at the bottom of the screen. This means that you can easily share your coding strategies with others if you share a class login. There are two further examples to look at on the chapter padlet.

In the activity above you will have had the opportunity to explore making art on a computer screen using tools also used in the computing curriculum in primary schools. Within Scratch you can go further if you enable the video sensing tools, which allow the onscreen sprite to react to your hand movements using the webcam on a laptop.

You might extend your exploration of art and computing to include painting or drawing with robots. A popular activity is to program Sphero robots to create abstract painting. These spherical robots come with a removable shell that can be used with paint to create abstract artworks reminiscent of the work of Jackson Pollock.

Link: https://youtu.be/obw31l-onFU

Link: https://youtu.be/EncR_T0faKM

Many of these computing-based art activities offer opportunities for children to experiment with colour and tone as their work evolves, and reflect on the role of line, shape and form. They might think about the rhythm and movement of the finished pieces and even add sound to emphasise this. Gradation is the key concept in generative art and we can consider how to control tempo, with which the generative art builds up to a climax.

Working in augmented and virtual reality

Most people are familiar with augmented reality (AR) apps that insert images into a real-life view of the world through a phone or tablet, and virtual reality (VR) apps that entirely replace what you can see using a headset. AR and VR are often referred to as two ends of the mixed reality spectrum. Familiar examples of augmented reality include Pokemon Go!, which allows you to see characters in the same space as yourself, the Merge Cube and Google AR animals, which brings creatures such as a tiger or a panda into your living room. These apps add to the reality that we ordinarily see.

Try for yourself – creating an environment for augmented reality animals

Exploring augmented reality on your table top

You will need: a mobile device, the Google Chrome browser, the screen recorder on the device, card, paper and pens

First explore this ThingLink to learn how to access and use Google AR animals:

Link: www.thinglink.com/scene/1334903388625698817

As you play with the animals try to work out how to place them on surfaces and interact with other objects to give a sense of scale and watch how they move. Practise using screen recording to capture the scene. This can be edited later to tidy up the beginning and the end.

When you are familiar with the animals choose one and use paper, card and pens to create an environment for it. You might research your animal and use this to make a realistic environment or you might play with scale, narrative and expectations to create more of a story. Film your AR animal in the environment you have created and edit the video to add music, sound effects, speech or text in any combination.

In the activity above there is a connection between making physical art and using digital devices and tools as part of the outcome. Working with the two modes allows you creativity in both and the outcome exists as a complete piece only in the digital world, as a short film that can be shared on screens, websites and social media. It can serve as an introduction to the world of augmented and virtual reality in art. Another way into this is to reverse the relationship by creating digitally drawn objects in the app AR Makr and display them with real objects. In the example above toy animals could be the 'real' objects set in an environment with digital trees, rocks and other objects. Creating these and placing the two worlds together can be an opportunity for creativity and imagination. The outcome can be screen-recorded directly within the app.

Virtual reality consists of computer-generated environments that replace what we can see with a simulated immersive experience. This can be achieved through a phone inserted into simple cardboard or plastic goggles, or through much more expensive video-gaming headsets with high quality sound and handheld controllers or gloves. Both AR and VR offer engaging experiences which can be entertaining and educational. However, they also have the potential to become environments for creating artistic content.

CoSpaces combines a free web-based application with a phone or tablet app. It enables the maker to create and engage with interactive media content by building their own virtual worlds on a computer, and then viewing and sharing them in AR or VR via the app on a mobile device. The web application includes a library of 3D objects and backgrounds to choose from, as well as tools for creating your own objects. Creating in CoSpaces can be as simple as dragging and dropping objects to create simple scenes for others to explore using the app. A visual programming tool can also be used to add animation and sound to the environments, making them more immersive.

Link: https://cospaces.io/edu

There are AR and VR options for viewing the CoSpaces creations within the mobile app. In the example on the chapter padlet, a real-life view of a virtual plate of food is shared in AR.

Alternatively, scenes can be explored using virtual reality goggles in split screen mode by clicking on the icon on the bottom right of the app. The CoSpaces website includes free resources and lesson plans, such as the virtual plate project, which aims to connect students around the world by sharing plates of food. Another CoSpaces web resource demonstrates how you could showcase students' artwork as a virtual exhibition. The free lesson plans also include a suggestion for creating an interactive artwork with sound and animation, inspired by Van Gogh's *Starry Night*. This could be extended to inviting students to respond to a range of famous artworks by creating their own interactive images. Another idea might be to create a VR sculpture trail to explore in an imagined world, or to place virtual sculptures in real world environments using the AR option.

Link: https://cospaces.io/edu/projects.html

If you are lucky enough to have access to a high-end VR system with a headset and handheld controllers you can draw, sculpt and paint in 360 using an exciting app called Tilt Brush. Tilt Brush integrates with CoSpaces and the 3D sculpting tool Blocks so that you can paint on a blank canvas or remix other people's scenes and objects. It is simple enough for children to use, offering a palette of brushes and colours that enables them to paint with a range of effects such as stars, lights, fire and rainbows as they move the handheld controller around themselves in a 3D space. You can jump to a new space in your scene and walk through and around your own artwork. Once you are finished, you can export images or animated GIFs, upload videos of your work to YouTube or even render your own 360 videos. Although primary schools are unlikely to have this equipment (as yet!) it can be accessible through secondary schools; colleges and universities; makerspaces; and as a part of projects and exhibitions in galleries.

Link: www.tiltbrush.com/

Link: https://arvr.google.com/blocks/

Figure 4.4 Drawing in a virtual reality environment with Tilt Brush

Digital technology in the classroom

There is great potential to both view and create digital art in the classroom using the devices and tools that are available in school and beyond. It can also be used to support your planning, during your teaching and as a way of recording outcomes and sharing them. In the classroom it can be integrated into each phase of a unit of work: inspiring and preparing; making; and later evaluating and reflecting on learning. This section looks at some of the issues to consider when planning to teach digital art. These include working responsibly, planning, teaching and assessment, supporting research and collecting ideas, recording and evaluating work, accessibility and using digital art within cross-curricular work.

Working responsibly

As a user of digital technologies yourself you will have developed an awareness of the need to be a responsible and safe user of the tools and resources available to you. When you are working with pupils you will be a role model and seek to equip them with the knowledge and skills to be "responsible, competent, confident and creative users" (DfE, 2013, p.230) of technology across the curriculum and in their day-to-day lives.

This will be a part of a whole-school policy and approach. It may be that particular approaches or schemes are used to underpin e-safety. There are two listed below that you can explore:

Link: www.nspcc.org.uk/keeping-children-safe/online-safety/
talking-child-online-safety/

Link: www.thinkuknow.co.uk/

You should ensure that you know the policy, approach and resources of any schools that you work in.

There are a number of safe searching tools that you can use with children, guided by the school approach and alongside your own selections of appropriate material. When looking for images to use in research or making, for example, the search tool 'photosforclass' provides access to age-appropriate visual material and YouTube Kids provides safer access to video material.

Link: www.photosforclass.com/

Link: www.youtube.com/kids/

Alongside safety, the need to learn to respect the intellectual property of users is important and can be addressed in the context of art. As a student you will be used to protecting academic integrity by using a system such as Harvard to cite and reference your sources, both written and visual. As a teacher you can apply the same principles of respect to the work of others. When you are searching for material to use your search should be modified to find only sources that can be reused with or without modification and you should search only for images that are licensed through Creative Commons. The image search mentioned above (photosforclass) only searches Creative Commons images and a citation providing source information is embedded in each image. When you use material made by others it is essential that you acknowledge the maker and not just take the resource and use it as if you had made it yourself. Sometimes this will mean that you have less choice available to you but it is vital that plagiarising the work of others is avoided in all situations.

Many schools and educational institutions now engage in the world of social media. At its best it can be a source of support, inspiration and collaboration. In the recent pandemic many educators and creative people generously shared ideas and resources to support schools, teachers and families working in different situations than usual. As people working in education and with the future users of social media, our pupils, it is vital that we are role models of using it for good. It will be important that you follow any policies or guidelines that your school or institution has developed.

Find out more – social media and art

Exploring social media and learning in art

You will need: the pro forma below and a mobile device to access the internet

Use the social media accounts you already have to find useful and inspiring accounts relating to art teaching. These might include Facebook (groups and pages), Twitter, Instagram, Pinterest, YouTube, etc.

Activity – Exploring social media and learning in art

	Names of accounts	**Notes**
Artists		
Art educators		
Organisations		
Schools		
Galleries		
Companies / businesses		

Guidance notes

As a user of social media you might have a professional online persona that you use for following and interacting with others as part of your work. Looking for interesting and inspirational people and organisations to follow can give you access to ideas, resources and advice that you could not access in any other way. Many artists share their work and information about upcoming exhibitions, as do art galleries and arts organisations. Some of these might be online or have related online resources and events. Many teachers and art educators share their work through social media, allowing you to expand your professional network way beyond your colleagues in school. As well as primary practitioners and schools it is also useful to follow and learn from secondary art colleagues, whose specialist subject knowledge can be supportive and a source of understanding of the next stage for primary children. If you are using specific tools, apps and materials it can be worth following the companies who make them for tips, problem-solving and support, and some have education programmes and ambassadors working with schools.

The activity above is applicable to all your professional activity online. In relation to art and digital technology it can be especially useful and supportive.

Find out more

A school: look up Gomersal Primary Art on Twitter (@GomersalArt) and find their blog.

Link: http://gomersalprimaryschoolart.blogspot.com/

Browse their interesting and inspirational art practice and consider how it might influence your own approach.

Planning, teaching and assessment

At the planning stage digital technology is a wonderful tool for research which enables you to find out more about artists, craftspeople and designers and choose examples of their work. Tools such as Padlet, Pocket, Pinterest and Flickr can be useful for collecting images together in groups to use in teaching. You can find out more about how colleagues in other schools are planning and developing learning in art through national and international subject associations (NSEAD, InSEA) and make connections with other teachers to get inspiration and support through social networking tools such as Twitter and Instagram. Many art galleries and arts organisations also have plans, demonstrations and activity ideas that you can download and adapt to enhance and develop your planning.

You might begin by thinking about evaluating the simple tools and resources that you already have at hand. For example, as part of your teaching you can use video clips of artists demonstrating media and processes or talking about their work. Hardware such as the visualiser or the digital microscope can be useful in art. The visualiser allows you to look at images or items with the image being projected onto the IWB and you can zoom in for a closer look. It can also allow pupils to see your own demonstrations close up. The photocopier can be a useful tool in teaching too. Making copies of children's drawings so several next steps can be tried, or resizing them to make them larger so additional detail can be added, helps preserve an original whilst developing and experimenting.

Digital photography and video can also be used to make supporting visual resources for teaching. This could include prompts and exemplifications to remind children of teaching points as well as step-by-step sequences of processes to help children recall what to do when. Labelled diagrams and layouts can help children organise materials and become more independent in choosing, setting up and clearing away. Using photos of the actual resources that children use in your classroom can make these prompts more meaningful and user-friendly to some children. Filming short sequences as reminders of demonstrations can also be useful to review at the start of the next lesson.

Digital media can provide a means of saving and sharing children's work for recording and assessment and is especially useful when work is of large scale, is collaborative or three-dimensional or consists of ephemeral pieces of art for which you might have little storage space. Taking photos and videos of outcomes and steps along the way and then storing these electronically can help overcome the challenge of storage and can also facilitate online or IWB sharing and feedback.

Research and collecting ideas

Today's devices make it easy for children to work with digital images and videos and these can then become versatile and useful resources or forms of expression in their own right. However, when working with media it is important to focus children and ensure that they know what they looking for as it is all too easy to take many photos at random. When taking photos with your class, aim to identify a specific focus such as collecting bright and dull colours or examples of different types of leaves, so that children observe and select carefully. It can be useful to set a certain number of photos so that children make three good choices rather than ten less useful ones – perhaps choosing those to keep and those to delete.

Bear in mind that the camera on a device itself offers opportunities such as zooming in and later cropping and changing images.

LEARNING IN ACTION

A class of Year 5 and 6 children are going to be making art based on faces and portraits. Their teacher has collected a large selection of images that the class can browse through at the preparation stage. Each child is asked to choose three images that catch their attention and save them to look at and talk about. Each child identifies what it is about the image that engages them in a conversation with peers: the media used, a visual element such as colour or shape or the subject matter itself. Later these ideas may form part of what each child goes on to make in their own art. It is this stage of selecting and talking about the images that is important in learning.

In the experience above older children have had the opportunity to choose images that interest them from a larger range, rather than being presented with the work of one artist chosen by the teacher. Using digital media in this way can give children wider opportunities to develop their knowledge and follow their interests, selecting and explaining their choices. An extension from this activity might be to look at the work of Eadweard Muybridge, an early pioneer of photography who captured people and animals in action. Muybridge is known for his experiments in photographing motion, which showed that a trotting horse lifts all four legs off the ground at once. Children can explore the idea of stop-action photography by looking at Muybridge's sequences of animal locomotion images, relating the images of birds to our understanding of early aviation and thinking about how we can understand motions such as dance differently through the lens of a zoopraxiscope. They can set a self-timer on a mobile device to take a sequence of photos of a physical movement and then use a GIF maker to upload the photos and adjust the delay to create their own Muybridge effect.

Link: https://imgflip.com/gif-maker

Link: www.youtube.com/watch?v=2KnnGeNrvdE

Choosing tools

As we have seen, digital media can support the creation of art in other media or it can provide an exciting medium in its own right. When working with other media and processes in art it is important to consider how some hardware and software can make life easier and allow children to be more independent. Teaching children to use a computer or photocopier to copy, expand, reduce and flip to mirror images can be very useful. When children choose images or create their own, resizing or having several copies to experiment on knowing that the original will not be lost in the process can help them make more adventurous choices of next steps.

Most schools have software specifically for creating images on computers as well as apps that involve drawing or manipulating images on mobile devices. Using tools to create and manipulate images can allow children the opportunity to make something they could not make in any other way. When planning a digital learning outcome it is important to consider how the qualities of the tools provide a unique contribution to the learning for the individual child or class, beyond that of being merely a different way to paint or draw. This will be explored more fully in relation to painting in chapter 8.

Digital technology gives both us and children different ways to see the world. On many mobile devices there is a magnifier present as part of the camera and apps can be downloaded that magnify even further. Looking at common materials and items close up can be interesting both scientifically and for art. Clip-on lenses can be bought to attach to mobile devices that distort and create new views and we can use Google Earth to access an aerial view of the world that provides another way into responding to the landscape.

As part of evaluating, recording and sharing

Digital technology can be a useful tool for allowing children to record progress and consider next steps. Taking photographs or scanning work at significant moments can allow older children especially the opportunity to articulate their decisions and evaluate their work. They can keep a record of each step of a shared project and identify their role in its creation and take photos of several views of a three-dimensional work before taking it home. When creating an image onscreen this can be saved under the same title but a different date each time it is worked on, so next steps can be seen by the child and by adults supporting and later assessing progress over time. It is possible to add a spoken commentary to photos of artwork in PowerPoint and this can allow for reflection and explanation from the child without the need to write.

It is relatively straightforward to share children's art work on school screens, school websites and through school social media accounts, respecting school policies that relate to these locations. Google Slides, PowerPoint and other software and apps can be used to create slideshows. Specific tools and sites, such as ArtSteps, allow you to create virtual reality exhibition spaces and populate them with photos and video of children's art that can be viewed online, through apps on Google and Apple or through VR headsets.

Link: www.artsteps.com/

Digital technology and accessibility

Digital art has much to offer pupils with special educational needs and disabilities (SEND). It offers an alternative means of expression for exploring and communicating issues and personal reflections, and the opportunity to be expressive in an accessible medium can diffuse frustrations. For many students who struggle to communicate their thoughts and feelings through words, digital art provides non-verbal modes of expression. For those with physical disabilities, accessible tools such as switches, eye gaze or touch screens provide alternative input devices and a motivating context for learning. Virtual reality software such as Tilt Brush offers immersive art opportunities, as does the use of technology-enabled sensory spaces described earlier in this chapter (Learning in Action).

LEARNING IN ACTION

An international group of children with special needs visited a class of children in England as part of an exchange programme on the theme of 'Sounds Around Us'. Inspired by the idea of noisy paintings promoted by the National Gallery and Henri Rousseau's jungle scene, Cornelia Parker's exploding shed and David Hockney's water scene, children used the app Keezy to record sounds onto coloured tiles which became a keyboard to compose music in response to the paintings, using trays of sensory and sound equipment. They used coloured cards to create a notation for their compositions so that they could read and repeat them. They then videoed their performances of the sound compositions representing their responses to the art. The video performances and compositions were swapped so that each group could use them to create a collaborative collage in response to each other's sounds, inspired by Kandinsky's images. In this way the Keezy app enabled pupils to respond to an artwork through sound and then use the recording as an impetus for more art.

To extend this work, pupils might listen to a voice recording of a peer describing an artwork and their response to it, and then respond or reconstruct by creating a new artwork using Sketchnote.

Link: Accessible digital art tools: www.ldonline.org/article/30245/

Conclusion

There is so much creative potential available to us through using digital technology in the art curriculum. As readers you will all be in different situations with regards to the technology you own yourself or have access to through your work or locally through organisations such as galleries, makerspaces, universities and projects. It is important to use what you have to its full potential yourself as well as with the children you work with, keeping alert to the possibility of accessing more cutting-edge technologies. If you look back on your own education and compare what was available then technologically to what you now use day-to-day, the difference will be clear. Keeping up with change and development will help you equip your pupils for the world they are moving into at secondary school and beyond.

Next steps

Explore this Padlet of resources for using augmented and virtual reality in education: https://uon1.padlet.org/jean_edwards/ARVRJE

Look out for examples of art created or shared using digital technology local to you and on social media.

Talk with the computing subject leader and others with an interest and expertise in this area of the curriculum about the devices and tools available to you and support with using them.

References

British Council. (2020) *Inside the world's first digital museum.* [online] Available from: www.britishcouncil.org/anyone-anywhere/explore/digital-creativity/first-digital-art-museum [Accessed 21/07/2020].

Bryant, R., Weiss, R., Orr, G. and Yerion, K. (2011) Using the context of algorithmic art to change attitudes in introductory programming. *Journal of Computing Sciences in Colleges.* **Vol 27**, No 1, pp.112–119.

Cohen, H. (1974) On purpose: an enquiry into the possible roles of the computer in art. *Studio International.* **Vol 187**, No 962, pp.9–16.

Cornock, S. and Edmonds, E. (1973) The creative process where the artist is amplified or superseded by the computer. *Leonardo.* **Vol 6**, No 1, pp.11–16.

DfE. (2014) *The national curriculum in England Framework document.* [online] Available from: https://assets.publishing.service.gov.uk/government/uploads/system/uploads/attachment_data/file/381344/Master_final_national_curriculum_28_Nov.pdf [Accessed 23/09/2020].

Edmonds, E. (2018) Algorithmic art machines. *Arts.* **Vol 7**, No 1, p.3.

Gayford, M. (2011) *A Bigger Message. Conversations with David Hockney.* London: Thames and Hudson.

Gollifer, S. (2000) Artist Space 4 'Tradigital imaging'. *Digital Creativity*, **Vol 11**, No 4, pp.234–248.

King, M. (2002) Computers and modern art: digital art museum. In: *Proceedings of the 4th conference on creativity & cognition* (pp.88–94). ACM.

Tate (2020a) *New Media*. [online] Available from: www.tate.org.uk/art/art-terms/n/new-media [Accessed: 20/07/2020].

Tate (2020b) *Digital Art*. [online] Available from: www.tate.org.uk/art/art-terms/d/digital-art [Accessed 20/07/2020].

Further resources

Caldwell, H. and Cullingford-Agnew, S. (2017) *Technology for SEND in primary schools*. London: Learning Matters.

Dede C.J., Jacobson J. and Richards J. (2017) Introduction: Virtual, Augmented, and Mixed Realities in Education. In: Liu D., Dede C., Huang R. and Richards J. (eds). *Virtual, Augmented, and Mixed Realities in Education*. Singapore: Springer. Pp.1–19.

Dunleavy, M., Dede, C. and Mitchell, R. (2009) Affordances and Limitations of Immersive Participatory Augmented Reality Simulations for Teaching and Learning. *Journal of Science Education and Technology*. **Vol 18**, No 1, pp.7–22.

Edwards, J. (2014) Inspired by Digital. *AD the NSEAD magazine*. **Issue 11**. Pp.24–25.

Chapter Padlet:

https://padlet.com/Jeanne/Chapter4

05

Chapter Five

Planning and assessing art

Introduction

As with any area of the curriculum, planning supports learning and allows us to organise content, ensure progression and consider the breadth and balance of the learning experiences. Most schools will have some or all of their planning for art in place and often plans will be reused and adapted for teaching from one year to the next. Whilst having plans in place is supportive and timesaving, retaining some flexibility can allow you to include new and different resources and events that can enrich learning, as well as respond to children's and the school's interests. At the early stages of teaching it is likely that the reassurance of having plans in place will be essential for your confidence and workload but as your teaching skills and experience develop you will increasingly value the freedom to follow your own creative ideas. In this chapter the following areas will be explored:

- The curriculum map
- Planning for a half term
- Assessing learning in art

The curriculum map or long-term plan outlines the content, indicating what will be covered and when. The expectations for a half term, a unit of work or a sequence of lessons provide more detail and indicate resources. There are aspects of good practice in learning and teaching across the curriculum that also apply in art lessons and there are some aspects of art that generate additional and different considerations that can be explored in planning.

The curriculum map

The curriculum map outlines the overall content of what will be covered and often it allocates content to specific terms or half terms in year groups across the school. The school's art policy underpins this and gives you an understanding of the bigger picture of art in the school. Looking at this curriculum map allows you to understand what the children have already experienced and what they will go on to explore in art in future years. It can give you a sense of the progression of skills, knowledge and understanding throughout the child's experience in the subject at the school, which will be invaluable when you are planning and teaching your part in this overall learning continuum. As a student, new teacher or teaching assistant (TA) this is likely to be a document that you use, but if you have the opportunity to be involved in writing one it will help your understanding of the overall curriculum enormously. It is likely to be in the form of a grid, although it is increasingly common to map out the journey through a subject in a more visual form, which makes it more accessible to the user.

It is at this stage that links can be identified between two or three subject areas where these will enhance learning. Out-of-school visits, visitors to the school and participation in local and national events can also be planned well in advance using this framework. The curriculum map should provide a guide for the content of your teaching. When you consult it to find out more about the next half term it is most unlikely to be in a form that you can pick up and teach directly from. It might indicate the media or process, a digital tool, one or more visual elements and the work of one or some artists that may form part of the learning.

The elements in a curriculum map

In a curriculum map you might expect to find some or all of the following elements:

- techniques or processes

You will need to know which media, techniques and processes you will be supporting or teaching throughout the year so that you can ensure you have the appropriate subject knowledge or identify gaps that you need to address. In addition to this you will need, within the broader headings of 'painting' or 'printmaking' or 'sculpture', more detail about what is expected. If the long-term plan states 'painting' you need to know what sort of paint and how this experience builds on previous use of paint. If it notes using digital tools you will need to know if you are introducing a new app or tool or developing the use of a familiar one. You can also use this to check that you have the required resources available at the time that you will be teaching the unit.

- subject knowledge and vocabulary

It will be important that you know which one or two visual elements (line, tone, colour, pattern, texture, shape, form and space) will be underpinning the learning and teaching in the unit. You will need to be sure that you make coherent connections between the specified visual elements. If no visual elements are noted you need to check which ones would best fit the media or process and artists' work stated in the long-term plan and will build on children's prior experience. These will also have implications for the vocabulary and the activities that you plan to use with children.

- works of artists, designers or craftspeople

If the work of an artist is specified it is important that you can access resources to use in your teaching. You may need to check that there are good reproductions available in school or that they are available digitally. If the artists, designers or craftspeople are unfamiliar to you, you may need to do some personal research so that you know some background information about them and their work and how their work relates to the techniques and visual elements you are teaching.

- strong and meaningful links to other curriculum areas

When you look at the overall long-term plan or curriculum map for all subjects, cross-curricular links may be identified or you may be able to move content around to enable productive links to be made. It will be important that you retain the integrity of the learning in art for the children you are teaching. When considering using digital tools and techniques within art and design it is important to identify how these connect to the computing curriculum across the school.

- Your questions to follow up

Depending on the detail available you may have some gaps and questions that you need to follow up. Colleagues teaching the same year group, the teacher who taught the class the year before and the art coordinator are all people who could be of help with this.

Find out more

Search for examples of long-term plans, curriculum maps and curriculum overviews for art.

These will vary in the level of detail supplied.

Consider what would be helpful to you in terms of understanding what a child would learn and experience in art as they progress through the school and how you, in your year group, would plan and support that in a sequence of lessons and a series of half terms.

Building on prior learning

Looking at the curriculum map can give you an understanding of the techniques or processes, artists' work and inspirations or contexts for previous learning in this area. When planning a sequence of lessons, it is important to consider the prior knowledge, skills and understanding of the children you will be working with. Asking yourself some questions may help you make some decisions about what you are planning or adapting. It may be that with some small changes you can have a unit of work that advances learning more effectively. The chart below outlines some questions you might consider when building on the prior knowledge, skills and understanding of the children you teach. It gives some examples in the context of printmaking.

Using prior knowledge to support planning

Questions	Considerations for your planning – could you...	Examples (context of printmaking)
Which aspects of the technique / process have the children experienced before?	introduce a new aspect of the technique / process?	The children have printed with objects, used polystyrene tiles in KS1 and they will go on to make card prints in Y3.
How much independence did children have in using the technique / process?	expect the children to use the technique with more independence? give children more choice in the response they have or the outcome they make? give children more choice in which processes they use?	The children made pressprints with help in Y1 and go on to make and print with greater independence and complexity in Y2. Children have experienced pressprint and card printing in Y1 and in Y5 they choose between the two.
Which visual elements were the focuses of the units?	develop a technique / process experienced with a focus on different visual elements?	The children have explored pattern and line in printmaking in KS1 and go on to explore colour and shape in KS2.
What inspired the art work? (observation, experience, imagination)	aim for an outcome inspired by a different area?	Children have used natural forms as inspiration in Y4 and in Y6 respond to the built environment.
What scale did the children work on?	plan for a different scale of outcome?	Children have made small prints in KS1 and in Y3 make a large sheet of printed wrapping paper (A2).
Did the children produce individual, group or whole class outcomes?	plan an outcome that requires a shared response?	Children have made individual prints throughout KS1 and go on to make a large collaborative textile banner in Y4.
Which artists' work have the children looked at in relation to the technique / process?	inspire or relate to the work of an unfamiliar artist?	In Y3 four children look at the work of Norman Ackroyd when monoprinting. In Y5 they explore the work of a local artist who makes collagraphs.
From which places and times have children looked at art in relation to the technique / process?	use the work of an artist or art from a different place, time or culture to inspire a response?	Y1 children have looked at Indian fabrics and William Morris patterns. In Y3 they look at medieval clay tiles.

Questions	Considerations for your planning – could you…	Examples (context of printmaking)
Have the children experienced the technique / process linked to another curriculum subject?	link the art unit to another curriculum subject?	Y3 children explore rotation, transformation and tessellation of shapes in both printmaking and maths. In Y6 children scan their small prints into the computer and develop them further on screen.
Have children linked the technique / aspect to another art technique or process?	link two techniques or processes?	In Y2 children make wax resist backgrounds to print their pressprint animals onto.

As you plan, or consider adapting existing planning to meet the needs of the children in your class, you also need to ensure that you are clear about the progress they can make in the unit of work. You might ask yourself:

- What will the children know, or know more about, at the end of the unit of work?

- What will the children be able to do, or do better, at the end of the unit of work?

- What will the children understand, or understand more about, at the end of the unit of work?

In your school

Investigate the resources available to you to support planning:

- In school: published schemes that the school has bought in
- Online: websites of galleries, museums, arts organisations
- At university: in the art room and in the library

There is great potential in the art curriculum for planning learning experiences that allow individuals to respond in their own way, expressing themselves and following their own creative impulses. As teachers, our role in planning activities and units of work and working with children in art lessons to facilitate, encourage and value individual responses is vital. It is important that we try to avoid ending up with thirty outcomes at the end of a sequence of lessons or a unit of work that are largely the same or at best very similar, with no real personal expression in evidence from the children who made the art: what Barnes (2002) refers to as the "predetermined, end-product thought-trap" (p.29). Whilst teaching a new process step-by-step is important in skills development, application should be an opportunity to personalise the response.

There are a number of reasons why outcomes can become the same or overly similar. If we plan too tightly and restrict children's opportunities to explore, experiment and make their own choices at each stage of a unit of work any personal and individual response is squeezed out. At the early stages of learning to plan and teach art as adults we are often dependent on a scheme of work or tried and tested plans. It can be difficult to identify where to allow children choices and manage the divergent routes and outcomes that result from these. Time, space and organisation of materials and resources can be a challenge, as well as the pressure from other subjects in the curriculum. Although there may be challenges to the possibility of supporting and encouraging personal expression, in art it is vital to overcome these and aim to plan some opportunities for children to follow their own ideas and pathways. If we deny them this opportunity in their experience of art in school and focus solely on learning and using skills and making drawings, paintings and other outcomes their understanding of something vital to art – the impulse and inspiration that makes people want to create art – can be stifled. Drawing on these feelings of needing to experiment and make something in order to fulfil a personal drive rather than serve a function is important in education and learning overall and especially so in art. This drive or inspiration can lead children to be motivated learners, determined and creative in their approach and willing to persevere and work hard to achieve their goal. The sense of satisfaction from pursuing learning as well as being absorbed in a piece of work is an important aspect of being a learner.

In some other subjects there are predetermined learning objectives, sometimes supported with success criteria or learning outcomes. In art, the element of uncertainty when giving children choices and allowing them to pursue a more personal impulse can feel unsettling. It is important to use what we know about effective teaching combined with our understanding of learning in art to plan, support and teach the subject with sensitivity. For children, often used to being set a very clear goal and indication of what learning will look like in other subjects, having more freedom in their learning can be unsettling: some children may have had little freedom or control over their own art work since their experience of art in the early years. When everyone in the class is making basically the same thing some children are more likely to compare their own art to that of others and judge themselves harshly, leading to a loss of confidence or enjoyment of the process.

Planning for a half term

Following on from the overview discussed above, more detail is usually provided at the half term stage, perhaps through a school written medium plan or published scheme of work. The structure and content of this is likely to vary from school to school, especially in terms of format and detail. The plans are likely to be influenced by how learning and teaching is organised in the school. It may be that art is taught for one lesson a week, every week, or art may be taught in a series of lessons in one week or linked to another subject and these two taught together. There are a range of sources of planning available to use or adapt. These include units from published schemes of work that the school has collected or bought, school-devised units of work that relate to the school's interests and local activities and resources collected from an online source. Schools may draw upon any or a combination of these sources for planning learning and teaching in each half term. Where there are resources available to you at this stage this is supportive of your workload, but if there are fewer resources you could view this as an opportunity to experiment and be creative with what you plan for the children.

The structure over half a term

One approach to the structure of a unit of work at the half term stage can be outlined following these phases: firstly, inspiring and preparing to create art; secondly, making art; and finally, reflecting on learning. These can be followed through a sequence of weekly separate lessons over a half term or a continuous experience over a shorter, more concentrated period of time. They are a useful of way of helping you to think about the sorts of learning and teaching experiences that are appropriate throughout an art unit of work. The length of each phase will depend on what you plan to teach and the time available overall and is likely to vary from unit to unit.

There is more than one way of organising learning and you should be flexible so that the sequence of learning that you plan will support learning rather than fit into a predetermined pattern. Alternative approaches include blocking together the time available for art into a compressed period of time to allow for more intensive work. This can be especially useful when using materials that are difficult to get out and put away on a weekly basis. It can also allow for children to become more absorbed in their exploration and learning because they don't have to stop and start. You might also consider pairing learning in art with another subject, as long as this supports learning in both. Within lessons, you should consider how time can be used effectively and give thought to the balance between your teaching and the children working practically. You should also consider how long clearing away and reorganising the classroom might take. Considering approximate timings can guide you and ensure that any supporting adults know how much time is available for different parts of the lesson.

Inspiring and preparing

At the beginning of a unit of work you will be starting to explore an aspect of art with the children you are supporting or teaching. This may be a new technique or a different approach to a familiar technique. It may be introducing a different source of inspiration, starting point or work of art, design or craft. It could be a different sort of outcome involving size or scale or an individual, group or whole class collaborative outcome. If you have considered the children's prior knowledge, skills and understanding from the curriculum map you will have a clearer picture of the new learning planned for this unit.

In the early stages of a unit of work you could be planning to collect ideas in sketchbooks and be researching from books and online. You might be encouraging children to explore how to use unfamiliar tools and materials freely or teaching an entirely new technique or process. You could be planning for children to refine and consolidate skills in using a known technique or reminding them how to use familiar tools and develop their precision and independence of use. You will probably recap on previously learned vocabulary as well as introducing new vocabulary.

This is a vital stage in a unit of work. It is very difficult for anyone, child or artist, to create a meaningful piece of art from nowhere. In this stage the exploration and development of ideas allows children time to become inspired, to gather the ideas and explore the tools and processes that will contribute to the art they will make in the next phase of the unit. I know myself that my finished prints evolve over time from ideas in my sketchbook, responses to classes / workshops I attend, visits to exhibitions and the impetus of sharing work with others. Imagine if you were given a set of watercolours, for example, and asked to make your piece of art immediately. Your response would be quite different than if you had been shown how to use the watercolours, been allowed to experiment with them, looked at the work of an artist who uses watercolours and then been given some choices and ideas to inspire your painting.

Try for yourself – starting points

Exploring the range of responses that can be inspired by the same starting point

You will need: the pro forma

What to do: Take the starting point 'in the woods' and the technique of making collages. Identify as many different ideas as you can for using collage techniques to respond to this starting point. Look at the list of collage techniques in chapter 10 to support you in this task. Explore the links relating to Eva Jospin and the exhibition 'Among the trees'. Aim for giving children opportunities to respond individually and creatively.

Activity – Starting points
In the woods

Guidance notes

When you are working from a starting point that you have chosen or that has been chosen for you there can be scope to inspire a wide range of personal responses even when children are using the same media to work with.

If you are able to take children to the woods or a group of trees on your site or nearby some children will want to respond to what they see by making quite representational collages using digital photos; collecting woods / forest type images from magazines or from online images; using papers of different sorts to recreate the scene; or combinations of these. You can encourage children to go beyond the representative by getting them to sit and listen to sounds around them or lie on the ground and look up at trees and the sky as well as feeling tree trunks. This can lead some children to make more abstract collages based on their response to senses other than their vision. Also, looking close up at tree trunks, bark and leaves using a magnification app on a mobile device could lead to collages that take a tiny part and enlarge it or recreate the texture. Recording of sounds could also be included, to make the experience more multisensory and lead to a more installation type response.

If you are unable to visit the woods or trees you could make a sequence of images of woods and forests using photographic images and images from art, such as the work of Eva Jospin, and including illustrations from children's literature. The images that you select to develop the starting point can inspire different responses than had you visited the wood. You might choose images suggestive of the mysterious and dark quality of woods in fairy tales; the stillness of winter; or the bursting to life that happens in the spring. This can lead children to respond imaginatively by trying to convey a sense of time or atmosphere in their collages.

Taking this one starting point, there are many possibilities for children making collages individually or together. You will probably have identified different ideas than those discussed above, depending on your experience and interests.

In the exercise above you were encouraged to approach a starting point with the idea of allowing children to express themselves in their work. With younger children this could be within the same technique, such as collage; with older children you might go beyond this, allowing choice between several techniques or processes or combinations of two perhaps. As well as constructing individual and small-scale collages there is scope for planning work on a larger scale and work that is made, appreciated and then deteriorates naturally or is deliberately removed, perhaps inspired by the work of artists Andy Goldsworthy or James Brunt. This can also provide an opportunity for children to work together in groups, making decisions about designs and allocating tasks amongst the group.

Making art, craft and design

In the middle of the sequence you will be planning for the children to work towards making art by using their inspiration and experiences in exploring and developing ideas. By this time the children should know whether they will be working individually, in pairs, in small groups or as a whole class. They should know the scale they will be working on. Perhaps each child will make a small individual piece that will contribute to a greater whole, such as making a square of fabric work that will become part of a collaborative wall hanging. Alternatively, each child may make a larger individual outcome. There are opportunities in art to create temporary outcomes that exist for a short time and then are gone, after being captured by photography and video, so it may be that this allows a greater range of responses.

Evaluating and reflecting on learning

Opportunities to stop and reflect should be planned in at any stage of the unit to help children make decisions and think about their art. Towards the conclusion of a unit, as children begin to come to the end of making their art, work plans should include opportunities for children to talk about it as they complete it and after it is finished.

At Key Stage 1 children may either be self-assessing by thinking about what they have learned and produced freely or supported by using prompts or shared success criteria. They could be describing their own work and be beginning to peer assess by talking about and asking questions about the work of other children. They could be considering what they would have done next or what they might have changed, without actually making these changes. It can be useful to capture these comments by annotating them or making a short screen recording of a photo of the piece of art and the child talking about it.

At Key Stage 2 children will be building on this supported self and peer assessment by having the opportunity to make changes to their work in order to develop it further. This will need to be structured and supported, as it is easy to do something that changes the piece of art irrevocably and leads to disappointment. Strategies leading to evaluating and developing work could include stopping just before the piece of work is finished and reviewing it whilst there is still scope for making change or making a copy or taking a photo of the work before changes are made.

At both key stages deciding on a title for a finished piece of work can be a purposeful final activity. This can also include a short explanatory statement about the art and how and why it was made. It is important that you consider when it is appropriate to evaluate and develop work within the unit and leave enough time to do this. It is easy for children to finish their piece of art towards the end of the last lesson and have no time to stop and think and enjoy and appreciate their art and that of others. One of the purposes of art is to be shared with an audience and responded to by viewers, so this should be part of the experience that you plan for children.

LEARNING IN ACTION

In a mixed Year 1 and 2 class children look back at the collages they have worked on over several lessons. They use a short list of prompts that their teacher has prepared for them to help them consider their finished work. These prompts include:

- What are you most pleased with about your collage?
- What did you find most difficult?
- What did you enjoy?
- How would you change your collage if you could?
- What have you learned about making collages?

The younger children think about their checklist with a teaching assistant to support them and scribe their responses. Some children write their own thoughts down. The teaching assistant and the teacher make some suggestions for children to choose from where necessary and children also have their own ideas. Their evaluations are placed in their sketchbooks to mark the end of the unit of work. Their teacher photographs each collage and displays them on a series of slides and each child is given the opportunity to say a couple of sentences about their slide using screen recording. The slideshow is displayed on the school screens around the school and is shared with parents on the school website.

Figure 5.1 Children make evaluative comments in conversation about their art

In this case study younger children are supported to evaluate and changes are discussed but not made. With older children this evaluation stage could be planned at an earlier stage, leaving time and scope to make changes. Questions and prompts would ask more of the children in terms of analysing their own work and making connections to the ideas that had led to it. In both cases the learning objectives can be taken as an initial guide for the evaluative questions or prompts.

Within this stage the children's art can be shared with an audience. This is another aspect of evaluating the work – people other than the artists themselves looking at the art, making comments, asking questions and showing that they are interested in and value the children's art work. This could be through display within school or outside school, taking photos of the art and showing the photos on the IWB for parents to see either in the classroom, in an assembly, on the school website or shared on social media. Staging a mini exhibition by displaying finished pieces and sketchbooks at home time, so that parents can come in and see the work, can also be an exciting end to the unit.

An alternative approach

You might consider an alternative approach to the one outlined above. The Studio Thinking Project presents eight studio habits of mind that we can use to help our pupils think and act like artists. These are: develop craft; engage and persist; envision; express; observe; reflect; stretch and explore; and understand art worlds (Hogan *et al.*, 2018, p.4). They are deliberately listed by the authors in alphabetical order as no single habit of mind is considered to be more important than any other and they overlap and interact with each other. The eight habits were derived from research into what art teachers teach and how they organise their teaching. Considering your planning in relation to each of these can provoke different insights into what you might make available for children to do in their art learning. It can be useful to consider different pedagogical approaches, especially those focused on the subject itself and not derived from teaching all subjects generically.

Reflect and extend

Find this website: www.studiothinking.org/the-framework.html (Studio Thinking, 2018).

Read about the framework in the 'about' section. There are some useful diagrams and charts that summarise it there.

Browse the other materials on the website.

Lesson planning

The approach to lesson planning will undoubtedly vary from school to school and the presence or absence of some elements may well depend on the level of detail available in other areas of planning. In this context we are referring to anything that you have in front of you in the lesson that you are using for teaching or supporting children. The format you choose or that is used by the school should be one that supports your teaching or support and the children's learning. It must be shared with or be available to all adults working in the lesson before the lesson occurs. If you are a teaching assistant who supports groups or individuals with particular needs within the lesson you are likely to need the lesson information in time to be able to suggest and make modifications to meet the needs of the children you work with. The lesson could include: what the children will learn and how this will be demonstrated; resources; vocabulary; health and safety information where relevant; inclusion, with a focus on the pupils in the class; classroom organisation and timings.

Schools usually have a policy that guides learning and teaching, including the way learning objectives and success criteria are constructed and shared. This should be followed in your planning and teaching of art lessons whilst taking into consideration the way children learn in art, which perhaps requires a different approach than in some other subjects. The Assessment Reform Group (2002) included learning goals and the sharing of the criteria by which they will be assessed as one of the ten principles of Assessment for Learning, noting that : "Understanding and commitment follows when learners have some part in decid-ing goals and identifying criteria for assessing progress" (ARG, 2002, p.2). Wiliam (2011, p.69) acknowledged the complexity of devising these, noting the role of teacher expertise and the need to consider how best to formulate and share them with children to avoid a formulaic approach. This approach can be applied when planning for learning in art, although it is also important to allow space for other important aspects of the art experience to be pursued by the learner.

When you are identifying learning objectives you may be guided by suggestions in published materials, but it is likely you will need to modify these to make them more focused on the learning of the class you are teaching. You may also need to make some of them more small-scale, or break them down into a series of smaller steps related to each lesson. It is likely that you will need to express them in more accessible language for the children you teach. It is most important that you devise learning objectives that are expressions of what you plan for the children to learn, not what they will do or the context of the activity. This is a vital distinc-tion to understand. As Clarke (2014, p.81) suggests, this allows children to begin to understand that what they are learning may be applied beyond the single activity or context that they are currently working on and make connections between the skills, knowledge and understanding they are learning.

Try for yourself – expressing what children will learn

Considering effective learning objectives in art lessons

In this task you will look critically at learning objectives in order to think about how to write clear and effective learning objectives for your lessons.

You will need: the pro forma below or a copy of it

What to do:

Use the learning objectives suggested below or replace them with learning objectives from your own planning. Consider each learning objective against the questions listed on the pro forma.

Activity – Expressing what children will learn

	Learning objective (LO)	Is the LO focused on what the children will be <u>learning</u>? If not, rewrite it so it is focused on learning	Is the LO written in language accessible to the children? If not, rewrite it so it is accessible to children
A	To draw what you can see through the window		
B	To explore how to create tone using drawing materials		
C	To develop the skills of observation and recording through drawing in a variety of media		
D	To draw what you can see using lines		
E	To paint the flowers		
F	To collect ten digital images that represent the word 'identity' to you		
G	To explore the colours you can make with red and blue		
H	To use Sketches Pro to make a picture of a landscape		
I	To combine the visual and tactile qualities of materials and processes and to match these qualities to the purpose of the work		
J	To make and decorate a clay pot		

Questions to consider:

- Some of these learning objectives are very firmly focused on the completion of one specific activity. LOs A, E, H and J merely describe the activity that the children will do rather than what they will learn by doing the activity. In rewriting these you have to identify what skills, knowledge or understanding could have been learned and write a learning objective based on this. Clearly, there are many opportunities for learning within these activities so you must select and prioritise on the basis of your unit for the work and the children you are teaching. Possibilities for A could include 'to use line in your drawing' or 'to explore what a 4B pencil can do'; for E they could include 'to paint from observation'; for H they could include 'to explore the tools of Sketches Pro' or the tools could be specified; and for J they could include 'to join clay coils' or 'to carve into a clay surface'.

- Some of these learning objectives are expressed in language that is too complex to be easily accessible to most children. LOs C and I are especially challenging. These are similar to those that might appear in published schemes of work. In rewriting these you need to take into consideration the age and language levels of the children you work with. As well as rewriting, consideration about the possible learning must be identified. LO I should be considered in relation to the visual elements and processes that the unit is based on. LO C can be more clearly connected to the visual element/s that could underpin observation, such as 'to draw what you see using lines and shape', or could focus on the exploration of drawing tools in 'to choose drawing tools that will help you draw what you see'.

- LOs B, D and G are clearly written and are focused on what the children could learn. They are not specific to a particular activity in terms of context and this allows them to be revisited and developed over key stages. LO B for example (exploring tone in drawing) will recur as children draw in different contexts, such as from observation, imagination or experience. The use of the word 'explore' suggests that children have some freedom to find out and experiment. As their experience and mastery of drawing tools such as a range of B pencils, chalk and charcoal, pastels and pens develops they will learn more about representing tone. They will also have other opportunities to explore tone in painting, printmaking and collage perhaps. Your use of success criteria can modify this learning objective so children can understand some of what they might do to show learning in relation to the objective.

When you devise learning objectives it is useful to have already written them in child accessible language so that as you talk about them in your teaching and share them for children to refer to you are prepared. It can be challenging to try to rephrase learning objectives from plans on the spot during your teaching.

In this activity you have evaluated learning objectives. Learning objectives can be considered alongside success criteria, allowing you to work with the children to clarify what the learning will look like. Your school may have a policy or guidance about how you express success criteria, steps to success or 'what a good one looks like'. You might have in mind what you consider the outcome for learning but it is important that you include the children in discussing this and formulate it in child-friendly language. One way of checking that the children understand what they will be learning is to ask them (before they go off to work) what they will be saying and doing to show you that they are learning. In some instances this will correspond with your expectations and if it does not this is a signal that your teaching has not had the impact you intended. In other instances, where you are encouraging children to respond openly and creatively, for example, what children will suggest will be much more diverse and open to personal interpretation and this is to be valued and encouraged.

A clear outcome can be used as a focus for feedback and support whilst the children work and to structure discussion in a plenary or review at the end of a lesson. You can also use this as reminders and prompts as well as including differentiation where appropriate. In art it may well be the case that 'what learning looks like' encompasses a wide range of possibilities, especially where children are exploring and expressing their personal and creative ideas. Devising success criteria or guidance for learning outcomes can make reference to this, indicating to children that whilst they are all, for example, painting using watercolours and exploring the use of colour, there may be other areas where personal choice will have led to some significant differences in outcomes – size of work, the way the paint is applied, the use of colour and subject matter perhaps. The various ways individuals have responded can be highlighted in discussion, emphasising how sometimes unplanned and unexpected things happen in art as part of the process.

LEARNING IN ACTION

Year 1 and 2 children are drawing from observation in their sketchbooks outside in the school playground. Their teacher has shared the learning objective with them. It is 'I am learning to draw what I see'. She has demonstrated how they can look for significant and striking shapes of buildings and how they could use line to draw these and to add detail. The teacher has taken a series of photos of what can be seen from the playground and taped these together into a panaromic view that the children can look at later. On the planning, success criteria are related to using the visual elements of line and shape and being able to identify what has been drawn, because some key features are clear on the drawing. With the children's help the success criteria have been expressed as:

- I have used the shapes and lines that I can see on buildings.
- My friend can take my drawing and find what I drew on a photo or in real life.

The teacher and teaching assistant use these success criteria as they work outside with the children. They use them to question, prompt and comment, saying such things as:

- 'Can you show me the shapes you have used?'
- 'I can see you have drawn the triangular roof that you can see.'
- 'Can you see any details that you could add to the wall?'

When the children come back inside they swap their sketchbook with a friend and try to identify where the drawing was made. The children enjoy giving clues and feedback in this part of the lesson. The teacher and teaching assistant are ready to prompt by pointing to a key feature in each drawing that will home the viewer in on what was being drawn.

In this case study a clear shared learning objective and some accessible success criteria are used to help focus children on their learning in the art lesson. This activity is a relatively short and self-contained activity. For some learning in art you might have one or more challenging learning objectives and success criteria or learning outcomes that children work on over several lessons or weeks. It is important that we convey to children how their learning connects up and for what purpose they are learning. In relation to the case study above, the children had been to see two paintings that represented scenes that could be identified as well-known buildings. They would be going on to make their own paintings based on observation. The drawing activity helped them to begin to focus on the key features and shapes of buildings that they would go on to paint. Sharing this 'bigger picture' was motivating and supported children in working purposefully, rather than seeing the activity as a disconnected one-off.

Vocabulary

Identifying the key vocabulary that you will be using within the unit of work and in individual lessons will allow you to be clear about the meaning of the words you are using when they are used in the context of art. This has been explored in relation to vocabulary relating to visual elements in an earlier chapter and will be considered in relation to media and processes in later chapters. When you identify key vocabulary you should think in terms of words and sentence structures. This is an area that will be of particular significance when planning to meet the needs of children learning English as an Additional Language (EAL) or children with a special educational need or disability (SEND).

As a student or teacher you should have an overview of the whole class as well as ideas about differentiation, in order to include children with EAL or SEND and extend the more able. Many published plans identify key vocabulary that you can use as a starting point. As a teaching assistant you can use the identified key vocabulary on the plan as a basis for thinking about the needs of the group or individual you are supporting. You may need to take advice from the class teacher about which words are most important, so you can focus your support on these. You may be able to use visual clues, labels, symbols and other aids to understanding.

Assessing learning in art

You will be familiar with assessment in subjects such as English or mathematics since these subjects are the focus of much assessment activity and training, but you may feel hesitant about or lacking in experience of making assessments of learning in art. If you have trained or been working in schools in the last few years you will also be familiar with the principles of Assessment for Learning. In addition to this, it is likely that your school will have a policy that will guide your approach to assessment in relation to types, strategies and subjects.

Your approach to assessment in art should be informed by your school policy and your own understanding of assessment and Assessment for Learning (AfL). Features such as giving formative feedback including using success criteria, offering useful and accessible advice about what children have done well and specific advice about how they might improve and encouraging self and peer assessment are aspects of Assessment for Learning (ARG, 2002). Assessment in art can be perceived as different to assessment in some other subjects because of the creative, personal and subjective nature of the subject. There are, however, aspects of art that are measurable such as technical skills and those that are less so, such as the individual outcomes of the children's own ideas, responses and creativity. As Bowden *et al.* (2013, p.24) state: "Artistic activity cannot be measured in absolute terms and this can lead to the view that Art and Design cannot be measured at all." It is important for you to remember that without feedback about how to develop and improve, learning cannot take place in art as in any other subject. OFSTED (2012) identified that good or outstanding lessons in primary schools were characterised by: "subtle and strategic use of assessment, focused on individual pupils' progress" (p.16). Your role is to plan, teach and support children so that they can learn and develop in art.

When intervening to teach or give formative feedback in art lessons it is important to be sensitive to the nature of the subject. Children can easily pick up if we as adults have an expected or 'correct' response in mind and will be quick to judge their own work against this expectation or standard. Giving more open-ended feedback can allow us to value and preserve children's own responses and avoid inadvertently pushing our own ideas and preconceptions at the expense of theirs.

Evidence of learning in art

There is a range of evidence of learning in art. The child's sketchbook is a valuable source of ongoing development and progress. Adding annotations on sticky notes and prompt sheets can add useful contextual detail, including scribed comments from the child. Photos of the child at work, art work in progress and finished pieces are also useful. Making screen recordings of the child talking about a photographed piece of art is a quick way of capturing thinking. In addition to this, observations made by the teacher and / or teaching assistant about the child at work, their attitude and their decisions enhance the quality of information available. Annotations on planning are useful reminders for future lessons or the next time the lesson or unit is taught. Displays of work also provide evidence of learning in art as do school digital portfolios of collected examples.

Formative feedback

Formative assessment is the assessment that we use day-to-day in the classroom to support children's learning and help them improve: a key part of your role. There are strategies that you can use to give feedback to children in art. You can also consider formative feedback in relation to children's skills in making, the attitudes they demonstrate in art and their knowledge and understanding of the subject.

Some of the strategies you can use when giving feedback include acting as an 'interested observer', watching and waiting rather than being quick to comment, or suggesting several alternative approaches, such as 'you could try… or you could try…'. If you are asked for help, demonstrating alongside the child and focusing specifically on an aspect of the skill that would be helpful to their next step or solving the problem they have is a useful approach. When talking with a child, using the opening 'tell me about…' rather than 'what is it?' allows the child to articulate and describe. Asking the child to talk about what the piece of work is called or what they would tell someone about it builds on this. Acting as scribe and making a transcription of the child's responses is a useful way of recording the child's thoughts and ideas at different stages of their work. You might also provide a structure for response based on success criteria or a checklist or ask a peer to show and talk through how they are working on a similar area.

Formative assessment – making art

Supporting children to develop their technical skills in using tools, media and processes with increasing control and confidence is a key part of formative assessment – what you say and do here can make a real difference to their learning. Using pieces of work that you have created to exemplify a technical point that children need to improve can elicit comments and give children the opportunity to look more critically and then apply what they have noticed to their own work.

LEARNING IN ACTION

A class of Year 5 children are working on printmaking. They will be revisiting pressprinting, an aspect of the printmaking process that they have used before. This time they will be expected to be much more independent, use several blocks together and achieve a better quality of finished print. Their teacher has identified some of the things that the children need to be aware of. These include:

- Moving the tile after initially putting it down, resulting in an unclear print
- Holding the tile with inky fingers so that the print is surrounded by fingerprints
- Not rolling ink across the whole tile and in particular missing out the corners
- Picking up the tile carelessly so that finger marks show on the print
- Rolling too much ink on the tile so that the marks cut into the polystyrene do not print clearly

The teacher makes prints that exemplify each of these possibilities. She asks the children to identify what went wrong and what advice they would give to someone to avoid each unwanted outcome happening.

These responses are shared with the whole class and used as a way of reminding and structuring feedback to each other. Because no individual child's work is picked out, as the feedback is applied to a set of generic examples, all feel free to say what they think and make suggestions. It gives some children confidence that whilst things can go wrong they can also be corrected.

As you work with children you will be able to identify where they need focused teaching in order to make progress; where they need time and opportunities to practise their skills; and what the balance between these two is. Taking care to give specific praise focused on what the child has done well and what they might do to improve or make the next step will be more effective than generic statements. You might also take into account how much support they need from adults, from using resources and from differentiation, when considering their progress in using tools, media and processes.

Formative assessment – attitudes

Noticing children's attitudes and personal qualities in the context of art lessons is another aspect of formative assessment. These have an impact on their learning and may well be different from subject to subject. Qualities such as independence, perseverance, questioning and enthusiasm play a part in learning to make art and enjoy the art made by others. You might notice how independent children are in their practical work and when they look at art; how long they are able to concentrate and sustain interest for; whether they are absorbed in their work or easily distracted; and how readily they engage with the new ideas and experiences that they are introduced to in art. You might find that some children relish the freedom that art gives them to respond in different ways and use their own ideas, or that some children find this very freedom challenging and worrying. Using your formative assessment in this aspect of art will allow you to gain understanding of individuals in a different way than in more formal and less practical lessons, as well as intervene sensitively to support their learning.

Formative assessment – knowledge and understanding

As well as technical skills and personal attitudes, children will also be developing knowledge about art through your teaching and their own exploration. Noticing what they remember and the connections they make from lesson to lesson, unit to unit and beyond will give you an insight into the depth of their knowledge and understanding. Some understanding on your part of their prior experiences will help you begin to make connections, comparisons and reflections through your questioning and conversation with them and your own planning of learning.

I like the way you have used the brush in sweeping smooth strokes.

You've chosen a wide range of different greens to put together in your photo collage.

If you try pressing on lighter or harder you can change the tone of your lines.

You've used shades of one colour here to suggest night time.

Figure 5.2 Giving formative feedback through focused talk

Using assessment formatively to help children improve their art is an integral part of teaching and learning. Much of the ongoing formative assessment that is built into lessons will be oral and part of conversations with children about their work as it progresses. It is important that this feedback is clearly focused on learning and is specific rather than general. Whilst general positive comments may appear helpful and reassuring, they can also be unhelpful in their lack of clarity about exactly what is being done well. Using your knowledge of the children you teach, their prior experiences as well as your planned success criteria, and thinking about the unit of work can focus your feedback, making it sensitive and effective rather than general and formulaic.

Self and peer assessment

Involving children in the assessment process is an important aspect of AfL. Helping children to assess their own work and supporting them in making peer assessments should be a part of art lessons as in any other lesson. Successful self-assessment begins with clear success criteria, steps to success or learning outcomes that are shared with the children. These should be expressed in language that is accessible to the learner and used as a basis for praise and feedback throughout the lesson or unit of work. With younger children it is likely that much of this will be oral, although it may be transcribed by adults so that the assessment information is not lost. It may be structured by using a short self-assessment checklist to structure the child's reflection.

Self-assessment strategies such as using sentence starters may help children to articulate their own learning in a more focused manner. These could include:

- I am most pleased with…
- I have got better at…
- I chose… because…
- Next time I will...
- I would change…
- I have learned to…
- I know more about…
- I like…
- This reminds me of…

It is important to give children a focus for their self-assessment because children are prone to be harsh critics of their own work or can make general comments that do not help them articulate their learning.

When moving on to peer assessment it is even more important to be aware of the need for tact and appropriate language when expressing oneself in relation to the work of others. Think back to comments that have been made about your own work and how poorly expressed comments might have made you feel. When planning peer assessment you might structure this by asking children to look for specific areas or features. Laying out all the pieces of work you might ask children to circulate and look for a painting where colour has been used in an interesting way, or look for a painting with detail in the foreground or look for a painting that makes them feel happy. You might practise giving positive peer assessment comments on the work of artists, craftspeople and designers and also ask children to consider the feelings of the person receiving the feedback.

End of key stage assessment

There is no formal requirement for teachers to record and report children's attainment in the form of levels for art at the end of each year or key stage.

This is an activity that you should participate in with colleagues in school – looking at and talking about the range of outcomes of children's learning in art and what it means for their progress and your teaching. It will help you to develop your expectations and ability to consider children's knowledge, skills and understanding as well as their creativity and attitudes. You can also look at examples of children's work in school portfolios if these are available, as well as using any pointers in the schemes of work that you are using to guide your evaluations.

Reflect and extend

Read chapter 6, 'recording progress', in John Bowden *et al.*'s book *Art and Design: Primary Coordinator's Handbook*, published by NSEAD in 2013.

Think about the ideas and points he and his fellow authors put forward in relation to assessing art.

Conclusion

In this chapter the stages of planning, strategies for teaching and supporting learning and formative assessment have been explored. Your own understanding of these areas as well as your developing subject knowledge will help you teach and support effectively in art lessons. Your personal enthusiasm and interest will also support effective lessons and bring about a positive approach from children. In the next chapter, strategies for teaching and supporting learning in art will be explored in more depth.

Next steps

- Look on the curriculum map to identify the techniques and processes that will be taught in the year you are working. Have you used these before? If not, have a go at them yourself so you can anticipate how to teach / support.

- Check that plans and resources are available in time for you to teach / support effectively.

- Look for plans available from galleries and organisations that could help to support, develop and enliven your planning.

References

Assessment Reform Group. (2002) *Assessment for Learning: 10 principles. Research based principles to guide classroom practice.* [online] Available from: www.aaia.org.uk/storage/medialibrary/o_1d8j89n3u1n0u17u91fdd1m4418fh8.pdf [Accessed 12/12/2019].

Barnes, R. (2002) *Teaching art to young children 4–9.* 2nd ed. Abingdon: Routledge.

Bowden, J., Ogier, S., Gregory, P. and National Society for Education in Art Design. (2013) *Art and Design: Primary Coordinator's Handbook.* London: Collins.

Clarke, S. (2014) *Outstanding Formative Assessment Culture and Practice.* London: Hodder Education.

Hogan, J., Hetland, L., Jaquith, D. and Winner, E. (2018) *Studio thinking from the start.* New York: Teachers College Press and National Art Education Association.

OFSTED. (2012) *Making a mark: art, craft and design education.* [online] Available from: www.ofsted.gov.uk/resources/making-mark-art-craft-and-design-education-2008–11 [Accessed 20/07/2020].

Studio Thinking. (2018) *The Framework.* [online] Available from: www.studiothinking.org/the-framework.html [Accessed: 21/11/2019].

Wiliam, D. (2011) *Embedded Formative Assessment.* Bloomington, IN: Solution Tree.

Further resources

Heaton R. and Edwards, J. (2017) Art. In: Caldwell, H. and Cullingford-Agnew, S. *Technology for SEND in primary schools.* London: Learning Matters.

Chapter Padlet:

https://padlet.com/Jeanne/Chapter5

06

Chapter Six

Teaching and supporting learning in art

Introduction

In the previous chapter aspects of planning were explored. The plans that you devise or adapt will underpin your teaching or support for learning. They give you the opportunity to think about what you will teach and how you will teach it or how best to support individuals and groups of children in lessons. As in any subject or area of learning there are a number of teaching strategies and ways of organising learning. When you are planning an art lesson you will choose the most appropriate strategies for what you are teaching and what will best meet the needs of the children you are working with, taking into account the distinctive nature of art as a subject. There may be some factors to consider that are inherent to the subject or related to your own confidence and expertise. As a student or teacher you should consider your own role and the role of any supporting adults. As a teaching assistant you should consider your own role within the team of adults in the lesson in order to support the learning of the class, group or individuals that you work with. In this chapter the following areas will be covered:

- The role of the adult

- Teaching art – some approaches

- Using a sketchbook in art

- Meeting the needs of a range of learners

- How can technology help?

- Classroom management

When primary aged children are involved in art lessons many of the teaching skills that you use all the time will, of course, be relevant. Having said this, art lessons will be different because of the practical nature of the subject. The resources we use in art may require us, as adults, to give more thought to classroom organisation than when children are more contained at tables. Often the working atmosphere in an art lesson is different: sometimes the room falls silent because of the intense concentration involved in drawing whilst at other times there is an excited buzz from children following own their creative ideas and sharing those of others. One feature of art lessons that will be unlike that of any other lesson or subject is the use of a sketchbook to support learning.

The role of the adult

In the more distant past art education was focused on direct instruction and the idea that children should be taught the technical skills needed to use tools and materials correctly. The role of the teacher was to demonstrate and teach skills directly, with little scope for individual response and exploration. Later, this was largely replaced by the idea of a more 'child-centred' approach. In this view of how children learn in art the role of the teacher would be to provide contexts and materials and allow children to create in response to their own ideas and interests, with little if any direct teaching. Most schools would now include opportunities for exploration and expression in their art curriculum, as well as teaching children how to use tools and materials. However, teachers now also need to provide children with opportunities to be interdisciplinary, to collaborate, to connect and to themselves act as agents of change. Technology can be a facilitator of this in art because it can provide a platform on which to communicate with others; it can allow children to be active makers, inventors and problem solvers; and it can be a working space to disseminate process, product and change.

As with using planning in any subject, it is at the level of the lesson that the plan you have in front of you can become an invaluable support to what you do in the lesson. Translating the planning into action – actually teaching and supporting learning – requires you to choose from a range of teaching strategies. Plans vary in their format and content. A key factor is that you can use the plan effectively to help you support children or teach children. If you are using a plan from a published scheme or a plan given to you to work from it is likely that you will need to add details to help you use it effectively. If you are the class teacher or a student on placement, you may have to think through the plan in relation to your classroom organisation and class and the requirements from the provider. If you are a teaching assistant supporting a specified group or individual child you may have to think about the plan as it applies to their needs. Annotating the plan with reminders, adding post-it notes, writing on it or typing into it can help you prepare so that your teaching and support is more effective.

The number and roles of adults in an art lesson will vary from school to school. As the teacher you could be the sole adult teaching the class. You could also have the support of a teaching assistant (TA) who will provide general support, or the TA may be focused on supporting an identified group or individual. If you are an HLTA you could be teaching the class you normally support either with or without the TA support you would normally provide. If you are a TA supporting in art you may be providing general support as directed by the class teacher or you might be supporting a group or individual with specific needs. In all of these examples communication will be important. All of the adults working in the lesson need to know what will be happening and how learning for individuals and the whole class can be most effectively supported. There are some essential points to consider:

- Make sure that all of the adults have access to the plan in enough time to read it and think about it.

- If you are supporting an individual or a group with particular needs think through how the plan will support learning for them and whether you need to suggest any modifications in order to promote inclusion. Annotating teaching detail onto the plan at an earlier stage was suggested as a way of ensuring that you are prepared for the lesson – in this example you might annotate details about how you will support and include your pupils.

- Be prepared to be flexible during the lesson as it is sometimes difficult to anticipate how long practical activities will take.

- Think about your own subject knowledge in relation to the lesson. Do you need to have a go with the resources yourself before you work with the pupils?

If you have a positive working relationship with the team of people that you work with these points will perhaps be second nature to you. If you are a student in the setting you will need to develop this working relationship quickly and ensure that the adults are fully briefed, either by using the systems already in place or by devising ways of your own. In this instance, you should be alert to taking advice from the staff who know the children best, as they can tell you about how they will respond in art lessons and how their learning can most effectively be supported.

Reflect and extend

Read the article 'An exploration of primary teachers' understanding of art and the place of art in the primary school curriculum' written by Hallam, Gupta and Lee in 2008 and published in *The Curriculum Journal* (Volume 19, Issue 4, pp.269–281).

Think about the three approaches to art in the curriculum identified: art as a skills-based activity; art as an expressive activity; and art as a site for cross-curricular teaching.

What are the implications for the art curriculum, your teaching and the children's learning?

Teaching art – some approaches

Choosing from a range of teaching approaches will allow you to support learning in lessons. Across a half term you might be demonstrating how to use tools and how to work effectively, using some techniques or processes; you might facilitate learning by providing prompts, reminders and examples; and you might support free and independent working.

Demonstration

When you are introducing a new skill, medium or process or developing a familiar one in a new direction, one of the most effective ways to do this will be by demonstrating it. You must, therefore, be clear as to how best to model the most important features of the skill or technique, so that the children can draw upon this in their own learning. If you are introducing something that you are less confident or familiar with you should rehearse this before the lesson to make sure you can demonstrate it clearly and anticipate any points that need emphasising. In doing this you will also be able to identify useful tips and things to avoid that will help you demonstrate more effectively. When teaching some aspects of art it might be useful for children to have their sketchbooks out and work alongside you as you demonstrate. Using a visualiser with the IWB or screen can be very useful as it allows children to see exactly what you are doing close up. Making a short video that children can have access to or finding and using video demonstrations made by other teachers can also be useful here. Being able to watch and rewatch as and when they choose can help the learner focus in on what they need to know and develop. Alternatively, videos can be a source of developing your own subject knowledge before going on to demonstrate to children.

Another factor to bear in mind is that children can be eager to please adults and may want to reproduce what you demonstrate. When you plan what you will demonstrate you should focus on the skill or technique rather than the content, subject or outcome that the children will be working on themselves. An example might be if you are demonstrating how to vary the pressure on the pencil when drawing, to create darker and lighter tones. You may want to scribble or draw lines and marks rather than drawing a recognisable picture. If you are demonstrating how to use the paintbrush so that the bristles touch the paper but the ferrule (metal part) does not, again you can paint lines and marks rather than a picture that children may be tempted to try to reproduce. If you have time you might want to build in a step-by-step following along altogether instruction to learn from, followed by more free exploration and application so that you have the best of both approaches.

As well as demonstrating to the whole class you may also use these teaching strategies with groups and individuals to support them further. The same principles can be applied and working on the children's work should be avoided. You can demonstrate using the same tools and resources that the children are using but on another piece of paper or in your own sketchbook alongside the child's work, rather than work onto the child's work. For some children teaching assistants may be deployed to support within the whole class for part of the lesson, to help them focus on the main teaching, or to mirror the whole class by teaching alongside an individual. As you observe children working you can identify those individuals who can demonstrate to a friend, a group or the class: this can be a useful experience both for the child who demonstrates and the children who learns from this.

Using examples, prompts and reminders

When teaching art, examples of the skills and techniques that you have made for the purpose or that you have taken from the work of artists can be used. Depending on what you want to highlight to children it may sometimes be easier to make your own examples, whilst at other times examples from the work of artists may help children make an interesting and informative link between an artist's work and their own. When using an example to teach from it is important that you make a careful choice and that this does not steer children into copying the example. You might label the example with prompts to remind the children of the useful learning points.

Other useful visual prompts or reminders might help children who are working on their own to remember the purpose of their activity. An activity with a particular sequence of steps can be structured with a series of steps or instructions in words and / or photos or a short video as a reminder. Several key questions or a short checklist may remind children of what they could try out or how to overcome challenges.

You might plan to allow children free exploration of a material in order for them to find out what can be done and what the challenges are. Only after this more exploratory phase of learning, where you observe and identify key areas that children need help with, should you go on to teach directly and help children share ideas and approaches. This can also be useful when children return to a tool or process that they have not encountered for some time, as it can give you an insight into what they have remembered and where you need to work from and towards.

Adult-led, directed and independent activity

When you plan art lessons, the way you organise teaching and learning will vary. In some lessons you may follow a similar pattern to other lessons, where you begin with a whole class teaching input followed by some guided or independent work and ending up with a plenary session to finish the lesson off. This can be adapted to art by, for example, beginning with a short drawing starter that helps children settle into the atmosphere and expectations of an art lesson. It is important to consider the proportion of time that children spend actively working practically and making art, as this is a crucial aspect of an art lesson. If you find that you are talking and teaching more than the children are working, the balance will need adjusting. In other lessons a group rotation organisation, where some children work independently and others work with the support of adults, may allow for more teaching and practical work to take place. You should be guided by the organisation or management that will best fit the learning you plan to take place.

Try for yourself – organising learning

Evaluating different ways of organising learning

In this task you will have the opportunity to consider two main types of classroom organisation and they can support learning or be a barrier to learning.

You will need: the pro forma below or a copy of it to make notes onto

---

Activity – Evaluating different ways of organising learning

	Adult-led or directed learning	**Independent learning**
Advantages When would this type of activity support learning?		
Disadvantages When might this type of activity be a barrier to learning?		

What to do:

Make some notes in each box relating to the advantages and disadvantages of each of these ways of organising learning in an art lesson. When you have finished compare them to the discussion below.

Questions to consider:

•   When might adult-led or directed activity support learning?

When considering this you may have identified that demonstrating how to use a tool or follow a process step by step can give a clear model for children to follow. Tips and features that will support success can be clearly modelled. A familiar tool or process that is to be used in a new or different way can be explained. Having this clear model can boost children's confidence and reassure them before they go and try for themselves. It can also be an efficient use of time, tools and materials.

- When might adult-led or directed activity be a barrier to learning?

If adult-led or directed input is given to the whole class there may be some children who find the language or learning too challenging and some for whom it is not challenging enough. It may be difficult to use teaching assistants effectively in the whole class, teaching part of the lesson. For some children too much adult modelling can be discouraging as they can feel that their own efforts will not match the model they have been given. This approach can also lead to thirty similar responses based on the adult model seen by the children and little opportunity for individual and creative response.

- When might independent activity support learning?

Having the time and freedom to explore what tools will do or what effects can be created by processes and techniques allows children to develop their skills and creativity. It may be a more effective use of space and resources, especially if the activity uses specialist resources or is particularly messy. They will have more autonomy and independence in their learning and the outcomes they produce. It is also an enjoyable and positive experience.

- When might independent activity be a barrier to learning?

Having a go with insufficient guidance and support can be a waste of time and resources and lead to frustration. It can result in children repeating the same outcomes and not taking steps forward in their skills, knowledge and understanding. It can be a challenge to provide enough time for children to work independently for a sustained period.

It is likely that when you plan and teach art you choose from a variety of ways of organising learning according to the time you have available, the adult support at your disposal and the individual needs of the children and the learning that is planned. Ensuring that there is balance between adult-led and independent learning as well as opportunities for guided work where appropriate is something for you to aim for and monitor.

Working outside

For some units of work it will be important that children work from what they can experience and see outside the classroom, when they can collect ideas and images. This could be a relatively small-scale walk around the school grounds taking photos, sketching and making notes or it could be something more large-scale, like a half- or whole-day trip beyond the school that is entirely or partly focused on art.

When you plan for children to work outside, organisation of materials and resources is crucial to supporting learning. Useful resources include:

- Sketchbooks

Children might work in their usual, ongoing sketchbooks, especially if these are portable and have a hard back that can be leaned on. Alternatively, you might make small sketchbooks, just for this experience. These might be more portable and user-friendly for use outside, especially if you concerned about weather and potential loss.

- Clipboards

If the sketchbooks you are using are not hard enough to form a support each child will need a piece of stiff card or a clipboard to lean on as they draw.

- Drawing materials

Drawing pencils, pencil sharpeners, pens and any other tools that would be useful should be available.

- Mobile devices to take photos / record video with

Allowing children to use these will let them make their own decisions about what visual material to collect and will make the images more meaningful when back in the classroom.

- Bags, boxes or a trolley

It may be useful for children to collect things to bring back to the classroom to use. If so, having a bag for each child or a large communal bag is useful.

- Other art materials

Depending on your plans for the work outside you might take other equipment – watercolours are very useful, as they come in small light tins with a lid to use for a palette.

Using your school grounds and the immediate local environment as a source of inspiration for learning in art can allow you to establish behavioural expectations and teach children the skills they need to go further afield with confidence. In the case study below young children use their school grounds to observe and research when learning about pattern.

LEARNING IN ACTION

A teaching assistant creates a 'looking for pattern' trail for her Year R children to explore, in order to develop their observational skills and ability to recognise patterns in their environment. She uses a tablet to take close-up photos of ten patterns that she finds around the inside and outside areas. These include the pattern on a piece of fabric, bricks on a wall, a pattern carved into a wooden bench, some markings on a flower, and others. She has deliberately included patterns from nature and the built environment. Each pattern is printed out and strengthened by sticking it onto a 10cm square card, which is then laminated. She takes the children in groups of five on a walk around the setting to look for the patterns – each child holds two cards. She has planned out a route and places to stop and look as well as some clues if they are required. As the patterns are found each one is talked about and labelled, with a note of where it was.

Later, children will be asked to find and photograph some patterns that they have found, to add to the collection. They will use the PicCollage app to combine, label and share these.

In this case study young children are given the opportunity to match and identify patterns in the world around them. This inspires description and discussion and encourages them to look more closely and with more purpose at a familiar environment. Some children continue spotting patterns at home and on their way to and from school. Without these early experiences it would be much harder for children to develop an understanding of this visual element that they can build on in Key Stages 1 and 2.

Beyond the immediate school grounds children could have the opportunity to go on a trip that is solely focused on art, or it may be built into a trip that is also related to learning in one or more additional subjects. Trips to historic sites, places of worship and places of natural beauty have potential for art as well as history, RE and geography. This is a time when meaningful links between art and another subject can be made.

Participating in events

Connecting art in school to events taking place out of school can be inspiring and add to the art curriculum, as well as develop links to your local community and give you access to resources and ideas beyond the school. If you look around there may be local events such as projects, workshops and exhibitions that you can participate in. These might be through your local authority, secondary school, college or university, or local arts organisations and galleries / museums.

In addition to local events and opportunities, there are some national events each year that you can use to focus attention on aspects of art and develop its profile in school. Each autumn term The Campaign for Drawing organises events focusing on drawing called 'The Big Draw'. You can register on their website to get resources and information about events in your area or you can organise a Big Draw event of your own. Each year there is usually a theme and there are lots of ideas and resources available to support schools and other organisations.

Link: https://thebigdraw.org/

Increasingly, there are opportunities to take part in online collaborative projects and activities. These can give you access to resources from artists and institutions from around the world and create a sense of taking part in something bigger.

Using a sketchbook to research and collect ideas

The use of sketchbooks is common in Key Stage 2 and they are often introduced in Key Stage 1. If sketchbooks are to be used effectively in the teaching of art it is important that we understand what they are, how they can be used effectively and when they might be used. Keeping a sketchbook of your own alongside that of the children can allow you to model what you are teaching. Including examples of children's work and notes can also help your practice and be a valuable source of ideas and reflection for the future. As an artist, keeping a sketchbook is a tradition that goes back centuries and examples from the past and from living artists, craftspeople and designers can show children how they can be used to support research, thinking and making art. Each child's sketchbook is a personal record of their thinking and development as artists and can be a vital source of information about their progress and development.

What is a sketchbook?

The term 'sketchbook' can be used to mean many things. In this discussion a sketchbook can be likened to an exercise book for art – a book in which children explore, research and record both within and outside of art lessons. It is not a scrapbook in which children's 'best' work is presented, it does not contain only drawing and it is not necessarily a neat and tidy book. It could be used alongside a digital record of children's larger and shared pieces of art, kept through photos and video.

Sketchbooks are likely to vary from school to school. They tend to have pages of blank cartridge paper, often thick enough to allow children to work on both sides of each page. Some sketchbooks have pages of different colours and types of paper. If the cover is hard it can be useful as it makes the pad rigid, so it can be leaned on whilst working, but this can be prohibitively expensive. Sketchbooks may be any size, although if they are too large they can be unwieldy, hard to move around and hold and difficult to store. If they are too small they can be constricting for children, although small pads can be more portable and useful when used outside. The pages can be stapled, spiral bound or sewn together. Cost is usually a significant factor when sketchbooks are chosen for children. Making, or allowing children to make their own, small sketchbooks for a specific purpose can be an effective approach. Choice of papers (colours, types, weights) for pages and size can allow children some control over their collections of ideas.

Figure 6.1 Examples of sketchbooks

LEARNING IN ACTION

As part of a session exploring the use of sketchbooks, a group of initial teacher training students are asked to make their own mini sketchbook. They are given the choice of ten different A5 sized papers (brown parcel paper, white cartridge paper, tracing paper, newsprint, black sugar paper, two shades of sugar paper, squared paper, tissue paper and card). They collect five sheets and staple them into a card cover. Some students choose very much at random and others employ various criteria, such as trying to match tones and colours or trying to collect a variety of surfaces.

They use their mini-sketchbooks to collect research materials around the campus, including drawings, rubbings, collages of collected natural materials and photos. Later they refer back to the visual information to support the making of group images based on a chosen route around the campus.

They also consider the value and potential of the sketchbook for supporting learning and giving choice to children. The opportunity to choose the different pages was valued by many students. They could see the possibility of planning for children to do this as an opportunity to support a particular unit of work as well as a way of allowing them to explore different paper surfaces and colours. Some students suggested that instead of stapling pages into a cover, punching holes in the top of the pages and lacing them together would allow for additional pages to be added later if necessary. A number of students liked the idea of having a small sketchbook for a particular project and found it more portable to use outside than their full-size sketchbook. Others suggested the possibility of each child having a page or two to use and then making a class sketchbook for all to refer to on their return to the classroom.

When children first begin using their sketchbook by choosing the next page or running through pages, turning a new one over each time they perceive their marks as a 'mistake' can be a problem. To overcome this it can be useful to have a thick elastic band with each pad, to keep the pages together and prevent them from flapping, to identify the next page to work on and to stop children from moving through pages too rapidly.

As well as a paper-based sketchbook you might consider the uses of storing work digitally. As schools increasingly use mobile devices to take photos and video or use tools such as Seesaw, Google Classroom, etc., it is likely that some of the art, craft and design work that children make will be photographed, videoed and sent home rather than stored, especially work that is large, collaborative or temporary. Keeping a folder for each child, including photos and video of children's work and other research, can also be used in a complementary way to the sketchbook. It is not necessary to print everything out and stick it into the physical sketchbook – perhaps a note or a sticker at the relevant point in the paper sketchbook indicating that there is additional material available digitally can serve as a reminder of this. Alternatively, and for younger pupils especially, you might maintain a digital sketchbook shared by the class that you can then display on the interactive whiteboard and refer to in subsequent lessons, using it as a reminder of prior learning.

How can a sketchbook be used?

There is huge potential for using a sketchbook in art lessons and beyond. They can be used on many different occasions in art lessons, with children working directly into them and adding other material where appropriate. They might be used in other lessons and subjects or in cross-curricular projects. They can also be used outside school on visits, at out-of-school art experiences and at home, or children might have specific sketchbooks for these occasions, especially if you have concerns about the loss of a sketchbook that contains evidence of sustained work in art.

In your school: exploring sketchbooks

Finding out more about how sketchbooks are used in your setting.

Developing your understanding of how to use a sketchbook to its full potential in art lessons.

In this task you will have the opportunity to think in more depth about how sketchbooks can be used to inspire and support learning in art and consider these possibilities in relation to current practice in your setting.

You will need: a child's sketchbook. It may worthwhile to choose a Year 6 child's sketchbook or an example of any sketchbook that has been used for a sustained period of time.

What to do: Look for examples listed below.

Activity – Exploring sketchbooks

	Example found – note details	Comment
Experimenting with /refining skills with tools / materials		
Collecting examples / pictures / reminders / photos, etc.		
Exploring a visual element such as colour /pattern		
Collecting examples of artists' work, notes about		
Photos of child at work in art lessons, annotated		
Photos of child's finished pieces of art, annotated		
Self / peer assessment relating to an outcome		
Materials collected on a visit or when working outside		
A variety of techniques and processes		
Work starting from imagination, experience and observation		
Assessment by pupil / pupil and teacher		
Work in art but related to other subjects		
Any digital material that goes alongside the physical sketchbook		

You might find a combination of these different types of uses of sketchbooks or a few that predominate, depending on your school's approach. A sketchbook can provide you with a fantastic record of a child's learning journey and be a reminder of prior learning and progress made. Looking at this task from another angle, you might consider what the opportunities are for using a sketchbook in different parts of a unit of work: examples of this can be found in subsequent chapters.

Some or all of the experiences related to the starting point or research would be recorded in the sketchbook, so that they can be referred to in subsequent practical work. Children can look back to materials gathered, notes made and photos collected and draw ideas and reminders from these. This is especially supportive for younger pupils or pupils who might find it harder to recall earlier lessons or experiences. Sketchbooks should, therefore, be kept with pupils in art lessons and be available to consult and return to. If you keep your own sketchbook alongside those of the pupils you can model this approach.

Reflect and extend

Search for the 'Access Art' website online and put 'artists' sketchbooks' into the search box. Here you can explore some examples and find ideas about using sketchbooks effectively and imaginatively.

Link: www.accessart.org.uk/?s=artists%27+sketchbooks

Explore *Think inside the sketchbook* by Robinson *et al.* (2011) for some inspiring ways of using sketchbooks, along with examples from children's and artists' sketchbooks, as well as practical ideas to use and develop for your own teaching.

Meeting the needs of a range of learners

All children must be included in art lessons in the same way that they would be included in any other subject or aspect of school life. Indeed, art may provide a context in which many children can succeed and enjoy learning, even if they find more formal and academic lessons challenging. How all children will be included in the lesson should be part of the planning decisions and this could draw upon ideas and strategies that are used across the curriculum or it may require some additional planning, depending on individual needs and the subject of art itself.

Some of the challenges you may need to consider are:

- Fine motor control, control of tools

- Organisation of space and resources

- Sequencing of steps in processes

- Subject-specific vocabulary

- Self-esteem, confidence, fear of making mistakes, perception of one's own skills

- Behaviour / concentration

The role of teaching assistant is vital when considering how to include and support all children. Deploying the teaching assistant effectively and ensuring he or she is fully informed about the lesson is crucial. As a teaching assistant supporting a child or group in an art lesson you should consider what you know about the children, the information on the children's support plans and any other information from the SENCo and other adults. You should then think about the lesson critically, with the needs of the children you are supporting in mind, in order to consider any changes or additional resources that could support learning. This will help you to anticipate and pre-empt any challenges or barriers to learning in the lesson.

Given the demands on the time of teaching assistants it may be that there is no support available in art lessons, despite the practical nature of art lessons posing a challenge. As a student or a teacher you may need to consider how you will meet the needs of all children without the support of an additional adult. Strategies may include the use of visual prompts and reminders, breaking down tasks and activities into small steps, using resources such as digital technology and peer support.

Try for yourself

Considering a range of strategies to include an individual or group

In this task you will consider how a range of barriers to inclusion might be tackled.

You will need: this pro forma or a copy of it

What to do:

Annotate the pro forma identifying the challenges faced by each child in an art lesson – these may be different to those faced in a literacy lesson, for example. Then suggest some ideas about how you could overcome the challenges faced by the children. You might consider one suggestion for if a TA is available and one for if there is no additional support at your disposal.

Activity – Considering a range of strategies to include an individual or group

	What are the challenges for the child in an art lesson?	How could these challenges be addressed?
A child whose expressive and receptive language is below that of most of the class		
A child whose fine motor control is less well-developed than most of the class		
A child who finds it hard to concentrate and has a short attention span		
A child who finds it hard to sequence and follow instructions		
A child who has just arrived in the UK and begun school		
A child who has low self-esteem in relation to his / her ability in art		
A child who is exceptionally talented at drawing		
A child who finds it hard to organise work space and tools		

Strategies to support inclusion:

- A child whose receptive and expressive language is below that of most of the class

In terms of receptive language (ability to understand language) the level of language that you are using to teach most of the class may mean that your teaching is inaccessible to the child. This may result in the child misunderstanding your expectations, becoming frustrated and disruptive or switching off. In terms of expressive language (ability to express oneself verbally) it may hard for the child to ask and answer questions and describe their work. The practical nature of art lessons may make your teaching and expectations clearer to children, since you are not relying on words alone but also demonstrating skills and techniques visually. You may need to consider the subject-specific language that you use and ensure that you identify the key words that are essential and concentrate on these. Giving children options to respond non-verbally, such as by using facial expressions, scale of one to ten and several statements to choose from may support response.

- A child whose fine motor control is less well-developed than most of the class

The use of tools such as paintbrushes, pencils, pens, needles, glue spreaders, scissors and modelling tools may be a challenge for a child with less well-developed fine motor skills, particularly when working on a small scale. This may result in the child being frustrated and unable to create the art they want to make and can see other children producing. Working on a large scale can help this child, as can allowing children some choices in their art so that they are not always expected to produce small and fiddly pieces of work. Supplying appropriate tools such as modified scissors and different sizes and handle lengths of paintbrushes can also be helpful. Providing opportunities to develop both fine and gross motor skills is likely to be a part of the ongoing support for a child with these challenges.

- A child who finds it hard to concentrate and has a short attention span

The challenges facing a child who finds it hard to concentrate may be that he / she tunes in and out of the main teaching and then has gaps in his / her understanding of what to do, how to do it and your expectations. He or she may also be distracted and be a disruptive influence in the class. Considering the length of time that you expect children to concentrate without doing and joining in will be important and again the practical nature of art lessons may be more inclusive to the child. Breaking activities and processes down into small steps and punctuating teaching with practical activity will also be helpful. Providing reminders and prompts and using peer support can also help the child who has not been able to retain all of the steps of a process in order.

- A child who finds it difficult to sequence and follow instructions

There are some processes in art lessons that require children to work step-by-step through a sequence in order to be successful and complete their work. For children who experience difficulties with sequencing and ordering, processes such as printmaking may be a challenge. Scaffolding the steps with photos and short instructions will be vital as will being very clear in the demonstration of the process and the layout of each step. Pairing the child with another child who has a good grasp of the process can also be helpful.

- A child who has just arrived in the UK and begun school

For a child who has just begun school in the UK, getting used to the new environment, possibly a new language, routines and expectations will be a challenge in itself. It may be that art lessons are a welcome relief in that the child can make and do practically, with clear visual clues from those around them. You will need to consider the child's different cultural experience and general knowledge about the UK and how this might affect the making of their own art and their response to the work of artists, craftspeople and designers. Their terms of reference might be very different to many of the other children.

- A child who has low self-esteem in relation to his / her ability in art

Some children have negative views of their own abilities to make art and may compare their own work harshly to the work of other children. They can be hesitant, unwilling to have a go, find it hard to move on from mistakes and be overdependent on adult support. With children like this it is important to have strategies for overcoming what they perceive as mistakes and promote a culture of having a go in order to learn. Thinking about how you praise and support is also important, as well as planning art activities that are not always centred on the ability to produce representative art work.

- A child who is exceptionally talented at drawing or another aspect of art

It is likely that you will have one or some children who are very good at aspects of art such as drawing and whose competence is beyond that which you would expect for their age. Ensuring that these children learn and develop is also important. You may need to plan an additional or different activity for these children, which allows them to take a next step or work with greater independence so that they can fulfil their potential and not feel frustrated.

- A child who finds it difficult to organise their workspace and tools

For children who find it hard to manage their workspace practical lessons can be much more of a challenge, as there is more scope for chaos when there are more tools and materials involved. The challenges for these children are that they can waste a lot of time searching for what they need, their tools and materials can impinge on the workspaces of others, especially if a group are sharing resources, and the quality of their work can be affected. Providing a well-organised working space that is clearly set up and supported by straightforward rules is essential and supports all learners. For some children, prompts such as shapes to return tools to, labelled trays and checklists are an additional help.

Figure 6.2 Photo prompts to provide scaffolding instructions

Reflect and extend

Find Helen Caldwell and Stephen Cullingford-Agnew's book *Technology for SEND in Primary Schools: a Guide for Best Practice*.

Read the chapter focused on art (pp.119–136, Heaton and Edwards, 2017) and browse the other chapters for useful ideas and resources.

How can digital technology help?

Using the devices and tools we have available to us in the classroom to support our teaching and children's learning can add more opportunities and choices to enrich art and support us in our role.

When you are planning, there are many ideas and resources available online to inspire you and help you bring creative ideas into the classroom. Art galleries and museums, educators and organisations all share their ideas for learning and activities, often with supporting resources. The greatest challenge can be to make good choices for you and your school and children. You are no longer restricted to the ideas and resources available to you in the books on your shelves in school or at university. You can add to these with ideas from artists, art educators, gallery staff and teachers, sometimes with opportunities to share and collaborate.

When teaching new processes or techniques, step-by-step 'how to' prompts can be made using the actual resources children will be using for their work. Video can be taken of the demonstration of a process or tool, which can be used to teach from and be rewatched by children as and when needed. There are many video resources available online to use in the classroom or to use as a model to make your own and since the pandemic there has been a huge sharing of online resources to support learners, which can be used in the classroom or as prompts for working elsewhere. If you are choosing material to use in the art classroom it is important to be aware of the continuum from 'how to make a ….' to the more open and creative demonstration, leaving the child to have a creative input into the end result.

Try for yourself

Choose a way of collecting links to useful online resources. This could be using the 'favourites' on your internet browser, using a tool such as Pocket or Pinterest or making a padlet.

Choose an area of art that you are going to be teaching in the future.

Starting with these resources, browse for activities, examples and demonstrations to save.

Start with:

The Arty Teacher: https://theartyteacher.com/

AccessArt: www.accessart.org.uk/

The Art Classroom: https://theartclassroom.wordpress.com/

Tate Kids: www.tate.org.uk/kids/make

Using photography and video can be invaluable for recording moments of change and progress in art learning. For adults seeking to capture learning a series of photos, a video of outcomes or setting up a mobile device to record what is happening in an art classroom on the timelapse mode can be useful and interesting.

Empowering children to take the photos and video can also be worthwhile, even more so when audio is added to the images as they can narrate what they did or their reflections on it. Screen recording in PowerPoint or using voice notes on a mobile device can be useful strategies to teach in practical subjects.

Organising the classroom

When you are teaching or supporting in art lessons it is likely that you will need to think through how you will organise the classroom in more depth, because of the practical nature of the lesson. Areas such as resources, health and safety, use of space, timing and the management of any adults in the room will be important to the success of learning and teaching in art. Ensuring that you have anticipated any challenges will help you provide a supportive learning environment.

Management of resources

Art lessons tend to involve tools and materials that are not always readily available in every classroom. It is likely that you will have to collect what you need from elsewhere in the school. Planning can be used to make sure that you have enough of the appropriate resources available to you. If you are teaching the lesson, including a list of resources can act as a reminder to you or it is something you can ask a teaching assistant to check for you. If you are supporting in the lesson a quick check of listed resources against what is ready for the lesson will allow you to do a final check or collect anything that is missing. In further chapters, specific resources for some of the commonly taught areas of art are considered in more depth.

Health and safety

In art lessons you will be using resources and tools that may at first be unfamiliar to children or that they do not use very often. Thinking through possible health and safety issues at the planning stage can help you to anticipate and avoid risks. When considering health and safety in relation to art you should be guided by your own school's health and safety policy and any specific guidance in relation to art and health and safety in the art policy. You can also seek advice from the art coordinator and the health and safety coordinator in your school.

Areas for consideration are:

- The materials you are using, especially certain types of felt pen, dyes, glues, scrap materials, plaster of Paris and clay
- The tools you are using
- Protective clothing that is appropriate
- The usual fire and first aid procedures

- The use of space, how activities are set up within it, how children move around it

- Supervision that is appropriate to the number, age and levels of the children you are working with

In addition to this, maintaining a tidy and well-organised working environment contributes to a safe and productive lesson and the purposeful working atmosphere that you create in your classroom is also important.

Find out more

Clarify your understanding of the health and safety issues related to teaching art by searching for the NSEAD website online. There is some detailed guidance on health and safety in the context of art lessons available there.

Link: www.nsead.org/hsg/index.aspx

Space

It is likely that you will be using more and different resources in art lessons, but in the same classroom setting. In order to avoid or minimise accidents with resources it is important to think about how you will set up the room and use the space you have available effectively. You will need to consider such things as:

- The location of the sink – Is this where children will change dirty water? Is this where children will wash their hands? Is this where children will wash up equipment? Can children get to it without colliding with other children who are working? How will you organise space and timing so that the sink is not required for all these purposes at the same time?

- Where will children put their finished work? Can children take their work there or will they need adult support? Is there enough space for all children's work?

- If your room is partially or fully carpeted how will you protect this if necessary? Is there any part of the lesson that must take place in a tiled floor area? Can some children work outside?

- Where are aprons kept? Are they accessible to children? Are they easy to put on for children or will they need adult support? Do they protect sleeves or do sleeves need to be rolled up? Do the aprons fit? Are there enough aprons?

Giving consideration to these basic questions can help you to organise materials effectively in lessons. Organising how the space and the resources within it can be used in an art lesson, and most vitally making sure all adults working in the room know this, can ensure that your lesson runs smoothly so that all children and adults can concentrate on teaching and learning. You may find it useful to express this as a map or plan of the classroom or by using labels and prompts around the room.

Conclusion

In this chapter some aspects of teaching and supporting learning in art lessons have been explored. Your own experience of these as well as your developing subject knowledge will help you teach and support effectively in art lessons. Your personal enthusiasm and interest will also support effective lessons and a positive approach from children. In the next chapter the teaching and learning of drawing will be explored in more depth – you may find that some suggestions in this chapter apply beyond drawing and can be used in other art teaching.

Next steps

- Consider any specific needs of pupils in your class. How will you ensure that you include all children? Are there any children who particularly excel in art? How will you extend and develop them within each unit?

- Observe an art lesson in your school or next placement school. Identify the teaching strategies used by adults. How are these specific to learning in art?

References

Heaton R. and Edwards, J. (2017) Art. In: Caldwell, H. and Cullingford-Agnew, S. *Technology for SEND in primary schools*. London: Learning Matters.

Robinson, G., Mountain, A. and Hulston, D. (2011) *Think inside the sketchbook*. London: Harper Collins.

Further resources

NSEAD. Health & Safety. [online] Available from: www.nsead.org/resources/health-safety/

The Art Classroom. [online] Available from: https://theartclassroom.wordpress.com/

Chapter Padlet:

https://padlet.com/Jeanne/Chapter6

07

Chapter Seven

Drawing

Introduction

Drawing is essential to child development and understanding life and is imperative in the art curriculum. Children today exist in a rapidly changing world where
drawing can provide multiple ways for them to understand, express, engage
with and contribute to development on personal and social levels. Drawing in
art education is an extensive area of study, incorporating many forms of art and
occurring in physical and digital domains. Drawing itself is a form of research and
it has many applications beyond art, some of which will be explored later in this
chapter.

As such, everyone who supports and teaches art in primary schools must have
some subject knowledge of and commitment to supporting drawing in children's
learning. Drawing is so fundamental to life and learning that charities exist, such
as The Big Draw, formerly The Campaign for Drawing, which advocate and run
projects that endorse drawing's life-changing capacity. In this chapter the following areas will be considered to support educators in understanding and teaching
the fundamentals of drawing in primary art: drawing tools, materials and surfaces,
how drawing skills develop, using drawing to explore the visual elements of art
and pedagogical strategies for teaching drawing.

Many children globally love to draw and will become absorbed in making their
own drawings at home and in school. Being able to draw to communicate,
explore and record (physically and digitally) is a skill that children will use across
the curriculum. Depending on career choice they may also go on to use drawing
in work. Even if they do not draw as an artist in an art or design context after leaving school it is likely that being able to draw and get information from drawings
will still play a part in their lives. Many children enjoy drawing and explore it as a
spontaneous process without always thinking about the end product. If you have
spent time with children at home or in school you will have noticed this. Children's
enthusiasm and need to draw can be harnessed in our teaching and we can
equip children with the skills and confidence they need to develop their drawing.

On the other hand, many adults lack confidence in their ability to draw and
therefore find the idea of teaching children to draw daunting. Sometimes adults
retain a hesitant attitude towards their ability to draw from their educational
experiences, when their own teachers perhaps gave them feedback that caused
them to give up. You might have heard adults openly belittling their own drawing
skills in a way that would be inappropriate were they talking about other forms of
communicating. Perhaps you have encountered situations when it would be useful to be able to draw but you have not been given the help and opportunities to
learn the skills that would enable you to do so effectively. This can cause reduced
confidence and a misplaced feeling that you cannot draw. Concerns have been
addressed by educational bodies that "the notion that everyone can draw is not

being kept alive beyond the early years of schooling" (OFSTED, 2012, p.52). There is also a new requirement for English schools to offer a broad and balanced curriculum provision (OFSTED, 2019). Drawing is not only fundamental to art but it is an interdisciplinary practice that facilitates learning connections and therefore needs to be central in education. As educators you play a vital role in supporting children's drawing provision and accessibility to it.

If you have experienced any of the negative feelings discussed above it is important that you do not perpetuate these feelings with children you are supporting or teaching. As Anning states: "An adult in a school setting may undermine the child's confidence in the efficacy of drawing strategies they have been using routinely at home, by at best ignoring or at worst responding negatively to them" (2002, p.198). Having a positive attitude about developing drawing skills and modelling that drawing is a skill that can be developed and improved is something you can do in your role, whatever your own drawing skills are like. Fabian suggests that children need to realise that learning to draw "will involve having a serious attitude, applying themselves and perseverance" (2005, p.11) and you can demonstrate this in what you say and what you do.

Tools and materials

There is a list of suggested tools and resources to explore in Appendix 2, along with additional detail about some of the more specialist tools, equipment and resources used in drawing. Developing an understanding of the wide range of tools and materials that can be used for drawing will support you in making creative choices when planning and teaching. Drawing will likely be woven through most units of art and so it may be that each classroom has a set of basic supplies, such as several boxes of drawing pencils and cartridge paper, and many digital devices have apps that allow drawing with a finger or stylus on screen. Other types of drawing tools, especially of a more specialist type, are likely to be stored in a central place and used when required in planned units.

In addition to the list in the appendices, it is imperative to include drawing using digital media in the learning opportunities we give to children. Digital applications and software that allow children to explore mark making and drawing are now readily available, and many schools have access to digital devices, static and mobile, where children can experiment and develop their skills in drawing by making marks with a stylus, mouse or finger. Many of these have the facility to record the progress of the drawing so it can be viewed as a process as well as an end product. As the accessibility and ease of use of digital drawing resources are growing, more educational settings are adopting them, so it is important for teachers to understand the advantages and limitations of these. Engagement with the connection and extension activity below will facilitate your knowledge of

these tools so that you can make a considered choice about what drawing imple-
ments to use in your classroom.

Reflect and extend

Read the article 'Young Children Drawing Together on the iPad Versus
Paper: How Collaborative Creativity is Shaped by Different Semiotic
Resources' by Mona Sakr, published in the *International Journal of Educa-
tion and the Arts* (Volume 20, Issue 20) in 2019.

In this article you can find out more about the advantages and limitations
of using mobile devices when drawing with children, specifically in relation
to enhancing collaborative creativity. After reading the article, consider a
physical drawing activity that you may do with a class of children and think
about how you could conduct this activity digitally to encourage pupil collaboration and thinking skills when using digital devices to draw.

Exploring drawing tools

When you introduce a new drawing tool or a tool the children do not use regularly
or have not used for a while, part of your planning at the earlier stage of a unit
of work should include opportunities to explore the potential and qualities of the
tool. If children have these investigative opportunities they are more likely to be
able to use the tool with increasing confidence and control in their work. When
you consider planning these opportunities your priority must be the exploration
of what can be done with the tool and how to get the best from it, rather than
to produce a finished outcome. This is a time when children could work in their
sketchbooks or begin to create a digital sketchbook/ folio.

Try for yourself – drawing tools

Exploring a range of drawing tools

In this task you will have the opportunity to explore the qualities of some frequently used drawing tools, including a digital tool. You will also be encouraged to consider how you can support children in exploring these tools.

You will need:

A pencil from within the B range (ideally 4B), black felt pen (fine, broad or
marker), a biro or ballpoint pen and cartridge paper to draw on; a mobile
device with a drawing app / tool of your choice; the pro forma below or a
copy of it.

Activity – Exploring a range of drawing tools

Drawing tools	What can you do with it? Is there anything you can't do with it?	What does it feel like to use? How could it support drawing?	What challenges does it pose? How might you overcome these?
4B pencil			
Black felt pen (fine / broad / marker)			
Biro / ballpoint pen			
Digital drawing tool			

What to do:

Try out the following exercises with each of the drawing tools.

- Scribble with the tool to get a feel for it in your hand and how it moves. Can you make marks with it at all angles? What happens if you use it on its side?

- Making lines – make some continuous lines, some parallel straight lines, some cross hatched lines (including parallel one way and then the other way on top).

- Making marks – make some dots, spots and short and longer dashes, nearer and further apart.

- Making shapes and patterns – make some circles, squares, triangles; try out some repeating patterns, colour in some of the shapes.

- Making lighter and darker marks – see what happens when you press on harder and more gently as you make a continuous line. Try to make some lighter and darker marks, draw some shapes and shade in one fully, try to make lighter and lighter shapes until you have an almost white / empty one.

Questions to consider:

- What can you do with each tool?

- Is there anything you can't do?

You will have found as you worked through the exercises that the tools responded in different ways.

The 4B pencil and the biro, for example, will have responded to the pressure you exerted on them so that you could make very light and very dark marks as well as many tones in between. Whereas the felt pens do not respond to pressure as readily and the digital drawing tool will not respond to physical pressure. You may have found that you could create darker and lighter tones by overlapping marks and lines and placing them close together and further apart, using all the tools. The digital tools will have allowed you to change the tone, making the marks lighter or darker within the choices available through the menu.

The biro or ballpoint pen allows you to make very fine lines and the felt pens come in different widths so that you can use three pens – fine, broad and marker – and choose within these. The pencil could vary depending on how often you sharpen it. You could start with a fine line just after the pencil has been sharpened and then as it is used it wears down, sometimes quite rapidly, to make a broader point. When using digital drawing tools, you often have to make selections for the type of pen/ tool you wish to use and also select its thickness, so having the knowledge of how to make these selections with physical tools first is often helpful.

Clearly, the pencil can be rubbed out if you make a mark that you do not like. When working with children this can be useful or it can be a problem. The felt pens and biros cannot be rubbed out. This can mean that we accept marks we do not like and move on with the drawing regardless, as there is nothing we can do about it. This can be a positive attitude to develop with children, who may then apply it to their work with pencil and other media. When working digitally you can use either of these approaches, depending on the app or software you use.

• What does it feel like to use? How could it support drawing?

As you investigated each drawing tool you may have enjoyed how the different media moved across the surface. Perhaps you haven't considered a biro as a drawing tool before, although you will have probably doodled with it as you talk on the phone or listen in a presentation or meeting. How each of the drawing tools moved will have been influenced by the surface you chose for the exercise.

The drawing pencil can allow you to explore and use line and tone by your own pressure on the pencil. It takes practice and experience to be able to control this and make the tone you want by exerting the appropriate amount of pressure. The felt pens and biro will support the use of line too but will also allow you to explore creating tone, not by pressing down harder but by placing and overlapping lines and marks. The biro can allow you to create very fine lines and sometimes the properties of a biro will vary as it responds to pressure and by incidental changes in the flow of ink. How your digital drawing felt will also be dependent on whether you used a finger, stylus or mouse. Consider how much control you had and how your tool selection influenced what was possible in your digital drawing.

- What challenges does it pose?

- How might you overcome these?

Some of the challenges posed by these tools might in other circumstances be advantages. A point made earlier about how the pens and biros cannot be rubbed out may at first appear to be a challenge, but it can also be an advantage, as we have to let go and just draw over marks we don't like. One of the challenges of the soft drawing pencil can be its smudginess. Again this can be an advantage, because it allows us to blend from lighter to darker and produce a large range of tones. Smudging a finished drawing can be overcome by fixing it or placing a sheet of tissue or tracing paper over it to prevent it rubbing against other pages. Soft drawing pencils can wear down quickly, so you may need to be ready to sharpen them or have more pencils than you need. You can then substitute a blunt pencil for a sharpened one without the break in concentration going off to find and use a sharpener might cause. Felt pens can make marks on children's hands and possibly their clothes. Nowadays the ink in felt pens tends to be washable – check this on the packets before use. Biros can become blotchy but are readily available and relatively expendable. When considering digital drawing think about what the children may need to know, or be taught, prior to engaging in the drawing activity – for example, do they need to be taught about how to access the app on the device, or how to select tools or clear their canvas?

Giving children access to a wide range of drawing tools, physical and digital, so they can experiment with the marks they make and develop control and familiarity with a few basic tools used regularly, is important in teaching children to draw. Teaching children to choose and use the appropriate tools in drawing, as in other aspects of art, will support children towards independence and control over their art work in future.

Creative combinations of tool and surface

At its heart, drawing is using a tool to make marks on a surface. The resulting outcome might be temporary or permanent depending on the combination chosen. Opening your mind to a wide range of tools and surfaces to use when drawing can include and excite more children. In the chart below there are a few suggestions. Some of these are more challenging to access than others, depending on where you are located (sand, snow) and some would be inappropriate to combine (a digital stylus with anything other than a device screen). Having said this, thinking beyond the combinations we most often present to children can lead to increased creativity and engagement, as well as present new challenges to overcome in terms of how to use the tool, how to make the marks and how to keep a record of the completed piece of art. If the tool and surface are temporary, video, time lapse or photography can be useful here.

Tools
Broom
Chalk / charcoal
Fingers
Paintbrush
Pen
Pencil
Stick
Stone
String
Stylus
Tape
Toes

Surfaces
Card
Condensation on a window
Glass
Painted surface (wet / dry)
Paper
Plasticine or playdough
Plastic
Sand
Screen (laptop or mobile device)
Soil or mud
Snow
Tarmac or paving stone

Older children could also be involved in making their own digital drawing tools – such as drawing robots. The Tate Kids website has a useful resource to facilitate planning such an opportunity.

Link: www.tate.org.uk/kids/make/art-technology/make-drawing-robot

In chapter 12 you can find out more about using GPS technology to 'draw' virtually on the landscape and you will have read about drawing with light in chapter 4. Expanding how we view making marks and lines, and tools and surfaces, into the digital environment can provide new and interesting ways of exploring drawing.

Subject knowledge

When you are planning to teach drawing, understanding about the development of drawing skills as well as identifying the relevant visual elements can help you be clear about planning and learning. As with any aspect of art there will be subject-specific vocabulary as well as words used with a specific meaning in this context.

The development of drawing skills

You will have noticed through your experience of working with children or by thinking back to your own childhood that children's drawing develops and changes over time. As someone who supports or teaches children as they draw it is important for you to know about stages of development and how you can support and teach children as they learn. If we do not pay attention to the development of children's drawing skills it may be that we do not give them the support they need to overcome the challenges they face as they develop their skills. If we abandon the teaching of drawing too early it can have serious consequences for children's later feelings about and confidence in their drawing skills. As an adult you may look back and feel that your drawing skills are frozen in time and you have never moved on to a stage that you would find useful in your adult life. Anning points out that: "Many children learn in the first years at school that they 'can't draw'; and many adults remain arrested in the drawing capability they assumed at the age of six or seven" (2002, p.198). You can play an important role in avoiding this for the children you support and teach.

Early mark making

Children pick up tools and make marks with them on surfaces or use their fingers on a screen, at first accidentally perhaps and then later exploring what happens when they move those tools up and down, sweeping from side to side and pushing and pulling. They may be exploring how to hold the tools they mark make with and which hand to hold them in. Sometimes children will indicate what their marks relate to by naming them. This is an important stage. Barnes writes that: "Scribble is to drawing what babbling is to talk" (2002, p.38). One advantage of digital technology is that you can also record how children create their drawings, collate their video and audio, and play this back to them to document and reflect on their drawing processes. However, it is useful to be aware that sometimes this may detract from the spontaneity afforded by the drawing experience.

At the early mark making stage of drawing we can support children by giving them a variety of tools and surfaces to investigate and by allowing them to make choices in what they will try and return to. We can talk about and describe colours, lines, shapes and marks as they make them. We can pay positive attention and encourage without always asking 'what is it?', as this can make it seem that drawings always have to be an observation 'of' something, rather than enjoying the process itself, or being inspired by imagining or remembering something. Research is now also taking place into the role of digital devices in children's mark making development (Price *et al.*, 2015) and it is likely that such research will continue and filter into art practice, providing information about how best to support children to use digital practices, such as drawing, in the art experience. We feel such research is essential, as children need to dialogue with their current and future worlds in art, using tools and practices that are allied to their time.

First representations and schema

Children begin to remember and recreate the marks, lines and shapes and use them to represent things in their drawings and they tend to draw what they know rather than what they see. They draw about their experiences, paying less or no attention to actual colours, shapes and scale. Children use their drawing to tell stories and explain the world around them. They may initiate and respond more to talking about what the drawing is about. Over time, children develop ways of drawing things that appear in their drawings and this becomes the way they draw a house, a tree or a car; these are personal and relate to their experience. As time goes on the schemas become more developed and detailed. Space may be represented in ways that to adults appear unconventional, including views from inside, outside or above, and the ground and sky may be represented by lines or colour at the top and bottom of the paper.

At this stage we can continue to ensure that children can draw with a variety of tools on different surfaces, both physical and digital. We can help them make choices and allow them free choice of tools, surfaces and what they draw. We can guide them in learning about the qualities and properties of a variety of mark making tools. When drawing from observation we can help them to look and talk about what they are going to draw and touch before they draw. We can encourage children to choose to draw from memory and imagination as well as from observation.

Reflect and extend

Read the article 'Young Children Talking and Drawing' by Elizabeth Coates and Andrew Coates, published in the *International Journal of Early Years Education* in 2006 (Volume 14, Number 3, pp.221–241).

After reading the discussion section towards the end of the article, think about the implications for planning drawing opportunities for children.

Developing realism

Later, children include more and more detail in their drawings to make them appear more 'real' and representative. This can lead to frustration with the results when they compare what they were aiming to draw with what they have drawn. This might be when they begin to express a feeling of 'I can't draw'. Creating an illusion of space by using perspective can emerge as a challenge here and it should be remembered that this is an aspect of Western art and not a feature of art from other places and times.

It is at this stage perhaps that the role of adults is most important. As children begin to realise that the way they always draw something is not realistic and abandon their schemas the challenge is to find other ways of drawing. If no guidance is given at this point it is easy to give up. We can support children by helping them to look in a way that will support their drawing. We can continue to talk about what they will draw first and help them develop ways of approaching their work. We can also help children accept that when we draw we make mistakes that we can learn from, or incorporate into the drawing, and that we need to persevere in order to improve. Most importantly, we can introduce children to artists whose drawings are non-representative and for whom drawing something that looks real is not a primary aim. Here, digital tools can be useful in that children can use reference material on screen, drawing on top of it to gain confidence and a feel for shape and layout, then taking the photo away and continuing to develop the drawing for themselves. Exploring 'Everyone Can Create: Drawing' on the Apple Teacher website can provide some useful starting points for this approach.

Find out more

Look at The Art of Education University resource 'The Stages of Drawing: Development Reference Guide', to explore drawing development phases.

Link: https://artofed-uploads.nyc3.digitaloceanspaces.com/2015/12/The-Stages-of-Drawing-Reference-Guide1.pdf

---

Stages of development in drawing have been researched and written about in much greater detail than above (Cox, 2005; Deguara and Nutbrown, 2017; Rose and Jolley, 2019) and you should learn more about the stages, connecting them to the children's drawing that you encounter. Rough age ranges can be attached to drawing stages, although individual children will spend a longer or shorter time in each of them. They may move around between stages or may miss stages out. As an educator you need to know enough to support and teach the children you are working with effectively. This includes knowing them as individuals and not making assumptions about where they are with their drawing. As Barnes suggests: "The stages they have been through – scribble, symbols, schema and visual realism – are each important experiences which a teacher could impede" (2002, p.43). In order to avoid impeding them by what we say or do or what we fail to say and do we must use our subject knowledge to underpin our planning and teaching. Barnes goes on to say: "Knowing the stages gives us the opportunity to match activities to what the children are capable of producing, and avoids forcing upon them those images for which they are not yet ready" (2002, p.43). Drawing should fundamentally be an enjoyable and developmental experience for children.

Drawing, cognition and the brain

Vast research has developed about how the brain and cognition impact think-ing, children's art learning and drawing (Eisner, 2002; Efland, 2002; Heaton and Edwards, 2017; Heaton, 2019). The brain has a right and left hemisphere and sci-entists continue to investigate how these hemispheres work together. Generally, the left side of the brain deals with language, maths and logic and the right side of the brain deals with spatial relationships, facial recognition, visual imagery and music. Fabian (2005) suggests that when we see a familiar item such as a house, a tree or an animal the left side of the brain supplies a name. Thereafter we stop looking at what is in front of us and rely on our internal knowledge of what the item looks like. Edwards explains that: "We tend to see what we expect to see or what we decide we have seen. This expectation or decision, however, often is not a conscious process. Instead, the brain frequently does the expecting and the deciding, without our conscious awareness, and then alters or rearranges – or even simply disregards – the raw data of vision that hits the retina" (2012, p.xxiv). In order to develop our ability to look and then to draw we can try looking from different viewpoints, so that our brain does not immediately think 'a tree' and then draw our schema for tree – our internal tree picture. When drawing the human figure or face, for example, make a conscious effort to look for lines, edges and tones rather than a face or features. As soon as an awareness of the face takes over, the ability to look changes and can become less useful for drawing. Fabian (2005) suggests looking from unusual angles and viewpoints, looking at the space around the object instead of at the object itself or looking at reflected images.

Find out more

To find out more about how thinking (the brain and cognition) and drawing (visualisation) connect, explore visible thinking routines and practices on the Harvard Project Zero Website.

Link: www.pz.harvard.edu/projects/visible-thinking

Exploring the visual elements through drawing

When the learning objectives are focused on drawing it is likely that you will be exploring one or at most two of the visual elements. The chart below suggests some opportunities for exploring each of the visual elements when drawing with children in physical and digital forms.

Line	Tone
Exploring marks and continuous lines with a wide variety of drawing tools, both physical and digital Drawing outlines, overlaps, shapes next to each other, etc. Using marks and lines to create areas of tone, pattern, texture Making lines slowly, quickly, carefully, wildly, etc.	Exploring making light and dark marks using a variety of drawing tools Exploring lighter / darker tones and contrasts Using tone to create areas, objects, textures, shapes Using tone to create an illusion of three-dimensional form
Colour	**Pattern**
Exploring applying colour using a variety of physical and digital drawing tools Exploring blending tones within colours using drawing materials such as pastels Exploring making light and dark marks using colour	Making pattern using drawn marks Making pattern using lines, outlines Making pattern using tones Making patterns using combinations of marks and textures Drawing from pattern observed around us Drawing on top of patterns from digital images/ photographs/ prints
Texture	**Shape**
Representing texture using drawn marks, lines, areas of tone Exploring texture through photography and drawing layers on top of these textures	Representing 2D shapes using drawing tools to create outlines, shapes, etc. Placing drawn shapes on a surface spread out, next to and overlapping Using CAD software to draw and represent 3D shapes

Space	Form
Representing 3D space in 2D using drawing tools – composition, viewpoints, creating an illusion of space	Representing 3D solid objects in 2D using drawing tools
Representing 3D shapes on a 2D surface	Drawing onto forms to decorate them
Playing with space, unconventional viewpoints	Using 3D print technologies to turn 2D drawings into three dimensions
Drawing in 3D space using virtual reality software	
Using AR and VR technology to see drawings in digital space	

Through each year group and key stage you will revisit visual elements through drawing in different contexts, allowing children to build on their drawing skills and experience of drawing tools and surfaces. This is an area that should be thought through at the planning stage so that progression is clear and can be used as a basis for planning and teaching. You may need to think beyond the half term that you are working in now, and even the year group within which you work, to get a feel for the key stage so you can appreciate the child's experience as a continuum. A number of organisations like the NSEAD and Access Art provide primary art progression plans, which can be used as a guide and tailored to your context, school and pupil needs.

Some drawing materials will lend themselves to developing skills in a particular element more so than others. When we think about exploring tone, white chalk and charcoal might be a popular choice as these will allow us to make a dark black tone and a bright white tone and we will be able to blend to create grey tones between black and white. Choosing a mid-tone paper will allow the white and black at each end of the tonal scale to stand out more clearly. Some apps and tools allow children to experiment with materials such as charcoal and other media on the screen, leaving visual marks that somewhat replicate what charcoal would look like when blended.

Tone in terms of creating dark and light marks can be explored when drawing, using pencils such as 4B and 6B. These soft pencils will allow children to vary their pressure and make distinctly darker and lighter tones in the marks and lines that they make. The physical control of tools in order to make lighter and darker marks is a skill that requires direct teaching and opportunities to practise and consolidate. For some children it is a challenge that also has an impact on their writing, where perhaps they press very lightly so it is hard to read their written work, or they press so hard that they indent pages as they write. When using digital drawing tools tone can be often altered using a menu of choices, which might at first be less intuitive but later can provoke conscious choices.

Artists, designers and craftspeople

There are many artists, craftspeople and designers who have used or currently use drawing and whose work can be used as inspiration for children. Some recommendations follow but you can pursue your own and your pupils' interests, as well as what is available in galleries and through local artists in your area. When you choose a type or style of drawing or drawings by a particular artist it is important to choose with your objective or learning outcome in mind, whilst considering how looking at and talking about the example/s will support learning.

If you plan for children to explore the marks that can be made by drawing tools, look for examples of a range of these. The pencil and ink line drawings of Van Gogh are a wonderful example of detailed and repetitive mark making, whereas the shelter drawings by Henry Moore use light, dark and contrast of tones, often using not just pencil but wax crayon and ink wash. Children's book illustrators are a great source of examples of drawing. John Burningham often uses dynamic lines and marks; Raymond Briggs uses line and colour, sometimes (as in *Jim and the Beanstalk*) representing one thread of the story in black line drawings and one thread in coloured drawings; and many of Shirley Hughes's illustrations are line and colour wash / coloured pencil drawings. Children's authors and illustrators such as Oliver Jeffers are also embracing digital software to create and enhance their drawings.

It is also interesting how artists and illustrators have responded to the current pandemic by opening up their practices through technology, allowing children in to ask questions about the artistic processes they use in their work. Podcasts exist such as 'Kids Ask Authors' with Grace Lin, where children can submit questions and listen to responses through different episodes about artists' practices – this is great for children to understand the cognitive and physical processes of drawing and art making that can also lead to artistic products. Authors are also promoting drawing by running online sessions on platforms like YouTube, which make contemporary drawing practices open and visible to young learners, such as Jarrett Krosoczka's 'Draw Everyday with JJK' and Rob Biddulph, who gives live step-by-step demonstrations that children can join in with and then share what they did on social media, creating a sense of fun and community.

Finding examples of where artists, craftspeople and designers use drawing to collect visual information, practise their skills and work through ideas is also useful – you may have followed a suggestion to visit the Access Art website, where there are some examples of artists' sketchbooks to look at. Many exhibitions include artists' preparatory work, which can be interesting in itself and remind us that drawing, sketching and doodling are a way of capturing fleeting ideas, making plans and leading us towards pieces of art made in other media.

Increasingly, we can find examples of artists drawing using digital tools and media as part of their repertoire. Hockney's use of the Brushes app, leading to the Royal Academy Exhibition in 2012 and beyond, is a useful example of using digital drawing to capture observations of the weather and the environment around us. One of the interesting features that we can explore with children when looking at artists' digital drawings is that if the process has been recorded we can see them unfold chronologically. Indeed, drawing is often a feature of digital animation. For example, the 'Simon's cat' animations by Simon Tofield are an example of apparently simple line drawings brought to life and contemporary artist Jen Stark creates colourful interactive animations from drawings.

Teaching

Drawing techniques allow children to explore and make choices, leading to personal creative outcomes. When you are teaching you will be able to use some of the learning and teaching approaches discussed in chapter 6 and there are some aspects more specific to drawing that you will need to consider, such as how to support children who feel they have made mistakes, how to support at different stages of the drawing process and which resources can be helpful.

Rubbers and what to do about 'mistakes'

It is likely that you have rubbers available for general use in your classroom. Perhaps there is a school policy that guides the use of rubbers or maybe you have your own classroom rules and conventions about when and when not to use them. As with other work, it may be that some children often rub out evidence of their trying, so thinking and investigating becomes absent from the page. The surface of the paper may then become rough or even ripped. This can result in evidence of learning being erased.

In art lessons you may need to think more specifically about the place of rubbers and make this clear to children in your teaching and support. You can explain to children how important it is to try out and make marks to find out what they look like on paper – some of these might be 'right' and some might not be what we hoped, but this does not make them 'wrong' if we can learn from them. If your classroom culture values making mistakes so that we can use them to learn from, the children may more readily understand your approach. Sedgwick suggests: "Tell the children that wrong lines might come in useful later – please leave them there and then do the right line, or even another line that seems even more right." (2002, p.14).

When you are modelling drawing you can include making a false start or a mark you initially don't want and talking through what you will do. Perhaps if it is early in the drawing you might move on to another area of paper on the page, leaving the false start behind. You could continue drawing over the top and show how the earlier line becomes less noticeable as you continue to draw. For children who cannot live with a perceived 'mistake' on the page that they are working on you might have some small pieces of the same type of paper to stick over the area like a flap, so that the first try is retained but covered up. It can also be useful to show children pages from artists' sketchbooks to make it clear how often they try something and move on, including several first tries on the same page.

Before beginning to draw

When you are planning drawing as part of a unit of work there are a number of things that you should consider doing with the children before they put their pencils on the paper and begin. One of the most important (and obvious) is looking. There are a number of ways in which you can help children to look purposefully to support their drawing. Looking in art is different to just looking around the room to see if someone is there or glancing around to check out what is happening around us.

Looking in art is more about exploring what is going to be drawn. It will be important to bear in mind the learning objective/s that you have for the task. If your aim is for children to learn more about how to use line it is important to choose things to look at that will support this objective, whereas if attention to tone or pattern is your objective you might make a very different choice of what to draw, what to draw with and what to talk about before drawing. You can then decide which features you want children to notice and lead them through a process of 'guided looking'. Fabian (2005) states: "Children find it hard to believe that as artists their eyes are more important than their hands" (p.10). She goes on to suggest that we can guide children to look "with purpose and develop different ways of looking". With the increasing use of multimedia technologies in art education and drawing, one could even go as far as to say that teaching consciousness of and understanding all of the senses is becoming even more important. Listening to sounds that can be interpreted as marks and feeling surfaces and materials to create drawn textures which may form backgrounds for animations, as an example, are also progressive acts that teachers need to guide learners of drawing through.

LEARNING IN ACTION

A class of Year 4 children are drawing from observation. They will be looking at house plants from the classroom and around the school. In this lesson the objective is for them to look closely at the shapes of leaves and draw them with a focus on line. The children have the choice of using fine black felt pens that they have used before in art or a black pen on an iPad and stylus. Before beginning, their teacher asks them to walk around the classroom looking at the plants on the tables. She asks them to look for leaves with straight edges, curved edges and spiky edges and guides them to describe the shapes they see. Then she encourages them to choose to sit near a plant they are interested in, rather than sit in the first available space. Once all the children are settled she asks them to move their eyes to a leaf with a shape that interests them, and then point to where it joins to a stem. She asks them to follow the outline of the leaf with their finger in the air to get a feel for the shape. It is not until the class have looked, talked and looked in more depth that they get their sketchbooks or iPads out and begin to draw. The children begin by drawing the leaf they traced in the air and continue moving to the nearby leaves as the teacher and teaching assistant encourage them to look at the outlines they see. The emphasis is on leaf shapes rather than drawing the whole plant. After drawing for a time the children have another look around, this time for a plant with contrasting leaf shapes, and the procedure is repeated.

In this case study the teacher has used the learning objective (exploring shape in outline) to guide her choice of physical or digital drawing tool (pens that make clear, strong, fine lines on paper and fingers / stylus on screen) and stimulus (plants with interesting and varied leaf shapes). She has helped the children to focus their observations through talking about what they see and following the outlines with their fingers in the air to support successful drawing. This gives a clear starting point and guidance for children who could otherwise be distracted into trying to draw a generic picture of a plant. Children are also given choice over their drawing material, affording ownership and breadth of experience of contemporary ways of working, and are able to make comparisons between physical and digital drawing practices, particularly the sensory differences afforded by the two tools – friction is apparent when drawing on paper, but gliding occurs on a smooth screen.

Viewfinders and other viewing aids

A viewfinder is a piece of card with a hole cut through it in the middle, which can be used to isolate a part of a picture or object. It allows us to concentrate on one small part or area without being distracted or overwhelmed by the whole of what can be seen. It is a useful tool that can help children focus or organise their observation and drawing. It can support hesitant children by giving a boundary to what they are looking at and it can help children who find it hard to keep track of where and what they are looking at, by bringing them back to the same area each time they look and look back.

When you are making viewfinders for use with the children you are supporting or teaching take into consideration the size of the card. You need enough card around the hole to block out the rest of the visual information from the child's field of vision, but it should not be too big and unwieldy, especially if each child is using a view-finder. Think about the size and shape of the hole the child will look through. If it is too small, what the child can see may be so limited it may be lacking in interest, whilst if it is too large it defeats the purpose of a viewfinder. The colour of the card you use should also be thought about – a contrast to what is being looked at or a neutral colour so it is not distracting to the eye. It can be useful to make over time a selection of sizes and shapes of hole and colour of card so that children have a choice.

When you are using a viewfinder, it is important to help the children to appreciate that the viewfinder can help them look but it is they that have to make a choice of what to look at. You can model how to place the viewfinder in different positions, so the child can look first before definitely deciding where it will go and starting to draw. It is unlikely that the first place you happen to put it will be just the right place. For children who may move around a lot you may need to help them by taping the viewfinder down once they have decided on their placement, so it does not get bumped and displaced by accident.

Figure 7.1 Examples of viewfinders

In addition to viewfinders you might sometimes consider using magnifying glasses when drawing from observation. These can support children in drawing close up and aiming for detail. Looking at items or surfaces using a visualiser or a micro-scope connected to the IWB or laptop can also be an effective way of taking a closer look. Clement and Page (1992) suggest using mirrors and other reflective surfaces as a way of looking at familiar items from new and unusual viewpoints.

Supporting and teaching as children draw

As you support or teach children whilst they draw there are some strategies that you can employ to help them. Some of these are approaches that you may use in many learning situations; others may be more specific to drawing. It is important to make sure that the adults supporting the class understand and agree how children will be supported so that there can be consistency. This may extend to a school-wide policy or it may be something you implement in the classroom you work in. You will also need to consider the needs of individual children within the general classroom approach and there may be aspects you approach differently to meet individual needs.

A first principle is that you show that you respect children's work and outcomes by never drawing onto their work. If a teacher has ever drawn onto your work you may remember feelings of unease, frustration or even anger. Clearly there will be times when a child is struggling and needs suggestions of what to do to improve. You can do this by talking and making suggestions or by drawing on a piece of paper along-side their drawing, rather than onto it. If you or the child is concerned that trying out the next step might spoil the drawing you could photocopy the work and work onto the copy, so that the original is not lost. This can allow children to take a risk they may otherwise be unwilling to take. If you do model by drawing alongside the child try to show them just enough to help, or one or two alternatives to choose from, and put your modelled drawing away so that they are not tempted to copy it.

When you are giving feedback to children to help them improve their work always acknowledge the motivation, effort and perseverance that they have put into their work. We need to help children to appreciate the challenge of learning to draw. It takes hard work and regular practice to develop drawing skills, just like any other area of learning. Giving children a positive attitude is crucial. If you were not given a positive attitude about drawing it is all the more important that you do not allow this feeling to seep into your own support or teaching of drawing to children. If you subtly communicate that learning to draw is an impossible task, or that not being able to draw does not matter, you will be denying children the opportunity to develop an important way of communicating with, making sense of and responding to the world.

Reflect and extend

Read the article 'Responding to Children's Drawing' by Robert Watts, published in the journal *Education* 3–13 in 2010 (Volume 38, Number 2, pp.137–153).

Think about the implications for your own learning and the way you support and teach drawing to children.

Connecting to other parts of the art curriculum

It is likely drawing will be part of most units of work in art, particularly at the exploring and developing ideas stage. Sometimes it may be the main focus of a unit, leading to an outcome that is a drawing or has drawing as a main part. In addition, developing children's drawing skills should be planned for as a continuous thread throughout all units. Drawing is an interdisciplinary practice, just as reading and writing are, and these continue throughout the English curriculum. It is important that drawing is taught directly: following a scheme of work such as that written by Fabian, (2005) or the teaching ideas available through the Access Art website and The Big Draw, will support you in terms of your subject knowledge and teaching.

Starting points for drawing

Children should have the opportunity to draw for different purposes and reasons and their drawings should be inspired by a variety of starting points. It is important that we consider these areas when we plan drawing experiences for children. If you reflect upon the experiences that are given to children in their drawing throughout a year or key stage you can evaluate how they match to the areas discussed below. It may be that one area is used as a stimulus or context much more often than the others and this imbalance is something to consider in your planning.

Drawing from observation is often a large part of the planned drawing experience in school. This can be an increasingly challenging area for children as they may be matching and judging their own drawing to the 'real' object, person or scene that they are trying to record on paper. We need to support children to develop their skills so that they can begin to explore, record and dialogue what they see. Ensuring we choose or help them to choose appropriate tools to draw with, guiding them to look in ways useful for drawing and giving them opportunities to look at the different ways artists have drawn can be helpful.

When we ask children to draw from observation it is important that we give them interesting starting points so that they want to draw. Children need opportunities to draw from imagination or the world around them and should experience drawing relevant to their life experiences. Where possible we should try to give children choices within what we are asking them to draw, so that there is at least a possibility of being interested in the subject matter. We should also take account of children's previous experiences, so that they do not repeat the same tasks for the same purpose. If they do return to a similar or the same starting point it should be to explore it in a different medium, for a new purpose or in greater depth.

Drawing from experience allows children to explore their lives and memories and express their feelings using different materials. When children spontaneously draw they will often draw scenes of what has happened to them in their lives.

Their drawings tell stories, often including several scenes or viewpoints, and may convey their feelings through the way they use tools and materials and the marks they make. They may be less concerned with making their drawings look 'real' in the way discussed in the previous paragraph and this can give them more freedom and should be encouraged. For younger children, drawing can be an easier way to communicate than writing. Drawing as a response to significant events in personal, school, national or spiritual life, such as celebrating festivals, can often allow children to convey much more than they could if asked to write about the experience or memory. Talking about experiences may help children recall details to develop their work further or a spontaneous response focused on what was significant for the child may be more appropriate.

Drawing from imagination is perhaps an area that we find more challenging to plan for in the art curriculum. Starting points for stimulating imaginative work may be responses to music, poetry or stories. Many children are interested in fantasy in literature, television, film and computer games, so they have a visual vocabulary to use in their drawing. This could be seen as a hindrance to the child's individual imagination or as a wealth of imagery to draw upon when starting out on their own imaginative drawing. It may also be more motivating for some children and boost their confidence. Drawing from imagination may also allow us to make links to many other subjects, such as English, and the children's own story illustrations and animations.

As well as drawing to explore and represent observations, experience and imagination, children should have the opportunity to use drawing to explore and record in a more abstract way. In this type of drawing, their outcome will not 'look like' what they are drawing and the drawing itself may not be the end product but rather the experience of making the marks in the moment. Drawing to respond to and convey a sense of movement, atmosphere or feelings is a way of approaching this.

Changing the way children look at and record the familiar can also help them move from figurative to abstract work: asking them to isolate small areas and draw them much larger; asking them to experiment with rules such as only lift the pencil and replace it five times before you have to start a new drawing; or asking them to make a rubbing and draw from it using the marks they see in their drawing. Look for examples of where artists are drawing to explore drawing and not to make a finished representation of something to get more ideas about this approach to drawing. Even connecting drawing practices to those working in other mediums, such as Alison Goodyear, is useful because children can see how drawing techniques translate across art disciplines – in this example into paint and virtual reality. The idea that drawing is a relevant, contemporary and interdisciplinary practice is also reinforced.

Drawing used alongside digital tools can give children opportunities to explore the connections between the physical and digital worlds. Creating a hand-drawn environment in which they place a Google AR animal, or using digital drawing tools to create a digital environment for animal ornaments or toys, can both be examples of this approach. Drawing digitally onto photos or scans of their own art work is another way to experiment with this combination, as is drawing into photos they have taken themselves or collected.

Figure 7.2 Working with a combination of digital and physical tools

Drawing within units of work

In the early stages of a unit of work there will be many opportunities to include drawing as a means of observing, researching and gathering ideas and visual information, which can be used towards making a finished outcome that in itself might not include drawing. At this stage children could be working in physical or digital sketchbooks. They could be exploring and learning about a visual element through drawing before going on to develop it in another medium or process, or experimenting with drawing tools, including digital, to learn about their potential. When drawing to research we might encourage children to annotate the drawing with descriptive words and phrases, written independently, scribed or audio recorded. We can encourage drawing from several viewpoints, then zoom in and look at the details. Drawing to investigate and research may be an important part of the exploring and developing stage of a unit of work and these drawings may be less a finished outcome and more of a learning process.

Some units of work may be entirely focused on drawing, or drawing along with another related medium, with an outcome that is primarily a drawing. In these units of work you have the opportunity to pay more in-depth attention to children's drawing. Perhaps these are opportunities to tackle challenging areas such as representing space or combining drawing with watercolour, ink wash or printmaking. This might also be an opportunity to use digital media and in particular drawing software on the computer screen, large-scale on the IWB or on mobile devices. Drawing may also be embedded into interdisciplinary schemes of work which focus on learning approaches like STEAM (Science, Technology, Engineering, Arts and Maths). As in the light trails example discussed in chapter 4, drawing can be a central element in establishing learning connections which concern the arts and interdisciplinary teaching and learning practice.

Connecting to other subjects in the curriculum

There are often opportunities to draw in subjects other than art. We need to think about the purpose of these drawings, the skills that are required for these types of drawing and how they relate to learning to draw in art. As mentioned in earlier chapters, if learning objectives are firmly related to the skills, knowledge and understanding of the art curriculum then the activity can be defined as art. If the learning objective is related to illustrating within another subject – drawing a labelled diagram of a flower or drawing a Tudor house showing the construction clearly – it is not.

In your school: when do we draw?

Exploring drawing across the curriculum

In this practical task you will be asked to consider when and why children are asked to draw in their school life and how the skills for different types and purposes of drawing will be different.

You will need:

the pro forma below or a copy of it and a medium or weekly plan that you have worked from

What to do:

Look back over plans that you have observed, supported or taught from. Identify when drawing has been part of an activity. Note this onto the pro forma in the appropriate subject row. Then look again at the activities that included drawing and identify the features of the drawing that were important in the activity. Note down any other thoughts that occur to you, perhaps other ideas about when drawing is used in the subjects you support or teach. Focus on subjects other than art as drawing in the art curriculum will be discussed below.

Activity – Exploring drawing across the curriculum

Subject	From your planning	Features
Computing		
Design technology		
English		
Geography		
History		
Languages		
Mathematics		
Music		
PE		
PSHE		
RE		
Science		

In this exercise you may have identified that children are often expected to draw as part of their recording and communication across the curriculum. As a student, teaching assistant or teacher who may support or teach some or all primary subjects, it is useful to have thought through how drawing in these lessons may have some different features to drawing in art.

Children may be asked to draw diagrams and charts in maths and science and in these contexts the emphasis will be on accuracy and the recording of details that can be labelled and there may be some attention paid to scale. In design technology, children may be drawing designs for something they are going to make. These drawings will need to convey aspects of the design, such as how parts will be joined or decorated, and may show how the object looks from several viewpoints. Again clarity, labelling and measurement will be important. In geography, history and RE, children may draw to record narratives about people and events, observations of places and artefacts and maps. Drawing maps in particular may employ specific conventions such as the use of colours to indicate geographical features, the use of line to show height and the use of symbols. In music, children may be asked to draw what music makes them think and feel and also draw symbols to represent music they will play. In PE, children may draw out sequences of movements they plan to make in gymnastics or dance and diagrams of how games work. In English, children may illustrate stories and poems to enhance their work or draw out storyboards to plan the overall structure of their story.

When you stop to reflect on the various types of drawing for different purposes across the curriculum it will become apparent that you need to make the features of each type clear to children through your teaching. You also should make it clear when each type is required. In a science lesson, for example, you may model and teach about drawing with clear lines so that the features of what is being drawn can be identified. You will show good examples of this type of drawing in your teaching so that children can see what they are aspiring to.

Some consideration should also be given to how drawing is used around us in day-to-day life and by people in their work. Adams (2006) lists many examples of trades and professions that use drawing and explains how they "use drawing to help them understand, to help them to think, to work out problems or to enable them to communicate ideas and information to other people" (p.1). Even if you rarely make drawings of your own you will often look at and get information from drawings in the world around you. When you use a map or look at a diagram, when you watch a cartoon or animation or identify a logo or symbol you are using your ability to interpret drawings to help you or for enjoyment. As Adams points out: "In everyday life, we cannot function without drawing. It underpins our material culture. It enables us to make things. It makes things happen" (2006, p.4). Involving children in making and interpreting drawing in all its forms beyond its inclusion in the art curriculum is significant to their lives now and in the future.

Reflect and extend

Have a look at Paul Carney's book *Drawing for Science, Invention and Discovery*, published in 2018, and explore how ideas can be represented in drawing.

Look up sketch noting or visual note-taking for children and consider how this might relate to drawing and thinking across the curriculum.

Conclusion

For many adults, drawing is the stumbling block that makes them think that art is not for them. When we have talked with adult students their answer to the question 'How do you feel about art?' will refer to drawing firstly, as if drawing is art, and secondly they use a lack of confidence and under-developed skills as a reason for disliking an entire subject. We all have skills as teachers and learners that we find challenging, but it is helpful to work hard at these and understand the challenges children may face when developing their own skills.

At the time of writing this book, amidst a global pandemic, all countries around the world are engaging in social distancing but drawing – as with other art forms – has a special capacity that can actually help children and young people make sense of situations and bring them together with others. The benefit of drawing, though, is that it is accessible to most people. Arts education organisations such as the International Society for Education Through Art (InSEA), the National Society for Art and Design Education (NSEAD) and the National Art Education Association (NAEA) have all responded to current changes in art education provision (see their websites) and have generated resources to support teachers and learners to engage with art education online and in alternative ways. In relation to drawing specifically, InSEA have initiated a project, #inseadrawcloser, which reflects the current place of drawing in art education. The #inseadrawcloser project reinforces this in that it invites people to post drawings – made using all art mediums – on a social media platform (Twitter), which can be shared with people of all ages around the globe. It encourages visual responses, allows insights into how art/ drawing techniques and opinions are understood by others and models how virtual platforms and digital media now have a central place in art.

The key messages we would like you to take from this chapter are firstly that drawing is a fundamental part of art and there is more to art than drawing. As you read this chapter, we hope you see that there are many ways into art, including new and developing ones, and many different processes and techniques to explore. Secondly, that you can change your attitude to drawing and make sure that children develop a positive attitude to drawing through your example, teaching and support. And finally, that drawing experiences are necessary for children to dialogue, communicate and build connections in their learning.

Next steps

- Look for examples of drawing, physical and digital, across the curriculum and in day-to-day life.
- Sign up for updates from The Big Draw website.
- Look for drawing classes or workshops, on and offline, to boost your confidence and develop your drawing skills.
- Start keeping your own sketchbook with notes, sketches, ideas and examples.

References

Adams, E. (2006) *Professional Practices.* Lancing: Power Drawing.

Anning, A. (2002) Conversations Around Young Children's Drawing: The Impact of the Beliefs of Significant Others at Home and School. *Journal of Art and Design Education.* **Vol 21**, No 3, pp.197–208.

Barnes, R. (2002) *Teaching Art to Young Children.* Abingdon: Routledge Falmer.

Clement, R. and Page, S. (1992) *Investigating and Making in Art.* Harlow: Oliver and Boyd.

Cox, S. (2005) Intention and Meaning in Young Children's Drawing. *The International Journal of Art and Design Education.* **Vol 24**, No 2, pp.115–125.

Deguara, J. and Nutbrown, C. (2017) Signs, symbols and schemas: understanding meaning in a child's drawings. *International Journal of Early Years Education.* **Vol 26**, No 11, pp.4–23.

Edwards, B. (2012) *The New Drawing on the Right Side of the Brain.* 4th ed. London: Tarcher.

Efland, A. (2002) *Art and cognition.* New York: Teachers College Press.

Eisner, E. (2002) *The arts and the creation of mind.* New Haven, CT: Yale University Press.

Fabian, M. (2005) *Drawing is a Class Act.* Dunstable: Brilliant Publications.

Heaton, R. (2019) Digital Art in the United Kingdom. In: Hickman, R., Baldacchino, J., Freedman, K., Hall, E. and Meager, N. (eds). *International Encyclopedia of Art and Design Education.* London: John Wiley.

Heaton, R. and Edwards, J. (2017) Technology for the inclusive creative arts. In: Caldwell, H., Cullingford-Agnew, S. (eds). *Technology for SEND in primary schools: a guide for best practice*. London: Learning Matters: Sage. Pp.119–137.

OFSTED (2012) *Making a mark: art, craft and design education*. [online] Available from: www.ofsted.gov.uk/resources/making-mark-art-craft-and-design-education-2008–11 [Accessed 31/03/12].

OFSTED (2019) *The education inspection framework*. [online] Available from: https://assets.publishing.service.gov.uk/government/uploads/system/uploads/attachment_data/file/801429/Education_inspection_framework.pdf [Accessed 27/07/2020].

Price, S., Jewitt, C. and Crescenzi, L. (2015) The role of iPads in pre-school children's mark making development. *Computers & Education*. **Vol 87**, pp.131–141.

Rose, S. and Jolley, R. (2019) Children's Creative Intentions: Where do the Ideas for their Drawings Come from? *The Journal of Creative Behavior*. Pp.1–13.

Sedgwick, F. (2002) *Enabling Children's Learning through Drawing*. London: David Fulton.

Further resources

Briggs, P. (2015) *Drawing projects for children*. London: Black Dog Publishing.

Carney, P. (2018) *Drawing for Science, Invention and Discovery*. Loughborough: Loughborough Design Press.

Cox, M., Cooke, G. and Friffin, D. (1995) Teaching children to draw in the infants school. In: Gregory, P., March, C. and Tutchell, S. (2020) *Mastering Primary Art and Design*. London: Bloomsbury Academic.

Herne, S., Cox, S. and Watts, R. (2009) *Readings in Primary Art Education*. London: Intellect Books. Pp.153–168.

Hope, G. (2008) *Thinking and Learning through Drawing*. London: Sage.

Hughes, S. (2002) *A Life Drawing. Recollections of an Illustrator*. London: Random House.

Chapter Padlet:

https://padlet.com/Jeanne/Chapter7

08

Chapter Eight

Painting

Introduction

Painting can be both satisfying and challenging; it can provide opportunities to learn and develop skills, knowledge and understanding in art. Painting is often available to young children, but opportunities to learn and develop painting skills which foster increasing control and resources can sometimes become less frequent. Children can explore and spontaneously discover how to paint for themselves given freedom, time and access to a range of tools and materials. With guidance from their teachers and teaching assistants they can develop and improve their painting skills and knowledge of painting. It can be limiting if they only paint irregularly and to meet prescribed outcomes, so children need opportunities to play with paint, physically and digitally, so that they can dialogue with the world (Biesta, 2017) through this medium.

Throughout the primary years children should be taught and guided when painting. They should have opportunities to explore, experiment and discover the possibilities of working with paint. Painting in explorative ways, whether physical or digital, enables children to encounter resistance and exist in a middle ground between the world and themselves, in a position where they can figure things out for themselves and begin to make sense of materials, techniques, environments and their views and place in the world (Biesta, 2017). Art, or in this context painting, becomes a way through the world for children.

Tools and materials

There are many types of paint and ways of applying paint for different purposes that children should experience during their primary years. These are listed in the appendices, where paint types and painting tools are explored in depth. Paint can be applied with a variety of body parts and children can enjoy the feel of applying paint, or natural forms of paint like mud, directly onto different surfaces. Changing the texture of paint can be an interesting sensory experience. Some children dislike getting paint directly on their fingers or body so thin plastic gloves / aprons can be used and a range of tools for paint application can be provided. Letting children make their own painting tools also aids exploration. Painting devices can be made from natural materials (like twigs and feathers tied together with yarn) or manmade materials (like pegs, sponges, combs, balloons or cotton buds). It is also important to be experimental with the process of making paintings. Children can make their own spinning wheels or tops, so that they can create spin paintings like Damien Hirst, or use roll balls, tyres and springs to create action paintings like Jackson Pollock. They can also make simple robots to program and paint with, either by attaching painting tools to electronic toys or robots or by making simple kinetic devices that produce paintings. These types of immersive painting experiences also connect well to STEAM (Science, technology, engineering, arts and maths) opportunities for children, enabling them to build learning connections, transfer skills and engage in interdisciplinary experiences.

In the chart below, some of the most common types of paint available in the primary school are summarised.

Type of paint	Definition	In school	Useful for
Powder colour	Powder pigment that when mixed with water creates an opaque painting medium	tubs of primary colours, black and white	Mixing own colours Versatile – many colours can be made; adding PVA, wallpaper paste, washing powder, etc., can vary the consistency
Watercolour	A transparent painting medium	tins each with twelve hard tablet colours and a lid to use as a palette	Experimenting with building up layers Taking outside to use (very easily portable)
Ready mixed	Usually an opaque poster colour (opaque version called 'chromar' available)	squeezy bottles	Convenient to use in the classroom
Acrylics	Pigment in an acrylic polymer emulsion that can be diluted with water to various thicknesses	bottles / tubes	Can be used in different ways according to the amount of water used with it Can be used on many different surfaces
Drawing inks / Brusho	Based on dyes rather than pigments (use with care – some does not wash out of clothing)	bottles of ink or small canisters of powder (Brusho)	Making washes / wax resist Can be used to dye fabric as well as on paper

Painting is now available to us in digital forms, through using digital painting applications on laptops or mobile devices such as Sketches, Brushes, Paper 53, Draw and Tell, Adobe Photoshop, Corel Painter and the 3D virtual reality application Tilt Brush. More creative engagements with digital painting can also occur by becoming part of paintings using green screening techniques, by experimenting with adding sound to paintings and by manipulating or traversing between physical and digital painterly techniques. The Tate Gallery also have their own online resource, Tate Paint, where children can create their own digital paintings using a range of painting tools.

Link: www.tate.org.uk/kids/games-quizzes/tate-paint

Try for yourself – digital painting tools

Exploring and evaluating digital painting apps and tools

You will need: a laptop or tablet with a painting app or tool and the pro forma below

What to do: Systematically try out the tools in the list and make notes about them. As you do so, think about how they connect to painting using real materials.

Activity – Exploring and evaluating digital painting apps and tools

Look for and evaluate	Your notes	Comparison to 'real' painting
Painting tools: List the range of painting tools available in the app. Have a go with each one. What choices are available within each one (size of tool)?		
Painting surfaces: List the range of painting surfaces available in the app. Have a go with each one.		
Colour choices: What is the range of colour choices like? Can colour be mixed onscreen?		
Effects: What other effects are available?		
Saving and replaying: How is your work saved? Can you replay your painting to see the process unfold?		
Tools used with the app: Is a stylus or mouse necessary? Can the touch pad or screen be used directly with fingers?		

Look for and evaluate	Your notes	Comparison to 'real' painting
Other: Is there anything else interesting or useful about the way this app or tool works?		

Guidance notes

Painting tools: Apps and tools will often allow the user to choose different sorts of painting tools, such as different shaped brushes (round, flat) that are similar to those used in physical painting and items that look like brushes but produce effects (dots, rainbows, spatter, patterns). Sometimes the user can change the size of the tool and access other painting tools such as spray cans, dip pens, etc.

Painting surfaces: A range of different painting surfaces are often available, some of which might simulate real surfaces such as canvas or watercolour paper, including how the tools react on it. Some apps let you export a photo from your camera roll to paint onto.

Colour choices: There is usually a significant colour range to choose from, including lighter to darker tones of colours, and sometimes a pixel chart where specific colours can be pinpointed. Colours the user has chosen can often be saved to reuse, at least for the duration of the painting. This large colour choice and ability to find lighter to darker tones and change from opaque to transparent is useful for experimenting with how colours affect each other.

Effects: In addition to tools we would associate with painting in the real world there are additional effects we might use, such as drawing and filling shapes with colour and manipulating what is on the screen to copy and paste, change its size and scale and take out parts of it with the rubber.

Saving and replaying: Usually the finished outcome can be saved to the camera roll and as a .JPG and a .PNG. This can be useful for sharing, projecting and reusing in other apps and tools to go further, e.g. as a background for animation, green screen and further manipulation. Bear in mind that when a painting is created digitally, viewing it digitally will be the most effective way to appreciate it. Printing it out will not only be costly but will change its appearance to the viewer. To see the painting appear as the painter made it by replaying it can be an interesting feature for the child who made the picture, the adults who support the child and other viewers. Some more basic tools might require being able to take a screenshot, whilst others might be saving the image as a one-off, allowing the user to return and continue working.

Tools used with the app: Many apps and tools can respond directly to our finger moving on the screen or touch pad, giving us a sense of producing colour from our own hands. Others respond better to the use of a stylus or mouse, sometimes allowing more sophisticated results.

Other: Some digital painting apps and tools will have other features that may or may not be useful and some may seem gimmicky unless used for a worthwhile purpose. It is for you to evaluate their worth. The ability to zoom in to areas, work in more detail and then zoom out again can be useful, as can being able to undo and redo.

When you considered the similarities and differences between working digitally and with real paint there are, of course, some crucial differences in terms of the sensory nature of the experience, although some digital tools seek to include some additional sensory input by adding sounds to the tools. The key for you when supporting learning is that you give children experiences of both types of painting and that your selection is appropriate in relation to the task or experience. Sometimes you will combine both painterly means, so the advantages of each are utilised.

It is important that we do not consider painting onscreen as an alternative to applying paint to other materials, but rather as an experience with intrinsic qualities of its own. As Matthews and Seow (2007) comment: "although it is essential that children explore the messy gooeyness and splatteriness of real pigment, the smooth glide of electronic paint across a luminous glass screen is also a sensuous and enjoyable experience" (p.285).

Find out more

Have a look at the Artful Kids website: Digital Art for Kids: https://artful-kids. com/2010/07/02/digital-art-for-kids/

This resource will connect you to a range of experiences where you can explore Street Art paintings with children, engage in digital activities that explore the work of artists like Keith Haring or contribute creative outputs to an online gallery.

Characteristics of different types of paint

Knowing about painting can allow you to find out more about different types of paint and their properties and this will enable you to plan and teach effective lessons. Throughout their primary years children should investigate a range of paints as well as have the opportunity to use the same paints over time in order to progress their confidence and skills in one area. In the chart on page 189 some of the most commonly used types of paint, with an outline of their main characteristics, are listed.

Powder colour, watercolour, ready mixed and acrylic paints, as well as drawing inks or pigment such as Brusho, are perhaps the most commonly available in primary schools. Although the storage and management of powder paint can be challenging it does provide a great opportunity for experiencing the tactile satisfaction of mixing a colour from pigment and water. The consistency and quality can be varied by the amount of water added or by using PVA glue, wallpaper paste, washing up liquid or washing powder. Watercolours, ready-mix and acrylic paint can all be mixed to create new colours as well.

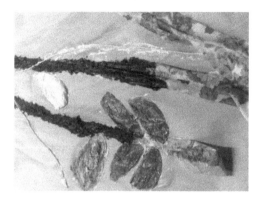

Figure 8.1 Applying paint

LEARNING IN ACTION

A group of undergraduate art education students explored techniques for applying and altering the texture of paint whilst learning about artist Henri Rousseau. The students were encouraged to paint large-scale, to experiment with different types of paint to explore their qualities and to use a range of tools to apply it, including paintbrushes, palette knives, strips of card, combs and sticks. The students took inspiration from Rousseau's work. They were encouraged not to copy it but to interpret it their own way as a collaborative group. The students encountered at first hand the challenges of painting collaboratively. They empathised with the way children may feel in collaborative situations and they considered how to deal with children showing signs of stress in similar situations. Some students suggested sharing strategies for effective collaborative working – like discussing what it means to be part of a team, showing respect and assigning jobs or tasks, whilst others suggested allowing children to create their own contributions independently, which could then contribute to the group painting. It is important to remember learners are individuals, so trialling a range of painterly and collaborative ways of working is important to see what is most appropriate for each learner in your class – art education should be a positive experience.

As the students painted they became absorbed in applying paint and exploring colours, marks and paint application techniques, which made them realise how diverse painting can be. Some enjoyed the unpredictability of flicking and spattering whilst others preferred the control of more carefully placed lines and shapes. Having time to experiment helped the students consider the range of ways of applying paint and how to teach children about these in art. Many realised that whilst children could be taught how to apply paint in these ways, perhaps by modelling techniques, they would also need opportunities to practise and progress techniques to develop them in their work – painting can also be scaffolded by teachers and peers.

Towards the end of the session the students identified challenges in terms of classroom organisation and resourcing and discussed how these might be overcome. They identified factors like having space to work, protecting clothes and classroom furnishings from paint and drying the paintings. They then discussed how too many resources may be overwhelming for staff and students and how these could be introduced gradually, depending on the age phase or skills of the children.

Once the artworks were complete the students explored how digital integration could occur in the painting session. Some students suggested that one member of the group could film or photograph techniques the others were using in order to document paint skills and means of application. Another suggested that time lapse films could record learning, whilst a different student spoke of how the paintings could be abstracted in digital apps to develop them or be used as backgrounds for animations or films. The students spoke of how it is important that digital integration is part of the art learning experience, not an add-on to it. It needs to be purposefully built into the learning scheme being followed, or be central to the learning connections being established.

In this case study paint and its application are explored by students. In this exploratory context the students experienced creative pedagogy (Lin, 2011) and they were engaged in creative teaching, teaching for creativity and creative learning. Creative teaching occurred when the students were given the freedom to explore leading their own learning through art making, teaching for creativity happened because the intention of the lesson was to learn about painting (applications, materials and techniques) through self-discovery and it appears evident that creative learning occurred because of the diverse range of visual outputs (creative painting techniques shown and produced) and explanations given by the students to reinforce their decisions and findings. The students used their creative acts to understand painting.

Subject knowledge

Exploring visual elements through painting

The chart below makes suggestions in relation to each of the eight visual elements. When you are planning and teaching a unit of work that involves painting it is important to identify one or two visual elements that you will develop with the children. It is likely that this will have been done at the long-term planning stage. Colour is the visual element that often springs to mind when we think of painting, although there are opportunities to learn about many others. The NSEAD web resource, 'Talk About a Painting', also offers support for thinking about the formal elements of art in relation to painting.

Link: www.nsead.org/resources/units-of-work/uow-talk-about-a-painting/

Line	Tone
Exploring making lines and marks with a variety of painting tools such as sticks, colour shapers, sponge paddles, brushes, fingers and styluses on digital device screens	Choosing, mixing and using various tones of the same colour / different colours Considering the effect that tone can have on the feel of the painting to the maker or viewer Zooming in to look at the tones shown in different pixels and on different parts of digital paintings
Colour	**Pattern**
Choosing, mixing and using a range of colours (primary, secondary, complementary, clashing, etc.) on real and digital paint Exploring the feelings the use of colours can evoke – warm and cool colours, dark and bright colours, etc. Combining and using colours to create different effects in paint and using filters and effects on devices	Using pattern within painting to create effects and cover areas – spots, dashes, lines, etc. Looking at the patterns artists use in real and virtual paintings Using simple coding software such as Scratch to make simple repetitive patterns
Texture	**Shape**
Exploring thin, thick, gritty, smooth textures in paint Represent texture in painting through marks or adding items to your paint Create digital texture paintings by building up digital layers in paint apps Using textures found in images of buildings – brickwork, objects – sponge or liquids – water effects	Exploring regular and irregular shapes in paint, dipping different shaped items into paint Use software like Pattern Shapes: https://apps.mathlearningcenter.org/pattern-shapes/ to create digital paintings made from shapes
Space	**Form**
Using paint to create the illusion of space through composition, perspective, etc. Using paint in the virtual world (Tilt Brush)	Using paint decoratively on 3D forms Use real objects and digital photography to create scenes that could become digital or physical paintings Applying colours, tones and textures, physically and digitally, to develop paintings

As you read the suggestions in the chart above you might notice that in some examples children are likely to be learning about painting itself – how to apply paint in different ways physically and digitally, the properties of paint and the tools that can be used. In others they are painting to produce an outcome – a painting or a 2D or 3D outcome in which painting is a part of the process; for example, painting to decorate a physical or digital 3D object they have made. When planning for learning it is important that you are clear about your objectives and learning outcomes and plan for some time in which to learn or refine the relevant painting skills.

Colour mixing and using their own colours was a part of painting for primary children, but with the development and ease of ready-mix paints and digital palettes, this opportunity is now not always made available. Where possible, allow children opportunities to experience the science of painting, engage them in mixing and controlling the consistency and colour of paint and let them experience the learning opportunities and satisfaction that paint offers. Let art making teach (Biesta, 2017).

Exploring colour mixing

When adults mix colours for children they can ensure that they are provided with a range of colours and consistencies to experience over time. When children have the opportunity to mix their own colours they are more likely to experiment and learn about colour. As they look at and talk about the work of artists it will become apparent to children that artists are not using a few standard colours but are using colour in a sophisticated and creative way. Children need the opportunity to explore this for themselves in their own work. Allowing children to mix colours can seem daunting in terms of organisation of materials, space and time but the learning opportunities it provides are enormous and outweigh organisational challenges.

When buying ready mixed paint or powder colour buy a range of colours or pigments that will allow you and the children to mix the colours that you want: this is known as the 'double primary system'. Barnes (2002) suggests that the following pigments are needed:

Red – crimson (a dark red) and vermilion (a scarlet bright red)
Blue – Prussian blue (a turquoise) and ultramarine (a brilliant blue)
Yellow – lemon yellow and brilliant yellow
Black – we recommend that you have less or no black pigment and encourage
    children to mix their own 'black' or dark shade from a combination of other
    colours
White – you will need more white pigment

If you plan to allow children to mix their own colours from powder pigment it is wise to develop a clear and organised work space and teach this to children. Pratchett (2007) presents an effective and well-organised system that can support children towards independence in their use of powder paint to mix their own colours. Using this as a basis for your own organisation can help you to pre-empt some of the problems you may be concerned about.

Artists, designers and craftspeople

When you decide to use a painting or the work of a painter to inspire or inform learning in art there are so many to choose from that it can be overwhelming – this can lead to safe and obvious choices being made. We are all dependent on our own knowledge of painters and painting, as well as the resources available to us, and we can develop this over time and in response to personal experiences and children's interests. The choices we make are significant, so it is important that we seek out interesting and varied paintings and painters to look at and teach with, such as those from different times and cultures, of different genders and addressing historic, present and future issues of the self and society. A current example of uniting physical and digital paint practices might be to explore the 'virtual Viral paintings' of artist Marc Quinn, who has used painting to create a personal visual diary of living through the Covid-19 health pandemic. As Biesta (2017, p.118) reminds us, learning art should help children feel at home in the world. With art education practices changing at this current time – for example, children are engaging more with art through home-based learning practices – as art teachers we too need to ensure that our art practices and those we engage children in, such as painting or exploring artists' work, are also developing and developing in ways that align to the present and future worlds on offer to children.

So, when using paintings and painters we might think about matters like:

Think about:	Type of paint	Example
The type of paint being used by the artist	Oil paint	Berthe Morisot
	Digital paint	David Hockney
How the paint is applied or manipulated	Careful lines and marks	Bridget Riley
	Series of washes	Elizabeth Blackadder
How colour is used	Bright colours	Chris Ofili
	Primary colours	Piet Mondrian
What the subject matter is	Urban environment	LS Lowry
	Animated films	Hayao Miyazaki (Studio Ghibli)

As your knowledge of art and its contribution increases, your confidence will develop and you will be able to go beyond the paintings and painters that you usually use and start choosing alternatives. Here are some suggestions, but there are many other great choices to be found if you want to tie your selections with your own interests and resources.

Artists who paint using watercolour include illustrators of children's books such as Jane Ray, whose paintings are delicate and vibrantly coloured illustrations of myths and legends, and Michael Foreman, who uses pale washes and deep colour to illustrate his own stories and myths and legends from around the world. Elizabeth Blackadder often paints using watercolours, painting still lifes of flowers, plants, objects and animals, often against white or plain backgrounds. From the past it can be interesting to look at the sketchpads and watercolours of Queen Victoria; examples can be found on the royal collection website. Links can be made to animation – search on the Teachers' Media website for the animation 'The Monk and the Fish'. The animation itself is accompanied by a short programme about the making, which includes the work of a watercolour artist who talks about how and why he painted as he did.

Artists who use watercolour or ink wash and line include children's book illustrators Quentin Blake and Brian Wildsmith. Botanical illustrators also often use watercolour or line and wash – you can find examples of the Victorian botanical illustrator Jane Loudon on the Victoria and Albert Museum website. Fashion designers too often use this technique in their work.

There are so many artists who paint in oils and acrylics. Paintings by Impressionist artists such as Degas and Monet are often used in schools and there were two women artists who are considered to be part of this group – Berthe Morisot and Mary Cassatt. Analysing the reason for your choice could lead you away from the usual choices into some more interesting and individual areas. If you had chosen Monet because he painted from the same view on a number of occasions look at the work of Japanese artist Hokusai, who made a series of prints of views of Mount Kilimanjaro. If you had chosen Monet because of his painting techniques think about other painters who applied paint in similar ways, such as Seurat and Signac, or in contrasting ways artists such as Bridget Riley and Mark Rothko. Remember that the painters that you choose should not all come from Europe – search the Ashmolean Museum website for Indian miniature paintings or look for the work of Chris Ofili, a painter of Nigerian heritage who began painting in the UK and now lives in Trinidad. As mentioned previously, Google Arts and Culture is a fantastic resource for accessing global and diverse art.

Teaching

If you are planning a unit of work that includes painting, be clear about the painting techniques and skills required to achieve pleasing results. The decisions you make will be related to what type of paint you are planning to use, the starting points and learning outcomes that you are using and the prior knowledge, skills and understanding that you will be building upon. Some areas for consideration are the use of tools and approaches to making paintings.

Use of tools

Some of the most obvious skills in painting are holding and manipulating the paintbrush or painting tool to make marks. When considering painting tools you should think about what will be appropriate for the children you teach and what works with the type of paint you are using. Factors to take into consideration include:

Gripping brushes

Long-handled paintbrushes may be unwieldy for some children and they often taper, making them harder to grasp securely and manipulate with control. Short-handled brushes with thick handles that are easily gripped may be a better choice. Alternatively, children could be allowed to choose the brushes that feel right to them from a range. Choice may allow you to encourage some children to select the brushes you know will suit them.

Using tools other than brushes

Earlier in this chapter we mentioned that there are many other tools that can be used to apply paint: paint shapers, palette knives, toothbrushes, sticks and sponge paddles. Giving children the opportunity to paint with a range of tools helps them develop their fine motor control. Using fingers, hands and feet to apply paint allows children to experience the tactile qualities of paint and a different kind of control in its application.

Pressure applied to tool

When you model painting techniques, it is important to allow children opportunities to understand how to make effective marks. Younger children and children who find the manipulation of tools a challenge often press down with their brush so hard that the bristles or hairs are pressed onto the paper and the metal ferrule scratches the paper. Children can be reminded in a tactile way to use the tip of the brush by asking them to practise stroking the palm of their hand with the tip of a brush to feel the pressure they are aiming for.

Digital painting

Some aspects of painting such as choice of colour, size of brush, type of paint and mark making can be explored through using art software, as you did in the earlier task. This is a different sensory experience for children and could be considered as an additional way to explore paint and painting. There are also opportunities now, as mentioned, to explore painting in 3D through virtual reality, which will be explored more fully in chapter 12.

If making a painting using digital media is your aim then you might consider how this can best be displayed, since the effect of the light can be dispersed when the painting is printed out. There are now lots of options to create online galleries using apps, or to post content on school platforms, such as websites, blogs or social media outlets. Such experiences not only disseminate children's artwork but enable children to understand how art is shared by artists in today's society. You need to adhere to e-safety regulations when doing this and it is also useful to teach children about how to talk about and give effective art feedback as explored earlier in chapter 5.

Making paintings

When planning for children to paint as the main part of a unit of work there are some areas to consider to support their learning and success. Considering the surface onto which children paint and whether and how they plan out their composition will help them prepare to paint. Ensuring that we teach what children need to know about painting techniques will also support them, as will planning to use different sorts of paint and painting.

The painting surface

It can be disappointing or frustrating for children to paint onto white paper, or a white screen – this either leaves a white background or children struggle to fill in around what they have painted. Thinking about the surface they paint onto at the planning stage can help overcome this. Building in opportunities for children to choose from coloured papers or textured materials on which to paint is one way to quickly and easily provide a more diverse background. Applying marks, rubbings, patterns or washes, or using digital prints or photos, are other strategies. These approaches also give you the opportunity to start children thinking about the use of space in their composition – what do you want the background to look like? Why?

LEARNING IN ACTION

After a visit to a zoo, a class of early years children are going to paint some of the foliage and animals they saw. Before painting, their teacher asks them to collect, think and talk about the animals and their habitats in relation to the colours (foliage – greens, browns, natural colours) and shapes they saw (ovals, circles, etc.). Each child paints a large background of greens and browns as their 'foliage' and these are allowed to dry – the background could take the form of a paint wash. As they make their background they talk with the teaching assistant, who is helping them about which animals they will go on to paint and where they will be in their painting. This allows them to begin to think about and plan out what they will paint and how they will use space in the compositions. They can give some consideration to the animals that will be in the foreground at the painting stage, without leaving a white area around all of their animals. Later in the week, when the children paint their animals, they paint them onto their background. Children can also use their paintings and the foliage they collected to engage in small world play, giving life to their artwork. Such experiences are also effective for developing speaking and listening skills, as the whole experience can be recorded using digital technology.

When we teach children how to use backgrounds or washes to contribute to their painting we allow them to consider the overall journey of their painting, learning how a painting can be built up over several stages. With older children, this can be developed as they gain more awareness of using space in their two- or three-dimensional work. This is quite a different approach to thinking of a painting as a one-off piece of work completed in one lesson or period of time. Although it has some implications for planning, classroom organisation and use of time it is a vital step towards developing independence and an evaluative approach on the part of the learner.

Another way of approaching this is to apply pattern or texture to the paper in a fairly random way and then paint onto it. This could be by making a wax crayon rubbing and then washing over it with ink or Brusho, or sticking ripped or cut papers of foliage onto the painting surface before painting onto it.

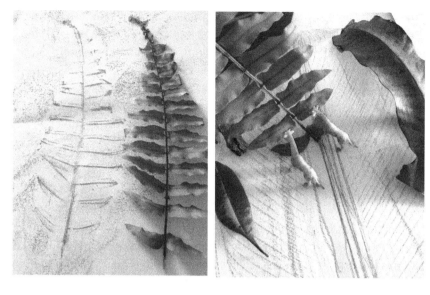

Figure 8.2 Creating backgrounds

Children can also be disappointed with their painting when they see it as a 'coloured-in drawing' approach. Perhaps you have experienced some of the difficulties that occur when children draw out their 'painting' in pencil outline and then try to fill in these often very small and fiddly shapes with paint. Working from a combination of sketches or a plan that is visible next to their painting is one alternative. If a child needs the reassurance of some guidelines on the page, painting some areas or rough outlines with a pale-coloured wash that will be painted over as the painting progresses can be helpful.

Painting with watercolours

Some ways of applying paint can be used no matter what type of paint you are using and others are more suited to certain types of paint. The type of paint that you choose to use should be closely connected to the painting technique you will be teaching. The practical exercise below is designed to help you explore the main properties and qualities of watercolour and to give a better understanding of some useful techniques and applications.

Try for yourself – exploring watercolours

Exploring using washes and painting on wet or dry paper

In this practical task you will explore the effects that can be achieved when using watercolours to paint with. Watercolours have some unique properties that can be introduced to children and will suit certain types of work.

You will need:

watercolour paints, the lid to mix colours in or a flat surface to mix on, thin and thick soft hair paintbrushes, a sponge paddle (optional), a pot of clean water and a large sheet of thick cartridge paper

What to do:

1. Dampen each tablet of colour with clean water and allow it to soak in, making the hard blocks a little softer and easier to use. (Avoid using the white tablet.)
2. Using your large brush or sponge paddle dampen a patch of the paper with some clean water. Using your smaller brush try out some spots, dashes and continuous lines on the damp paper. Take care to use the tip of your brush when painting.
3. Repeat similar marks on an area of dry paper.
4. Mix a thin colour wash of pale green and paint it onto your paper.

---

5. Using the palette mix some colours of your own to experiment with. Try to mix ten different greens to try out on your paper. Paint dots, dashes and lines onto the area that you applied the pale green wash onto earlier.

Questions to consider:

• What differences did you notice between painting on damp and dry paper?

When you painted onto the damp paper you probably found that the paint spread out in an unpredictable manner. When you painted on the dry paper you could create crisp clear edges to the marks you made. Perhaps when you painted onto the wet paper your marks were paler and more watery, whereas they were more vibrant and deep on the dry paper. As children learn about these possibilities they can use them purposefully in their work.

• How is painting with watercolours different to painting with other paints?

Perhaps you noticed that the colour of the paper is significant when painting with watercolours. Watercolours are transparent so the paper can show through the paint, having an effect on the colour. Areas of paper can be left unpainted to be white in the painting.

The amount of colour and water you mix determines the depth of colour, so rather than adding white to get paler tones you add water.

When you painted a pale wash over an area of your paper then painted onto it, this allowed you to build layers of colours and marks. With children you might consider helping them plan their composition so they can apply colour washes as a background and then paint details on to their work either when the paper is damp or when it has dried.

As you paint with so much water you may have become aware of the impact this can have on the paper. Paper that is too thin disintegrates whereas thicker paper is more likely to be a durable and effective watercolour surface. How you used the brushes may also impact the paper. Use soft brushes and their tips and avoid scratching the brush across the paper.

You may also have noticed that when your paper dried the paper was no longer flat. Finished paintings can be pressed flat under a heavy board. Alternatively, for the best work thick cartridge paper or watercolour paper can be stretched onto a board using tape. When the painting is complete it can be cut off the board.

Using watercolours to paint with is different to other types of painting. If you are going to teach children how to get the best out of these paints you must plan to teach some of the techniques discussed and demonstrate some tips to help them towards success. Look at some watercolour tutorials to assist you when learning about different techniques.

Find out more

Explore the Google Arts and Culture website https://artsandculture.google.com/ for apps like Art Transfer, to turn your world into paintings in the style of different artists or to view art in galleries using augmented reality. Play I Spy into Harry Potter paintings or search watercolour paintings to find out about artists who work in this medium, such as Georgia O'Keeffe and Lourdes Sanchez.

When you are choosing artists who paint with watercolours to inspire the children's own use of watercolour, you should consider exactly how their use of the technique will support the learning objectives you are teaching. It is important to be clear about the use of the technique and the effects that can be created, rather than the subject matter, if the learning objectives are focused on the process and the technique. Watercolours also tend to be relatively portable and easy to take outside the classroom. This allows children to mix and record colours, responding directly to what they see and experience. Using them directly into the sketchpad to develop colour on pencil or pen sketches can be an effective way of collecting and recalling visual information.

Painting with ready mixed / powder / acrylics

Using opaque paints that cover paper and other surfaces with no transparency is another very common experience for children in school. These paints come in many different forms – hard tempera blocks, powder paint, ready mixed paint of different types and acrylics. When you use hard tempera blocks, teach children to dampen the blocks and allow the water to soften them before beginning to paint. All of these paints can, of course, be mixed so that children can make their own colours – the type of paint will have an impact on the possibilities for colour mixing. Mixing colours from dry powder gives the most scope and control to children. Acrylics and liquid ready mixed paint can and should also be mixed by children. Hard tempera blocks are perhaps more similar to watercolour paint in their mixing and application qualities.

Having the opportunity to explore and experiment with paint mixing and paint application is vital to children's learning. As part of the early stages of a unit of work, some teaching and exploration of techniques will support what children can go to produce in their own work. Using the very wide range of ways artists have mixed and applied paint can help you in your teaching by providing examples and ideas, without copying whole paintings. One way of doing this is to identify some details (small patches or areas) from paintings and discuss them with children, focusing on what the paint is like and how it has been applied – interactive whiteboards, viewfinder tools and magnifiers provided on gallery websites are particularly useful for doing this.

Your choices of what to look at should be guided by what children will later paint. You might explore ways painters have applied paint by looking at natural colour use (greens, browns) by Kyffin Williams, John Constable and Henri Rousseau. The cool, muted colours of LS Lowry or Vilhelm Hammershøi, the bright, vibrant colours of Elizabeth Blackadder, Chris Ofili and Brian Wildsmith or the distinct blocks of primary colours used by Piet Mondrian. In these examples, the use of paint by the artist is the talking point rather than the subject matter of the painting. Children could try several of these techniques out for themselves, not aiming for a figurative or finished painting, in order to redevelop the ways they apply paint and use colour in painting.

LEARNING IN ACTION

In the autumn term a Year 3 class have visited their local art gallery, where they have looked at and talked about two paintings; Daubigny's *St Paul's from the Surrey Side* and Monet's *The Thames Below Westminster*, on loan from the National Gallery. The children talk about how it is possible to recognise landmarks in the paintings and infer that the artists must have worked from life and from drawings made in sketchpads. They discuss the colours in the paintings that make them think of winter – cold, dull and dark colours.

For their own paintings, the class are asked to work from their own sketches drawn around the school site. They are challenged to make sure that their drawings and the paintings that come from them will include recognisable landmarks and that their use of colour will make us think about the time of year – winter.

In order to manage the colour-mixing phase of the unit of work the class work in groups to mix a range of dull, dark and cold colours, which are stored in pots for use by the class as they make their paintings. This allows them to concentrate on colour mixing as an end in itself first and then concentrate on their paintings on a separate occasion. It also allows the teacher and the teaching assistant to organise resources and support the colour mixing for a short period and then move on to the paintings themselves.

The children go on to make their paintings and these are displayed alongside their preparatory sketches and scribed comments about what inspired their work and the challenges they faced.

In this case study children follow a unit of work leading to the outcome of a set of individual paintings inspired by environmental observation and informed by artists who have worked in a similar way. They have also exercised some control over the paint colours, using colours that may not have appeared in the paintings had the paint been used straight from the bottle, and this has caused the paintings to have a distinct winter character.

Older children, who have developed their painting skills over their primary years, should have opportunities to work on a variety of scales and have more control over how they make their paintings. Breaking down the painting into a series of steps and allowing time to review and reflect between each step supports children in evaluating their work and provides them with the time and opportunity to make decisions about the next steps. Alternatively, allowing children to choose between the latter way of working or making a series of two or three paintings to explore their response can be another approach for children who prefer to work quickly and instinctively. This also allows children the freedom they need to respond creatively and is less likely to lead to a set of similar paintings at the end of a unit of work.

Connecting to other parts of the art curriculum

Whilst children should explore and learn about painting regularly in their primary years, what they learn about paint and how to apply it should also be applied and extended within other areas of art. When children work in three dimensions, painting could form part of the decoration applied. This may also be the case when decorating functional objects made in design technology. Getting paint to adhere to a range of different surfaces can often be a challenge here and is something the teacher should prepare for. Sometimes it is easier to apply the paint to flat surfaces before the three-dimensional form is assembled. Making a connection between painting and drawing and when working in fabric, textiles and digital media can also enhance learning and allow children to use their knowledge, skills and understanding in other contexts.

When children work with threads, fabrics and textiles they might well use paint or painting techniques. Applying fabric paint directly to cotton will allow children to use their prior experience of and learning about paint. Applying wax or paste to make batiks will also include using tools such as brushes, sticks or more specific tools (a tjanting tool in batik). Including some painting experiences early in the unit of work can help children activate their prior knowledge, skills and understanding before going on to apply and develop it in the context of using different materials.

LEARNING IN ACTION

A class of Year 5 children will be going on to explore batik in a unit of work based around Adire cloth. This cloth is made in Africa by dyeing white cotton using an indigo blue dye. The children look at some examples of Adire that show the contrast of dark, deep blue and white and look at and talk about some of the patterns used on the fabric.

They begin by mark making freely, using white wax crayons on white cartridge paper and washing over it with deep blue ink. They recall the way wax can block out and resist the ink in the way that the wax will resist the dye in batik. This helps them think about how to make their own pattern for the batik they will make later.

They go on to explore making their own patterns on paper using white wax crayons to draw, creating lines, shapes and simplified natural forms, and then washing over these with ink. After making two or three versions, the children evaluate their ideas by considering the effect of their pattern or design, with a focus on the contrast of deep blue and white works.

(Batik – hot liquid wax is applied to cloth and when it is dry the fabric is dyed, creating a pattern.)

In the case study above painting is a minor but important part of the unit of work, leading to batik work on fabric. Nevertheless, children enjoy this part of their art and use the wax resists as a crucial part of their research, in that the wax crayons act in the same way that the liquid wax will when it resists and protects the fabric from the dye.

Reflect and extend

Find the article ' "It's Not For Real": The Tablet as Palette in Early Childhood Education', by Margareta Borg and published in the *International Journal of Education and the Arts* (Volume 20, Number 14). In this article Borg models and explores how a tablet can become a palette that enables young children to learn fundamental art skills using modern painterly techniques. The strengths and limitations of her digital approach are presented.

Connecting to other subjects and beyond

Painting can provide a worthwhile link to other subject areas. We also discussed how paintings can help us explore spiritual, moral, social and cultural learning. Making paintings can also connect across the curriculum, as long as we are careful to protect the integrity of the learning in art and avoid it becoming subsumed into the learning of the other subjects or activities.

When you see paintings displayed in art galleries and exhibitions they usually have a label. This tends to state the name of the artist, the date it was painted, the title and the medium it was painted in. Sometimes there is a statement about what inspired the artist to make the work. Engagement with artistic information is a valuable experience for children to have because they can apply such approaches in their own work. Learners can be encouraged to give their paintings a title whilst articulating their inspirations and aims for making the artwork. Formulating and communicating this supporting information can be part of the evaluative process towards the end of a unit of work and can be a meaningful connection with spoken language and writing in the English curriculum. This can be made digital and include speaking and listening by making a one-minute clip of the child artist introducing their work, or setting children up to interview each other.

Some of the experimental learning about colour and light that children explore when painting can connect to learning in the science curriculum about light and dark, reflection and shadow and the wider exploration of the properties of materials.

LEARNING IN ACTION

A group of undergraduate education students work with Year 2 children on a collaborative project based around light and dark. They show children some tiles with line drawings on them and ask them to explore the tiles in a darkened area with a range of torches, including some black light torches. It becomes clear that some of the tiles have additional marks on them made with luminous paint, which can only be seen in the dark with the 'special' torches. This feature of the paint and light working together is harnessed to make some art that at first sight looks quite monotone in nature, but when viewed in the dark with the black light torches comes magically to life. Along with exploring shadow-making the students and the children create some interactive mini environments for viewers to explore. They video their finished pieces and consider adding narrative and sound effects to the films.

When designing and making in digital technology, painting can be a useful way of decorating three-dimensional objects that are made, making them attractive and complete. This can also be a frustrating task for the child. Thinking ahead about what sort of paint will best adhere to the surface of the material being used (plastic, wood, card, fabric) and considering if it would be more effective to paint the surfaces before assembly, when they are still flat and unattached, can help address this.

Conclusion

It is likely children will paint at least once a year, if not more frequently, as part of the art curriculum. Given the complexity of the skills, knowledge and understanding involved in learning to paint, learning activities must be well planned to build on prior experiences and to support new learning and teaching techniques, such as those which involve digital and distance learning. Opportunities for exploration and direct teaching should be encountered. The adult role in planning, teaching and supporting cannot be underestimated here. Drawing upon both the planned use of media, physical and digital, and techniques, as well as accidental and unexpected effects, can be part of painting – this is an aspect of making art that will also be explored in the next chapter, which is about printmaking. Painting should progressively move beyond being expressive and enable children to dialogue with themselves, their experiences and their worlds.

Next steps

- Identify the key painters and paintings that children encounter through your art curriculum.

- Consider how these could be developed in interesting and creative ways, using physical and digital media.

- Think about trying colour mixing or incorporating a digital painting technique or support (such as a virtual gallery tour or gallery creation) the next time you paint with your class.

References

Barnes, R. (2002) *Teaching art to young children.* 2nd ed. Abingdon: Routledge Falmer.

Biesta, G. (2017) *Letting art teach.* Arnhem: ArtEZ Press.

Lin, Y. (2011) Fostering Creativity through Education – A Conceptual Framework of

Creative Pedagogy. *Creative Education.* **Vol 2**, pp.149–155.

Matthews, J. and Seow, P. (2007) Electronic Paint: understanding children's representation through their interactions with digital paint. In: Herne, S., Cox, S. and Watts, R. (2009) *Readings in Primary Art Education*. London: Intellect Books. Pp.269–286.

Pratchett, S. (2007) Powder and Paint. *START*. **Vol 23**, pp.8–11.

Further resources

Borg, M. (2019) 'It's Not For Real': The Tablet as Palette in Early Childhood Education. *International Journal of Education and the Arts*. **Vol 20**, No 14, pp.1–21.

Google Arts and Culture. (2020) [online] Available from: https://artsandculture.google.com/

NSEAD. (2019) Talk about a painting. [online] Available from: www.nsead.org/resources/units-of-work/uow-talk-about-a-painting/

Schumann, B. (2009) *13 Women Artists Children Should Know*. Munich: Prestel Verlag.

Water, E. and Harris, A. (1993) *Royal Academy of Arts Painting. A young artist's guide*. London: Dorling Kindersley.

Chapter Padlet:

https://padlet.com/Jeanne/Chapter8

09

Chapter Nine

Printmaking

Introduction

Printmaking is an exciting process with some intrinsic qualities that make it different to many of the other processes you will use with children in art. Many types of printmaking allow children to produce multiple copies of the same image, enabling them to investigate and experiment with the process and the image without obliterating their earlier work. This can allow them to feel freer to explore, to be creative and to engage in a space where they have freedom to figure out and be in dialogue with the world around them (Biesta, 2017). Printmaking can allow children to explore line, tone, colour, texture, pattern and shape. There is scope for progression towards increasingly more challenging use of the techniques and processes of printmaking. The possibilities for printmaking are opened up even further when considered in relation to digital technology. There are opportunities to work between physical and digital realms and we will share some of those throughout this chapter.

Printmaking techniques can be explored in connection with other areas of the art curriculum. Many can be applied to fabrics and textiles; others can be explored as part of developing drawing skills. Children can freely make printed paper or fabrics in order to use later when making collages or three-dimensional objects. Printmaking can be inspired by and explore the natural and manmade world around us or result from experimentation with materials and techniques to create accidental and deliberate effects. Different techniques have been used by printmakers from many cultures, times and places and these can be explored by primary children.

In addition to the practical process of printmaking, ICT and digital media can be used as part of the art process and as the outcome. Using the 'stamp' feature of art software can allow children to explore printed patterns across surfaces and some software allows choices and the opportunity to scan in your own items to stamp with. Prints can be developed by adding text or images that have been collected or made onscreen and printed out, or by app smashing – putting prints or print designs into one digital app, manipulating it and then transferring it into another app for additional manipulation.

You may be aware that many of the printmaking techniques that artist printmakers employ require the use of a press. All of the techniques used with children that are described in this chapter do not require the use of a press, although if you do have the opportunity to allow children to work with a printmaker and use a press this will widen their understanding of the possibilities available at secondary school and beyond.

Tools and materials

There is a list of suggested tools and resources to explore in Appendix 2, along with additional detail about some of the more specialist tools, equipment and resources used in making prints. Printing with objects is one of the first types of printmaking children encounter. Using objects either collected by the teacher or selected by the children themselves is an activity common in Foundation Stage or early Key Stage 1 and often abandoned later in Key Stage 1 and Key Stage 2. For younger children the excitement of pressing an object down on paper and lifting it to reveal the surprise of an unexpected shape or pattern can be absorbing and rewarding in itself. With older children it is possible to ask them to make and articulate their choices of objects, design images and patterns built from several objects and using several colours and take control of the process independently. This can allow older children to achieve complex and sophisticated results across a large surface area.

Try for yourself – exploring printing with objects

Exploring printing from objects

In this practical task you will explore one of the most basic printmaking techniques that many if not all children experiment with in their early years in school. It will allow you to find out more about how to make a successful print and how to avoid some of the typical problems that can arise when children use objects to print from.

You will need: a flat tray, a roller, printing ink, large sheets of paper

What to do:

1. Look around and collect ten objects that you can print with. You can consider completely varied objects or make your choices around a theme such as manmade, natural, toys, junk, household objects.
2. Put a small blob of printing ink onto the flat tray and use the roller to roll it out so the surface of the tray is covered in a thin, flat and even layer of ink.
3. Press each object into the ink and then press it down onto the paper to make a print.
4. You may do this several times so you can compare the difference between the first and last print – sometimes the print is clearer when there is less ink remaining on the object.

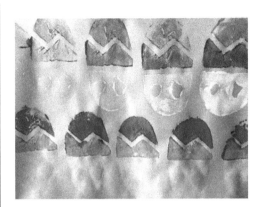

Figure 9.1 Building a print from repetition

Questions to consider:

- Did you get clear and interesting prints from the objects that you chose?

You may find that objects that have interesting shapes or textures on them make a more attractive image. Perhaps you will also discover that some objects do not print fully because of their shape or absorbency. This is a factor to bear in mind if you are choosing objects to put on the printing table for children to use.

- Were your objects easy to hold and manipulate?

If you, as an adult, find the objects difficult to hold it may be all the more challenging for children. Very small objects, objects that are slippery and objects that are soft may be particularly challenging to print from. On the other hand, the pattern that you get may be sufficiently interesting for you to find a way of overcoming these difficulties, such as by attaching a card or a plastic 'handle' to grip.

- Are your objects readily available in sufficient quantities for a class of children to use?

If you plan to print from objects with a whole class or a series of groups it is likely you will need to replace the objects as they get covered in printing ink. It can be frustrating for children to have to use objects already covered in ink and these may also give a less clear image than when they were clean.

- Are there any challenges when using this process that you can think of for the children you teach?

It may be that you have to demonstrate and practise how to press the object down into the ink and then down onto the paper without moving or sliding the object around in order to get a clear print. This can be practised without ink and perhaps with a shape or a spot on a piece of paper to 'target' the object. You may think of ways to describe the process that makes sense to the children that you teach. An example of this is to say that you must press down so hard that you can feel it all the way up your arm! Depending on the age and level of language of your pupils you may need to give some consideration to how to describe the process in a meaningful way.

• If you were organising this activity with a group or class of children, what are the implications for classroom organisation and management?

You should consider the size of paper so that each child's paper has space on the table and is not overlapping or flapping over the edge of the table. Alternatively, you could cover the table with paper and allow children to print anywhere. If each child is working on a sheet of paper of their own you need to consider where these will dry – is there a drying rack available? Is it nearby so children don't have to walk around with wet pieces of paper? After they have finished, where will the children wash and dry their hands? There will be other factors for you to take into consideration in relation to your classroom and the children you teach.

As with any process or technique, it is helpful to you as a teacher to try out any printmaking process that you intend to teach to children: this will allow you to identify teaching points, anticipate and pre-empt any challenges and find ways of organising the experience effectively.

Subject knowledge

When you are planning and teaching a unit of work that involves printmaking, it is important to identify one or two visual elements that you will develop with the children. It is likely that this will have been done at the planning stage.

Line	Tone
Drawing and mark making onto polystyrene tiles, into plasticine	Choice of tones within one colour of ink and / or paper when printing
Drawing onto a surface in monoprinting	Understanding the need for some light and dark contrast to make the image visible
Lines created with string on a tile	
Lines created with glue on a tile	
Blocking out with masking tape and rolling over	
Colour	**Pattern**
Choice of colour of ink and paper when printing – matching, contrasting, complementary, etc.	Exploring and creating different types of pattern – repeating, rotating, transforming, symmetrical, tessellating
Graduating colours on one roller / surface	Using single or combinations of objects / stamps / tiles to create patterns
	Using tiles to print with, physically and on screen

Texture	Shape
Exploring natural and manmade textures to make prints / rubbings from	Using regular and irregular shapes to create prints
Choosing textures to make planned effects	Using stencils / cut outs
Printing from collage tiles	Exploring mathematical aspects of shape – repeating, rotating, transforming, symmetrical in physical printing and digital pasting
Space	**Form**
Using the space of the printing tile / paper – composition	Printing to decorate three-dimensional forms
Printing around edges, in borders, across the whole surface, using a grid, in rows and columns	Using printed paper / card / fabric to construct three-dimensional forms
Placing on the surface – next to, overlapping, leaving spaces between	

There are some visual elements that lend themselves to exploration through print-making. The opportunities for repeating and reprinting allow children to explore pattern and pattern making in many different ways. Being able to take rubbings or print from textured objects, or create images and patterns from reassembling textured papers, gives much scope for exploring the texture of surfaces beyond merely making rubbings. Printmaking can also be a vehicle for exploring tone, line and colour as well as underpinning the exploration of form by allowing children to quickly create a lot of decorated paper, card or fabric with which to create three-dimensional forms.

LEARNING IN ACTION

In a unit of work on printmaking with a Year 1 class, two visual elements are identified in long-term planning as the main focus of the learning and teaching: pattern and line.

Pattern is at the heart of the unit of work and children are given the opportunity to explore and identify manmade patterns in the immediate environment; on Indian fabric; on reproductions of a range of tiles; and collections of images found online. They find, photograph, draw and talk about patterns in the exploring and developing ideas stage of the unit of work. The children's understanding of how patterns are designed is a focus for learning.

The other visual element that the unit focuses upon is line. Whilst exploring patterns the children are asked to draw using line, find examples of the use of line in patterns they are looking at, try out a selection of tools that make lines and explore straight, curved, continuous, broken and other types of lines.

The children draw upon their exploration of pattern and line and they each design and make a pressprint tile that carries a pattern created by lines drawn into the polystyrene. When they evaluate their work they are encouraged to look for how line has been used in the design of their patterns. They all print in black printing ink onto white paper to allow their designs to be easily compared and focus on the use of marks and lines.

Whilst working on this unit other visual elements such as shape, colour and space play a part, but they are not the main focus of learning and teaching at the early stages. Later, children go to freely print their polystyrene tiles using any colour of paper and printing ink to explore the variations and allow them to exercise more choice after the focused learning apparent earlier in the unit.

The learning experience in the case study above begins with a tight focus on two visual elements in particular and then allows more personal freedom to use the technique towards the end of the unit. The printmaking technique using biro line and mark making onto polystyrene supports this.

To extend the case study to integrate digital learning, or progress the children's awareness of printing techniques, the children could have their work photocopied. When photocopying or scanning work there are a number of opportunities to play with scale, size, colour, tone and repetition. With young children you could encourage them to cut out parts of their photocopied prints and rearrange them to experiment with space and composition. Children could also draw, paint or print onto the photocopies. The benefit of doing this is that the original print remains intact but the children still have an opportunity to be experimental and develop their work through different processes, making comparisons to their starting point. With older children, try playing with scale and tonal and repetitive tools on the photocopier or scanner itself, so that they engage with how the technological device helps them to achieve visually diverse print outcomes.

Key vocabulary

When you are planning for a printmaking experience or unit of work it is important that you identify the key vocabulary children will need to understand, respond to and use when working. This is especially significant for children learning English as an Additional Language (EAL) and some children with special educational needs and disabilities (SEND), who may be challenged by encountering new vocabulary or familiar words with different meanings when used in the context of an art lesson. Key vocabulary can be considered in relation to the printmaking process itself and the visual elements you are exploring – this model is often demonstrated on published plans and schemes of work. As an adult who knows the children in your class you should be able to identify a more precise and useful list of vocabulary, focused on the needs of individuals. You should also be able to make useful connections to vocabulary being learned and used in other contexts – in this example there is some mathematical vocabulary. This may be one of the factors that cause you to choose to teach this unit of work alongside or shortly after mathematical work on shape and pattern.

LEARNING IN ACTION

In the unit of work on printmaking with Year 1, discussed above, many of the children are learning English as an Additional Language (EAL). It is therefore crucial that the teacher identifies the key vocabulary the children will be responding to and are using in their art lessons. It will be important that the teacher is aware of words that are new to the children and words that they have heard and used in other contexts but may have a different meaning in art lessons.

In this unit of work she identifies the following:

In relation to visual elements:

*   Pattern – repeating, regular, decorative; words for shapes within patterns – square, triangle, circle, etc.
*   Line – straight, curved, curling, continuous, broken, thick, thin, (extended to wide, narrow, fine, broad, spiral, loop where appropriate)

In relation to tools and materials:

*   Felt pens (fine and broad), rollers, pencils, biros, trays, printing ink, pressprint

In relation to the process:

*   Press down, roll over, roll on top of, place, lift up

In addition to this the teacher thinks about when children will be talking about their work and identifies some sentence starters:

*   'I like this pattern because…'

- 'I chose this pattern because…'

- 'My pattern is…'

- 'I can see… in my pattern.'
- 'I could change my pattern by…'

A clear focus on the identified vocabulary will support the children's learning in art and in language development generally. This analytical approach to the vocabulary your pupils will learn and use is likely to be something you apply across the curriculum to support the pupils learning EAL in your class.

Printmaking processes

There are many printmaking techniques suitable to explore in the classroom with primary aged children. From the earliest years, children might place their hand flat onto some paint and then place their hand on paper to create a print or pick up objects to make prints with, as you explored above. But there is much more potential for pattern and image making with printmaking in the classroom. Vojvodić and Sredanović (2020, p.462) suggest a systematic approach to printmaking processes which are matched to the child's age and ability through media. One process that connects to printmaking is taking a rubbing by placing paper over a surface and rubbing over it with a broad crayon or wide piece of graphite. This can be a satisfying process in itself, as it reveals a pattern, images or lettering or combinations of these and can be a useful way of checking how a texture-based print plate is developing. A step on from this is to take the 'rubbing' using a roller and printing ink. Exploring the local environment to take prints from can be a way of evaluating the environment in a different way and creating visual material to use in further art making.

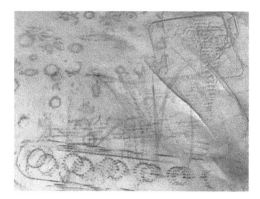

Figure 9.2 Capturing surfaces through rubbing

The chart below summarises those processes commonly used in schools, along with basic information about each.

Technique	Definition	Examples
Printing from natural materials	Placing natural materials such as leaves and grasses onto a flat surface, placing the paper over and rolling over with printing ink on a roller	Children collect fallen leaves and arrange these onto the table. A piece of paper is placed over the arrangement. A roller with printing ink is used to firmly roll over the paper revealing the texture and shape of the leaves below.
Printing from constructed tiles	Making a textured surface using card or textured collage materials, applying printing ink with a roller then pressing it down onto a surface	Children each choose and stick textured wallpaper onto a card tile the shape of a stone after observing and feeling the textures of weathered stone on an old building. They make prints from these to recreate a large collaborative wall.
Printing from drawing into a block	Drawing into a polystyrene surface, rolling printing ink onto it and then pressing it down onto a surface	Children create a linear picture by drawing into pressprint. They print these in a range of coloured printing inks onto coloured paper, experimenting with the contrast between ink and paper.
Printing from string	Making an image or pattern from string stuck onto a card	Children create a swirling pattern inspired by watching water in a stream. They practise making their pattern, then draw it onto a piece of card. The card is covered with double-sided sticky tape and then they place the string onto the lines they drew earlier.
Monoprinting	Rolling printing ink onto a flat surface, drawing directly onto it and placing paper onto it to take the print or drawing through paper onto the inked surface	Children create a monoprint of an imaginary creature – some children draw freehand having experimented in their sketchpads and others draw through a photocopy of their chosen drawing from their sketchpad.
Blocking out / stencils / masking tape	Rolling printing ink onto a flat surface, placing paper shapes onto the ink to block out, placing paper on to the ink and rolling to take the print	Children cut or tear long narrow strips of thin paper. They place these at random or by design onto the inked surface. A piece of paper is placed on top and rolled over. The process is repeated with another colour of ink and more strips of paper.

Technique	Definition	Examples
Making and printing from stamps	Creating stamps or using pre-made stamps with inkpads	Children use sets of stamps or create their own stamps, using inkpads to load colour onto the stamp and press the stamp onto paper repeatedly. This process is different from the others above as it is stamping onto a surface instead of placing paper over or onto the surface and lifting the paper to reveal the print.

Before you begin to teach children about a particular type of printmaking it is important that you try it out for yourself so you understand how it works and can identify ways of teaching and supporting children effectively. Anticipating any challenges that may occur and helping children overcome them through advice and organisation can help make the experience satisfying and successful. Alternatively, you may plan for children to experiment freely and then pick up what emerges: an example of this is when children print using letters or numbers and realise they must be reversed in order to print the right way round. Discovering this for themselves is often a powerful and memorable learning experience, but it should be discovered before a lot of time and effort has gone into designing and making a print block. The practical task below takes you through one technique – monoprinting – and also gives a structure that you could apply when trying out others.

LEARNING IN ACTION

A group of BA QTS students who are exploring drawing and printmaking explore monoprinting as a process that connects the two. They watch a demonstration of how to monoprint, noting the set-up of tools and materials. These include a flat smooth surface – such as a smooth table top, piece of perspex or MDF – flat trays, hard rollers, printing ink, pencils and biros, masking tape and paper to print on.

They watch as their tutor puts a blob of printing ink onto the flat tray and rolls it out so the surface is flat and even. She then rolls ink onto the smooth surface, aiming for an even covering. She places a piece of paper gently over the inked surface and tapes it across the top, then makes marks and draws onto the back of the paper, pointing out to the students that she does not rest her hand on the paper whilst drawing. She points out how the tape allows her to lift the paper to see the results and put it back down to continue drawing.

The students go on to explore this process for themselves to find out more about the practicalities of organising it and the potential for learning and creativity. Some students like the way that a drawn monoprint has a slightly 'fuzzy' residue of ink that adds to the attractiveness of the image. They also realise that it can be a great way of freely exploring mark making and drawing and that children could choose a drawing from their sketchbook, have it photocopied and then draw through it if blank paper worries them. Later in the session, the students experiment with layers of several colours on the same print.

Some students find that allowing their hand to press onto the back of the paper can result in too much ink getting onto the surface and almost masking out the drawing. They identify that when working with children they may need to demonstrate how to draw on the back of the paper without leaning their hand on it and allow opportunities to practise, perhaps on newspaper.

During the session students produce a lot of prints quite rapidly and so the space and supply of smooth surfaces to take prints from can be problematic. Cleaning the table or surfaces as you go along can help relieve this, as can using Perspex sheets that can be taken away, cleaned and returned. When using table surfaces that are usually reserved for 'clean' activities as a print surface a big clean at the end of the session will be essential. Organising the drying of a large number of prints must also be considered.

In the experience above students find that making monoprints is a completely different sort of printmaking in that each print is unique and a great many can be produced relatively quickly. This can allow freedom to experiment and explore the process, whilst immediately allowing learning from the experience to occur. This type of monoprint can be produced in several colours by drawing through the paper and using one colour of ink, then moving on to the next colour and the next. The colour of paper can enhance the print and then dry collage can be added to develop the image further.

Most of the other types of printmaking that we introduce to primary aged children will give them the opportunity to repeat their print many times. This feature of printmaking can be a wonderful way of allowing children to experiment with variations whilst using one block or tile. There are two main ways of making tiles or blocks to print from. One is to cut a shape and attach things to it to create a patterned surface from which to print. The other is to draw, cut or press into the surface to create the pattern. Experimenting with different combinations of these can range from the very simple to the much more complex, depending on the context and limitations the teacher plans for.

Surface	Attach to the surface	Press / draw / cut into surface
Polystyrene	x	Using a biro, pencil, sharp point
Inside of juice cartons	x	Using a biro, pencil, sharp point
Rolled out plasticine	x	Press natural and manmade items into the surface, draw into the surface
Cereal box card	Attach string by covering the surface with double-sided tape; attach textured wallpapers, cut and torn card, sticky-backed foam; attach varied found, manmade and natural collage materials	Using a biro, pencil or sharp point, tear surface away, scrape
Corrugated card	x	Draw into, peel away top surface
Foam tiles	x	Using a biro, pencil, sharp point

Figure 9.3 Monoprinting from natural materials

Artists, designers and craftspeople

Connections can be made between the work of printmakers and the printmaking techniques used in schools. When you are researching to find the work of artists to use you will come across the additional types of printmaking defined below. Although it is not necessary for primary aged children to know about all of these in detail both you and they will encounter these words when you explore prints made by artists. Some of these techniques or processes (but not all) have connections to the printmaking you will teach or support at primary school.

Term	Definition	Link to school printmaking
Collagraph	A print made from a collaged surface.	Using textured papers, card, fabric, string and glue to print from
Drypoint	A print made from scratching into the surface with a sharp point.	Drawing into polystyrene tiles
Engraving	The incising of marks, an incised block or the print itself.	Drawing into polystyrene tiles
Etching	Prints created on metal where the surface texture is created using acid.	
Intaglio	An imprint produced by rubbing ink into grooves (usually on a metal surface) and then printed through a press.	
Linocut	A print produced by cutting into a lino block with tools.	Drawing into polystyrene tiles
Relief	Impression produced by applying ink to the surface of the printing block or plate – the uncut surface prints and the cut areas allow the paper to show through.	Drawing into polystyrene tiles
Screen print	Printing using a frame covered in fine mesh through which ink is forced onto the paper below – areas are often masked off using stencils.	Blocking out ink on a surface using paper
Stencil	A shape used to mask out to create an image.	As above
Woodcut	A print produced from a block of side-grain wood or manufactured board.	Cutting into polystyrene tile
Wood engraving	A print produced from a block of end-grain wood using engraving tools.	As above

Definitions adapted from Desmet and Anderson (2000).

When you make connections to the work of a printmaker it is important to be able to choose one that relates to the learning experience. You could be looking for someone who uses the same or a similar technique: monoprinting, relief printing or collage printing, for example. Alternatively, you could be looking for someone who made / makes prints inspired by the stimuli you will be using: landscape, nature or their imagination, for example. As well as looking to the past and other places for examples of prints and printmakers there are many artists making prints now: the Victoria and Albert Museum (V&A) and other galleries have comprehensive modern-day print collections to explore. Prints are often more affordable as original works of art than paintings or sculpture, so it may be easier for you to have access to them and their makers.

A familiar starting point for finding prints is to look at the illustrations in children's books. Artists' prints have often been used to illustrate stories and poems. Edward Bawden made a series of linocuts illustrating *Aesop's Fables*; Patrice Aggs makes hand-coloured etchings such as the ones for Philip Pullman's *Count Karlstein* and Flora McLachlan makes prints inspired by myths, legends and fairy tales.

Exploring how printmaking has been used for decoration will allow you to study the technique in different times and cultures. Creating labels and looking into how prints are used in everyday contexts, like product advertising, are useful ways in which children can come to understand the purpose of prints, their relationship with digital developments and their provision of a means to dialogue with their own worlds in a critical way.

Indian woodblocks and fabrics created using print can be used to allow children to print with blocks, look at designs and then make their own prints on paper or fabric. William Morris designed handmade wallpapers inspired by nature. There are many examples of printed patterns used decoratively on the clothes children wear and the fabrics around them. Although these are now mass produced on a large scale, they are initially designed by someone.

Many artists working now work wholly or partially in print in varied and interesting ways. Lucy Skaer's prints from a deconstructed chair as part of her Turner Prize exhibit in 2009 can inspire children to think about viewpoints and the potential of everyday objects for printmaking. Ciara Phillips, a Canadian/Irish artist who was also nominated for the Turner Prize, in 2014, turned The Showroom Gallery, London into a community printmaking workshop, modelling how the process of printmaking can bring people together to build cohesion. Collaboration is central to Ciara's making practice, as it should be in the art classroom, where there is a need to dialogue with others. In the later part of 2020 Ciara will be contributing to an Open Studios residency in Toronto, Canada to explore printmaking in the contemporary art world. Children could practise in a similar way to Ciara, sharing printing techniques with and teaching them to their peers or school communities, to learn about the current practices of artists in society today.

Many of Banksy's works contain an element of printmaking: primarily using stencils. A notable work to share with children may be his 2020 *Game Changer* piece at Southampton General Hospital, which shows appreciation for the NHS. Sharing such a work with children may help them build a connection between art and contemporary events whilst also demonstrating how art can provide historical records, explore social issues and give voice and value to people and their communities.

Printmaking has also been influenced by digital media, with prints being created and / or printed using new technologies. There are some interesting examples on the website listed below.

Find out more

Find the Victoria and Albert Museum website. Click on the 'collections' tab, scroll down to 'explore the collections', select 'materials and techniques' then choose 'prints'.

Here you can explore different types of printmaking, be introduced to the practices of print artists from past to present and learn about how prints are used for commercial and technological purposes: www.vam.ac.uk/collections/print

---

Teaching

Printmaking is a wonderful technique to explore with children because there are so many possibilities – it can give you and the children a real chance to experiment, learn from accidental effects and make choices. When planning for a successful learning experience there are some significant factors to consider, including the organisation of space and resources and the use of physical skills.

Organisation of space and resources

For successful printmaking it is necessary to work in an organised space. As a teacher you should plan this in your classroom and, if possible, include a 'messy' table for children to apply ink at and a 'clean' table where children print onto their paper. The clean table should be near the drying rack or another arrangement you have for storing wet work. You may have a tiled or practical area available to use for 'messy' art and this may be equipped with a sink and a drying rack. The layout should be explained and modelled to children so they understand your expectations and how this organisation will help them produce successful art works and practice, like artists.

You should consider the tools and materials required at each table and the most efficient way of laying these out. An example of this is when you are printing from polystyrene tiles. You will need a roller in each tray of ink to ink up the tiles. You will also need to keep some rollers clean to roll across the back of the paper and onto the tile, exerting pressure to print. The easiest way to do this is to have an inking or 'messy' table, where the trays with ink in and the ink rollers are placed, and a separate printing or 'clean' table with clean rollers that can be used to roll over the back of the tile to make the print. It is again important that you explain and model this practice so children understand why they cannot grab any roller and use it for any purpose. Drawing a map or diagram for you and your support staff to follow or share with the children may help. You can also distinguish 'clean' and 'inky' rollers by attaching coloured ribbons or stickers to the handles of the rollers that will stay clean. Another consideration will be where to keep paper to print on so that it is accessible but stays clean. You should decide who will monitor and replenish the ink or paint trays. Older Key Stage 2 children could take on this responsibility, but adult support may be required for younger pupils, who may put out too much ink.

Figure 9.4 Colour variations using a block print

Physical skills

From printmaking experiences you may have had, or from undertaking the practical tasks earlier in the chapter, you will have begun to understand some of the skills that underpin printmaking. It is important for your planning and teaching that you identify the specific skills required within your unit of work or lesson and that you take into consideration children's existing skills and prior experiences in this area. At its most basic, the difference between many sorts of printmaking and other art techniques is the need to place the object or tile down on the paper, keep it still, apply pressure to it and then lift it up. In many other art techniques children will be, by contrast, moving tools around to make marks.

Within the various printmaking processes, children will be challenged to use their fine motor skills effectively in a different context than they are used to in the classroom. They may be using a pen or a pencil, but making marks into a surface that resists their tool – plasticine or polystyrene for example. They may be using tools they have never used before, such as hard or sponge rollers that require pressure to be exerted upon them to get the effect that they want. They may need to place objects or tiles precisely on a place on the paper without moving them around and then pick them up and replace them on exactly the same spot in order to get the effect they have planned. The knowledge that you have of your children will allow you to plan strategies to support some or all of the pupils in developing the skills they need.

It could be that you have to build in additional practice time for some skills, deploy support staff effectively or partner children with supportive peers. Digital technology can also support learning in this area and allow children to develop their understanding without the physical demands of printmaking. It is possible to scan one printed image and manipulate it in a 'printmaking like' manner on screen for children who find the physical process of printmaking challenging. Children can also manipulate stamp-like tiles on the screen to create patterns. There are several websites that allow children to create a pattern or design a pattern tile and print it out. Links to these are available in the list of websites at the end of this chapter. These activities can also be a useful part of the printmaking unit of work for all children and support connections between digital technologies, computing and art.

Even in the simplest of printmaking processes there are a number of steps that must be carried out in sequence to achieve a successful result. For children who find sequencing and remembering a series of steps in order difficult, printmaking can be a challenging process. Having said this, it can be an excellent opportunity to develop sequencing and instruction-following in a practical and purposeful context. Making sets of step-by-step instructions of some printmaking processes, a short video that can serve as prompts or models for you to use with the children or instructions matched to their specific needs can be useful. It can also be a context in which to apply the learning that takes place in English lessons on the non-fiction text type of instructions.

Developing an extended printmaking experience

When you plan a unit of work entirely around printmaking children will have an opportunity to create a print and experiment with it, building on their skills and developing their understanding of the technique more fully. As children move into Key Stage 2 it is important that they build on their prior experiences of printmaking and are challenged to achieve more complex and interesting results through an extended experience.

LEARNING IN ACTION

Children in later Key Stage 2 research African animals by searching online and exploring some Oxfam wrapping paper that features simplified animal shapes decorated with patterns. As part of their unit of work in art each child will design a two-plate card print to print individually and as part of a larger collaborative picture.

Each designs a simple animal in outline shape and creates two identical cards to use to make their print. One card is left plain and the other is decorated using card, string and collage materials. Some children base their patterns on their observations of animal coats and others choose a more decorative approach. Each child marks the back of their patterned and plain piece of card so that when they are printing they know which way round to place the cards they are printing from.

Initially, each child prints one print using a light colour for the plain shape and a darker colour for the pattern. All of the children evaluate their prints and consider any changes or improvements they wish to make. A few children decide to add more to their decorated card; several remake their patterned card so it is less 'full', allowing the patterns to be seen more clearly. At this stage, the children also refine their placement so they can print one card exactly on top of the other and use the marks on the back of the card plates to ensure that they put ink on the correct face of the card.

Next, the children print freely, experimenting with colour combinations and creating sheets containing three or four animals. They also make a wax resist background to print their animal onto as an individual outcome. Finally, each child prints their animal onto a piece of fabric to make a large collaborative hanging for the school entrance hall.

In this case study, older children used printmaking to follow through a number of steps. They draw upon prior learning and experience of techniques and can make a number of decisions whilst printing freely, evaluating and learning, leading to the creation of both individual and collaborative outcomes over half a term. At the planning stage breaking this unit of work down into a series of steps was crucial to classroom organisation, use of classroom space and time within lessons across the weeks.

Connecting to other parts of the curriculum

Some printmaking techniques are useful for creating backgrounds and interesting surfaces that can be used to work onto using paint, print or drawing. Prints can also be made in order to provide materials for use in collage. Using the whole surface of a large piece of paper and working individually or as a group can provide children with the chance to experiment freely, learn from each other and enjoy the sensory and creative experience.

Printing with objects across the surface is one way to create backgrounds and some of the other printmaking techniques that lend themselves to this are listed below.

Type of printing	How to	Example
Rolling over printing	Cut or rip shapes from paper. Place these below a large sheet of paper on a flat surface. Roll over with a hard roller and a little printing ink. Move the shapes and roll again, perhaps with a different colour.	Cut leaf shapes, some with patterned blade scissors and roll over in shades of green to create a background for painting, printing or collaging flowers onto.
String roller printing	Tie and knot string around a hard roller. Roll this through printing ink and onto paper.	Print in browns onto brown papers to create tree bark paper to use for collage.
Sponge roller printing	Use sponge rollers with patterns cut into them (stripes, spots, etc.) or put masking tape or string around a sponge DIY roller.	Use randomly onto white paper using pastel shades of paints, to paint onto later with bolder, brighter colours.
Marbling	Fill a large shallow tray with about 2cm of water. Drop marbling ink onto the surface. Place paper onto the surface to take a 'print' from the water surface.	Use as a watery background for printing, painting or collaging fish and sea creatures onto.
Bubble printing	Make a mixture of water, washing up liquid and paint, ink or Brusho in a container with no lid. Use a straw to blow into this to create bubbles that rise above the surface of the container. Take a print from the bubbles.	Apply silver and neon colour bubbles onto dark paper to create materials for using in fantasy and imaginative work.
Sponge printing	Use sponges cut into shapes at random or more purposefully to print with all over a surface.	Print brick shapes in purposeful patterns as a built environment background.

This may mean that you include some printmaking at the beginning of a scheme of work on painting or collage in order to allow children to create interesting surfaces to work onto, or you include these more independent activities within a printmaking unit and then keep the outcomes to use in later units: the overall plan can help you organise these connections.

Printmaking processes are the same or similar when printing fabrics and textiles but fabric paint or ink are used. These processes could include printing with objects, block printing and string printing. They could also include types of printmaking that relate more closely to use with fabrics and textiles, such as stencilling and screen printing. Trying out these processes on paper can be a useful way of allowing children to prepare and design before moving on to working with fabric.

Creative connections can also be made between printmaking and collage techniques. Prints can be taken from collage materials that have interesting textures and they can be enhanced by adding collage such as images and text, as well as natural and manufactured found materials, to the print surface either during or after printing.

LEARNING IN ACTION

A class of Year 3 children have been exploring stonework on some local buildings whilst on a trip to a field centre. Whilst outside the building each child focused on one stone and firstly looked at the size and shape, noticing that no two stones were the same. They were then guided to look more closely at what they could see on their chosen stone: marks, lines, patterns and colours. They felt the textures on the stones: there were smooth patches and rough patches as well as some pieces of fossil. They made rubbings from stones onto thin paper, using graphite sticks.

Inside the field centre, each child drew their stone shape onto a piece of card and cut it out, some with adult help. Using a collection of textured wallpapers each child ripped and cut textures to make up their stone and placed them until they were happy with the arrangement. When satisfied they glued the papers down to create a textures block from which to print.

Each child printed their stone several times on a choice of natural stone-coloured papers, using a limited colour range, to experiment with the interplay of ink and paper colour. They also printed their stone onto a whole class collaborative wall to display in the classroom. On their return, the children explored making prints from textured papers, learning about the parts of the surface that will hold the ink and print and the gaps that will reveal the paper.

In this case study children explore the creative possibilities of both collage and printmaking using collected, found and recycled papers to make printing blocks. On this occasion they have abstract and surface textures to choose from but if you look in DIY stores you will see that there are many wallpapers that have textures based on repeating patterns and natural motifs such as leaves, flowers and grasses. All of these are a great source for making print blocks with and lead to an interesting range of prints.

In this example, most of the possibilities have been explored around the shape of the stone. This gives you a sense of the various options from which choices will be made at the planning stage. Where children are given more time to play and experiment with effects, they are more likely to be able to plan to use what they've learned in more purposeful printmaking. Using card surfaces, or other materials that are easy to cut into shapes and are readily available through recycling, allows for experimenting without fear of wasting expensive materials – using found card shapes by deconstructing boxes is an effective surface to print from. Children can also make card pieces of a larger whole and print them together to make one large print, constructed almost like a jigsaw.

Reflect and extend

Read Anne Desmet's book *Primary Prints: Creative Printmaking in the Classroom*, published in 2010 by A&C Black.

Look at her project based around buildings as an example of a sustained printmaking experience.

Try out some of her ideas to extend the range of printmaking activities you plan for children.

Read Nicholas Leonard's chapter on 'Art, Media and Technology', which includes a section on printmaking, in the 2019 *International Encyclopedia of Art and Design Education*, published by John Wiley.

Connecting to other subjects and beyond

Meaningful connections can occur between printmaking and other curriculum subjects. In mathematics particularly, aspects of shape and space such as tessellation, symmetry and the properties of 2D shapes can be explored. Mathematical knowledge can also be transferred when exploring the characteristics of prints through digital codes. Print series are often created through repetition and children can code shapes and experiment with repetition to make digitally printed patterns or designs for prints. These prints could then be used in design technology work for example.

Connections between printmaking and other curriculum subjects can be made to strengthen learning in both subjects. Interdisciplinary practice in art, where two or more disciplines are combined, can be used so learners gain a deeper level of knowledge, understanding and exploration, but also have opportunities to apply knowledge and skills in different contexts. Interdisciplinary practice can also be useful to teachers, especially when they collaborate with colleagues or external partners, enabling them to explore, deepen, extend or see knowledge and practice differently or in new ways. Interdisciplinary working can be useful in professional development.

In the example below a connection is made to mathematics in order to put some mathematical learning into practice and explore it creatively.

LEARNING IN ACTION

A class of Year 2 children have been learning about two-dimensional shapes: naming them and exploring their properties, including the number of sides and the number of corners. They have been using mathematical vocabulary including: side, edge, corner, curved, straight, overlapping, tessellating and regular and irregular, as well as shape names.

The class are asked to draw and cut out two different shapes each from newsprint. The only constraint is that the shapes must all have straight sides and be of a size no smaller than their hand. This leads to children creating a variety of irregular straight-edged shapes. As the children make their shapes they sort them by the number of sides onto larger labelled sheets so that roughly the same number of shapes with three, four, five, etc. sides are made. They are aiming for a lot of shapes to use and discard in the printmaking activity.

For the printmaking activity a large piece of perspex (or a table top) is used. Yellow paint is rolled over the surface using a sponge roller. Ten children are asked to each choose a shape and place it onto the paint surface so it is not touching any other shape. A large piece of white paper is placed down onto the surface, taped to the table at one end and pressed down to take a print. Before the paper is lifted the children make a prediction – what colour will the shapes be? The paper is lifted to reveal white shapes where the paper shapes blocked out the yellow paint.

The paper shapes are peeled off the table and the surface is now rolled with orange paint. Another ten children each choose a shape to place down. The paper is placed down and pressed again. This time the children try to predict what might happen – when the paper is lifted there are some white shapes, some yellow shapes and an orange background. Some new shapes have been created by overlaps.

Finally, the paper shapes are peeled off, the table is rolled with red paint and the last ten children place shapes down onto the table. The paper is pressed down and then peeled off to reveal white shapes, yellow shapes, orange shapes and a red background. The paper is placed where the whole class can gather around to see it and talk about what they have noticed. In relation to shapes, children can see that new shapes have been created by overlaps, shapes within shapes can be seen and some interesting irregular shapes have been covered by others and are now lost to the viewer.

In the case study above this could be considered as an early approach to screen printing, where an image is created by blocking out and letting the surface show through. Children learn that when shapes are placed randomly some interesting parts of the print can be obliterated, later – they can be challenged to find out how to protect and retain these. Later in art, children can make individual or group prints based on different versions of the same shape or combinations of shapes, planning and predicting rather than working randomly as they were previously. It is an opportunity to teach children some of the basic possibilities of this type of printmaking before going on to explore it in more depth, on fabrics perhaps.

In terms of mathematical learning, children are more able to recognise irregular shapes and are more aware of how shapes can be created from overlapping or placing shapes next to other shapes. In the case study above the outcome is a large piece of printed paper to which all of the children in the class contributed. There are no individual outcomes to this activity. It is a relatively quick activity and creates excitement each time the paper is peeled off the surface to reveal a new image.

There are many opportunities to link printmaking to, and make prints in con-nection with, other curriculum subjects. Some of the experiences that children have in other curriculum subjects may inspire the making of prints as a response – poems, stories and the use of lettering and texts in English; visits to heritage sites in history; visits to other places in geography; visits to places of spiritual significance in RE; and close observational drawing in science. Also in science, the process of cyanotype printing can be explored using prepared paper, found objects and sunlight.

The sequential nature of some types of printmaking lends itself to stop motion animation. When building up a print from objects and tiles it is possible to record a series of images in a stop motion app, which will then play as an animated film with the print appearing bit by bit as the image is built up. Adding sound effects, music, speech or combinations of these in video editing apps or software after the film is made can enrich the learning experience and finished outcome. In Caldwell *et al.*'s (2019) example, Wilson Bentley's snowflake photographs are used as inspiration for a STEAM based printmaking project, using pressprint to explore mathematical ideas of shape and pattern recorded with print and photography. You can read more about this in the article on the chapter padlet. In the link below, a series of variations around the theme of block printing inspired by stones has been presented as a simple stop motion animation. This is a useful way of capturing work in progress and sharing finished outcomes. Another significant moment in printmaking that can be captured if technology is added is the moment of the 'reveal'. Unlike other types of art, it is not until we lift the paper that we know what the art will look like. Many printmakers film this moment. It is unique to printmaking and worth introducing children to in their own work and that of other printmakers.

Link: https://youtu.be/zzCp-dM7nrM

Link: www.instagram.com/p/CBh3THIIjWk/?utm_source=ig_web_copy_link

---

Find out more

Look up printmaker Wuon-Gean Ho's website and find her printmaking-based stop motion animations.

This is an approach to printmaking and digital technology that could be transferred to the primary classroom.

Conclusion

Printmaking is a huge area of art encompassing many techniques that can be used separately or in combination. It can give children opportunities to work as an individual and with others to create large-scale collaborative works where their own contribution can be identified. Accidental and unexpected effects are valued and enjoyed in printmaking so children can be surprised and excited by what happens as they work. We are surrounded by a developing plethora of prints and printmaking approaches used by artists and industry to voice, decorate, explore and express social, political and aesthetic discourses. Printmaking is a good opportunity to give children the chance to see original work, perhaps talk to the artists who make it and to dialogue with their own developing worlds.

Next steps:

- Look for examples of printmaking in your school, immediate environment and in response to issues in society.
- Find some useful websites and save them to your favourites to use for developing your subject knowledge or to use with children.

References

Biesta, G. (2017) *Letting art teach.* Arnhem: ArtEZ Press.

Caldwell, H., Edwards, J. and Grantham, S. (2019). The arts in STEM: STEAM. In: Caldwell, H. and Pope, S. (eds). *STEM in the primary curriculum.* London: Learning Matters. Pp.153–168.

Desmet, A. and Anderson, J. (2000) *Handmade Prints. An introduction to creative printmaking without a press.* London: A&C Black.

Vojvodić, M. and Sredanović. J. (2020) Methodological Aspects of the Implementation of Printmaking in Pre-school, Primary and Secondary Education. *Arte, Individuo Y Sociedadm.* **Vol 32**, No 2, pp.451–466.

Further resources

Desmet, A. (2010) *Primary Prints. Creative Printmaking in the Classroom.* London: A&C Black.

Desmet, A. (2010) DIY School Prints. *Printmaking Today.* **Vol 19**, No 4, pp.28–29.

Fowler, S. (2016) *Rubber Stamping.* London: Lawrence King.

Hickman, R. (ed.) (2019) *International Encyclopedia of Art and Design Education.* Hoboken, NJ: John Wiley.

Whittington, C. (2020) *Project: Print. 30 projects to spark your creativity.* London: Octopus Publishing.

Chapter Padlet:

https://padlet.com/Jeanne/Chapter9

10

Chapter Ten

Collage and textiles

Introduction

Working with collage and textiles gives children a wonderful opportunity to explore a wide range of materials and create interesting and diverse pieces of art by choosing, placing and arranging as well as making new art. This can be particularly engaging for children who are critical of their drawing skills and lack confidence in making art as a result. The characteristics of a range of materials and using them whole or remaking them can be a pleasing sensory and visual experience. Planning learning experiences based around these materials and the associated techniques can focus on the use of collected and recycled materials, making projects and units of work economical and responsive to the resources available locally. They can be an effective way of considering reuse, recycling, ideas of sustainability and impact on the environment.

Collage provides the opportunity for combining a range of paper-based materials and techniques in a mixed media approach. Collage techniques can be used as a way of creating types of decorated surface to paint, draw or print onto; they can be used to add detail and texture to a painting or print; or they can be a way of creating interesting papers to use in sculpture. Although collage can be regarded as an activity more suited to younger children it would be a mistake to dismiss it as just 'cutting and sticking' and restrict this area of art to the early years and Key Stage 1. Cox and Watts (2007) note that collage "can be perfectly simple or endlessly complex" (p.73). As children's abilities to use tools and make choices of materials and their placement develop, increasingly sophisticated and creative results can be achieved. Learning about threads and textiles and the associated techniques and skills can be an opportunity to explore traditional craft techniques as well as more contemporary approaches. There may be people connected to the school or in the local community who are practitioners that can share their experiences.

Taken together, collage and textiles can harness ideas from across the range of art skills, knowledge and understanding and can provide a context for giving children freedom to make their own decisions, using their prior learning.

Tools and materials

There is a list of suggested tools and resources to explore in Appendix 2, along with additional detail about some of the more specialist tools, equipment and resources used in making collage and working with textiles.

Collage

There are many materials that can be collected and used to make collage. Children can be given complete freedom or more focused opportunities to explore different types of collage techniques and use groups of materials depending on the unit of work. Using found and recycled materials can be both economical and alert children to the need to consider sustainability and care for the environment. Sorting these for the type of material; the properties of the materials; the tactile qualities; the visual appearance (colour, text, pattern) and other relevant characteristics can allow pupils to familiarise themselves before they make choices and use the materials to create art.

Textiles

The availability of materials will play a part in the choices that can be offered to children. There is satisfaction to be gained from using just the right texture, colour or pattern for their work. If you are lucky enough to have access to more specialist sets of materials and equipment, such as those for felt-making, batik or screen printing, it is likely that these will be kept together and used as a set – screens and squeegees for screen printing or tjanting tools and wax for batik for example. You may be able to learn how to use these and incorporate them as part of the curriculum, when working with an artist, craftsperson or designer or as part of out-of-school learning opportunities.

Try for yourself – stitching into paper

Exploring stitches and sewing

In this practical task you will try out some sewing of your own, considering the challenges of teaching children to use sewing in art and how to prepare for these.

You will need: a needle, some thread (several colours if possible) and a black and white photograph (original or printed out onto card)

Find examples of the work of contemporary artist Francesca Colussi Cramer to look at before you begin.

Link: https://colussicramer.bigcartel.com/

What to do:

1. Have a look at the photo and identify areas where stitching could be added. This might be to add or emphasise pattern, highlight a particular area of the composition or add something new to the existing composition.
2. Try out some different stitches on the photograph. You might try running stitches of varying lengths; stitches that overlap; straight stitches in groups; and any stitches you know or remember such as cross stitch,

back stitch, etc. If you were using stitching with children, what would you need to anticipate and plan for?

Questions to consider:

- Stitching – some of the points that you may have identified are starting off the sewing; not pulling stitches too tight or leaving them too loose; placing the stitches where you plan for them to be; and looping the thread around the edge of the surface from underside to topside. This can be easier when sewing into paper or thin card, as it is less floppy than fabric.
- Supporting children – how you do this will relate to their prior experience, their fine motor control and the task they are working on. When sewing it can be useful to begin with bigger needles, thicker thread and fabric with holes or an open weave that is easy to sew through. It can also be useful to practise on plastic or card sheets with holes punched in them (these can be bought or made). Allowing children to experiment and devise their own approach, as well as showing them how to place stitches to make patterns if appropriate, can help them decide what to do. Starting and finishing the sewing might be times when adult help is especially needed.

Find out more

About the resources available to you locally

Search online for your local scrap store. Identify:

- where it is
- the costs involved for joining / visiting
- the materials available and how they would fit into your teaching

Subject knowledge

When you are planning to teach collage or textiles, identifying the relevant visual elements can help you be clear about the learning that will take place. As with any aspect of art there will be subject-specific vocabulary as well as words used with a specific meaning in this context. There are specialist techniques and processes in both collage and textiles that you will need to know about.

Teaching the visual elements through collage

The chart below makes suggestions in relation to each of the eight visual elements. When you are planning and teaching a unit of work that involves collage it is important to identify one or two visual elements that you will develop with the children. It is likely that this will have been done as part of the curriculum map.

Line	Tone
Using linear materials such as string, thread, wire, wool, twine that can be manipulated into curved and straight lines Using linear materials that are straight such as twigs, sticks, dowelling, strips of card	Using tones of the same colour Exploring the effect of the contrast of tones – placing pale next to deep or bright next to dull
Colour	**Pattern**
Exploring the same, contrasting, matching colours Creating new colours from overlapping Choosing and placing colours next to each other for effect – contrast / clash / matching	Creating patterns from collage materials based on their colour, shape, tone, texture, etc. Creating different types of pattern – repeating, geometric, etc. Using collage materials that have patterns on them
Texture	**Shape**
Exploring textures of collage materials freely Making choices related to textural qualities such as smooth, soft, hard, bumpy Graduating textures from smooth to rough, from soft to hard Contrasting textures for effect	Using random and planned shapes Using regular and irregular shapes Creating shapes by choosing, cutting or tearing Exploring the shapes created by cutting away and leaving a hole (negative shapes) Exploring the new shapes created by overlapping
Space	**Form**
Exploring composition by placing and rearranging collage materials to create new images Experimenting with scale by reducing and expanding on the photocopier or on the screen digitally	Using collage to make or decorate 3D forms Creating relief images using layers of thick card

The visual elements that you focus on when making collage depend partly upon the materials you plan to use. If you have materials of many different colours, colour might be the focus of learning: children might choose and place materials of different colours to make varied effects or collect and arrange different tones of the same colour in their work. There is scope for exploring patterns through arranging collected items to make patterns as well as choosing from materials that are themselves patterned, such as papers and fabrics.

Another way of sourcing collage materials is using found materials such as photos, pictures and other graphic material (leaflets, flyers, maps, postcards, cards, text from magazines and books, etc.), which can be chosen, changed and used in combination to construct a new image or piece of art. Children can use resources brought from home or that are available in school or found online or images they have photographed themselves. This may support exploration of shape, space and form, which they would find challenging to represent in drawing or painting themselves.

Teaching the visual elements through textiles

The chart below makes suggestions in relation to each of the eight visual elements. When you are planning and teaching a unit of work that involves collage it is important to identify one or two visual elements that you will develop with the children. It is likely that this will have been done at the curriculum mapping stage of planning.

Line	Tone
Exploring using lines to make patterns, pictures and shapes (weaving, stitching) Constructing linear patterns (weaving) Using line in drawing / painting onto textiles	Using tones of the same colour / different colours in combination (weaving, painting, printing, sewing, appliqué) Exploring the effect of tones when dyeing and printing (moving from lighter to darker, contrasts)
Colour	**Pattern**
Changing the colour of fabric using dyes Choosing and using coloured fabrics and thread (weaving, appliqué, embroidery and stitching) Using crayons, paint and printing inks on textiles	Choosing and using existing patterns on fabrics (appliqué, patchwork) Making pattern whilst making new textiles (weaving) Making new patterns to decorate the surface of textiles (dyeing, printing, stitching, appliqué)

Texture	Shape
Choosing and using the tactile qualities of threads and fabrics when making or decorating textiles Exploring contrasts between textures of materials Choosing and using texture to create a feely fabric picture / pattern	Decorating fabric with shapes (pattern / pictorial) Exploring tessellation and geometrical shapes (patchwork) Exploring repeating pattern using shapes (borders, stitching, printmaking onto fabric)
Space	**Form**
Considering several viewpoints when making forms – (front and back of a hanging, inside and outside of a draped form) Exploring how textiles can be used to delineate and make new spaces Considering movement in space (hanging threading, banners, flags)	Creating and using textiles in three dimensions (weaving around a 3D shape, decorating fabric that will be draped to make a form, joining fabrics to make a patchwork) Creating new forms from thread (weaving, knitting)

Texture is a key visual element when working with threads, fabrics and textiles. Exploring and using the tactile qualities of the materials can encourage children to consider the choices we make with our clothes and in our homes as well as in craft and art. Encouraging children to touch materials, choose them on the basis of how they feel and use texture to evoke feelings in others who see and feel their work adds an extra dimension to their learning. Visual qualities such as pattern, colour and shape are also integral to many making experiences in this area.

Other visual elements will also be relevant, depending on the medium, the process and the outcome of the learning experience. Form may be important if the children are perhaps using weaving to create a three-dimensional form or a fabric that will be draped or stuffed, whereas line may be important if a flat weaving is made using lines of thread, wool and string, or line stitch is used to create a picture or pattern as part of appliqué or embroidery.

Key vocabulary

When you plan a unit of work based partly or wholly on mixed media techniques it is important to identify any words that will be used: these might be entirely new; familiar but used in a different context; or an opportunity to consolidate and re-enforce. Vocabulary could be considered in relation to, firstly, the materials being used and their characteristics and secondly, the technique itself and the tools and skills involved.

There are many opportunities for naming and describing materials. This could be in terms of collections and which materials fall within these – such as papers, including tissue paper, gummed paper, newspaper, shiny paper, wax paper. Alternatively, it could relate to characteristics such as thick, thin, silky, rough or smooth. Choosing and using materials can allow children to explore the materials and their characteristics at first hand so that when they are required, perhaps in science or DT, to explore and use materials in relation to their properties they have some experience of them. Whilst choosing and discarding descriptive and comparative vocabulary will be vital, ensuring that adults plan to and actually support children in articulating this should be a part of any plan.

Making collages will also involve vocabulary related to the type of collage: this is explored more fully below. The tools children use and the possibilities of the technique itself will also require some specific vocabulary. If children are making a decoupage, emphasis will be on words such as flat, smooth, next to and over-lapping, for example. In many different types of collage, placing materials will be a large part of the process and positional vocabulary such as next to, on top of, over-lapping, to the right of and many more terms will be vital when talking about the children's work. With younger children this may be used and modelled by adults: indeed, it would provide a good practical opportunity to consolidate these words.

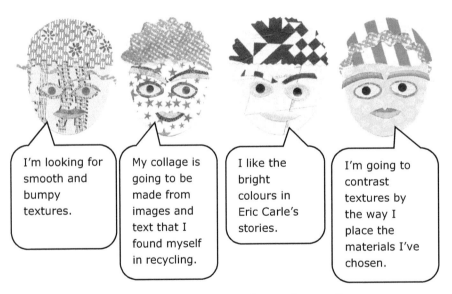

Figure 10.1 Using vocabulary when discussing collage

It is important to consider the general terms fabric, textiles, cloth and material – these can sometimes be used interchangeably, though in this context their pre-cise meanings could be explored. Fabric is a more generic term, with many dif-ferent types falling into it, including those made from weaving, knitting and felting and other processes; textiles are specifically those fabrics made from weaving or knitting thread together. Cloth and material are often used as synonyms.

Many fabrics are constructed from fibres, yarn or threads. These can be divided into natural fibres from plants (cotton, jute, etc.); from animals (silk from silk-worms, wool from sheep, goats, etc.); and synthetic fibres (nylon, polyester, rayon, etc.). The thread will be spun and often dyed before use to make textiles or could be decorated later. Other fabrics are made from non-woven methods, where the fibres are overlaid, entangled and then joined using thermal, adhesive or mechanical bonding. Examples of this are felting and creating synthetic fabrics with specific properties, such as being waterproof (laminated fabrics). These can be made from recycled materials or be used once and recycled themselves.

Another aspect of vocabulary to consider is the naming of different types of fabric. Although children may be familiar with a variety of fabrics, what they are used for and their texture, the specific names of many different types might not be part of their day-to-day vocabulary. Fabrics made from plants such as cotton, jute, and flax range from delicate materials such as gauze and voile to strong materials such as twill and denim. This group also includes canvas, corduroy, drill, gingham, jersey, muslin, lawn, linen, organdie, satin, seersucker, terrycloth, velour and velvet. Fabrics can be made from silk spun by the silk worm or spun from the wool of sheep, goats and rabbits. Those made from silk could include brocade, chiffon, crepe, damask, georgette, organdie, taffeta, tulle and velvet and those made from wool might include cashmere, chenille, felt, flannel, mohair, tartan and tweed.

Since the late nineteenth century, scientists have developed a range of synthetic fibres from which to make fabrics. These have been developed as replacements for natural materials or to have specific properties such as lightness, durability, strength or resistance to water and might include nylon, Lycra, polyester, rayon or vinyl. Some fabrics can be made from a combination of both synthetic and natural materials, or might be a manufactured version of what used to be a natural fabric.

As you plan and work with children on particular processes there will be useful vocabulary to teach them in relation to the tools and equipment that they are using. An example of this is in weaving, when they will need to know that the framework we weave on is called a loom; that the loom has two sets of threads – the warp threads that remain in place and the weft threads that are passed back and forth. Identifying these at the planning stage will allow you to introduce and model them as children learn and apply in the context.

An interesting aspect of language and vocabulary in the context of threads, fabrics and textiles is the number of words and phrases from this area that are used in day-to-day talk. Kapp (2010) suggests that this is an indication of the integration of making fabrics into our culture. We talk of weaving spells, stories, plots, bobbing and weaving and weaving in and out; we use proverbs like 'every cloud has a silver lining' and 'a stitch in time saves nine'. Exploring words and phrases in our language and where they have come from is a part of what older children learn in English.

Artists, craftspeople and designers

The work of many artists, craftspeople and designers who have used or currently use collage and fabrics can be used as inspiration for what children make. Some recommendations follow but you can follow your own and your pupils' interests, as well as what is available in your locality.

Collage artists

The technique of gluing papers onto surfaces was first named as collage in the early twentieth century, when artists such as Picasso, Braque and Schwitters began to incorporate fabrics, paper, text, pictures, wood and other materials into their paintings. Matisse also used cutting and placing later in his life. *The Snail* is a frequently used example of this aspect of his work, but also look for other examples of his use of the same technique to widen your and the children's experience.

In more recent times photographs and digital photography have been increasingly used by artists in collage or to make photomontages. The cover of the Beatles' *Sgt Pepper* LP is a very familiar example of using photos of people: collecting and arranging people who could not be present together in the same room. David Hockney's use of Polaroid photos of a landscape placed slightly separately in a grid pattern, or photographs overlapping to make a large composite view, are an example of the use of photos in collage. It is important to bear in mind that this is a difficult technique to allow children to explore on paper individually, unless you are prepared for the taking and printing out of many photos. It is something that could be explored in a digital context more economically and effectively using photo collage type apps.

There are easily accessible examples of the use of collage techniques in the illustrations for children's books. Polly Borland's illustrations for Lauren Child's retelling of *The Princess and the Pea* (Child and Borland, 2005), for instance, where three-dimensional dolls house room sets and two-dimensional collaged and drawn figures are photographed to illustrate the story. Jeannie Baker's illustrations for several children's books, including *Window* (1991) and *Where the forest meets the sea* (1987), feature the use of natural materials to create detailed landscapes, often with a theme of protecting the environment. Eric Carle uses collage constructed of papers that he has collected and made himself to make bold and brightly coloured illustrations for many stories familiar to younger children. There is an interesting video clip on his website, where he demonstrates how he works.

Link: www.eric-carle.com/photogallery.html

Collage techniques lend themselves to using one's imagination and sense of humour to enhance and alter existing images by adding, combining, covering or taking away. Jean McEwan is an artist who takes existing postcards and adds to them using material from other printed sources. Old postcards can be found in charity shops. Alison Sye is a collage artist whose philosophy is 'I don't add to the world, but use what is already here'. Look for her series called *Mostly Uninvited*, where she only uses flyers and junk mail that have come through her letterbox. *Kolaj* magazine is a source of interesting ideas and examples, including the idea of the 'cut out' page. This is a page of images based around a theme that can be exchanged with others, physically or digitally, and used to create new images.

Link: https://jeanmcewanartist.bigcartel.com/product/
a-month-of-altered-postcards-28

Link: www.alisonsye.com/

Link: http://kolajmagazine.com/content/?s=cut+out+pages

Find out more

Visit the Tate website and explore the 'art terms' section www.tate.org.uk/
art/art-terms and also explore some of the types of collage listed above.

Textiles artists

Examples of original textiles to explore may be more readily accessible to you because of their use for both decorative and functional purposes all around us, including clothes, toys and soft furnishings. Taking into consideration those examples available to use locally, which may be from a variety of cultures present in your community as well as those made further away in other countries around the world, can be a good starting point. Exploring those made in the past as well as those made by contemporary artists, craftspeople and designers working now should also be represented.

There is a lot of material available online that can be used in the classroom as sources. Look for examples from Africa and India on the Victoria and Albert Museum website as a starting point. Examples of crafts using threads and textiles from the developing world are sold in Oxfam shops as part of their support for Fair Trade in developing countries.

Another aspect that can be explored is work from the past. This can include fabrics with historical significance and those that give the children evidence and insights about life in the past: interesting links with the history curriculum can be made here. One example could be looking at samplers. These began by being a way of learning embroidery stitches, an 'exemplar', and became a part of childhood where children (primarily girls) practised sewing skills focused on letters and biblical and moral sayings. There are some links to more recent cross stitch on mesh designs still prevalent in the 1950s. Another example to research is that of military quilts that were made by soldiers in the nineteenth century. These tend to feature strong geometrical patterns and were made by the soldiers as part of their recuperation after injury.

As well as fabrics made in the past it is important to remember that there are many living artists, craftspeople and designers making work using threads, textiles and fabrics. It would be wrong to accidentally convey, by the choices we make, that this area is largely focused on small-scale, domestic work made by women. Explore the work of John Jones, who makes 'story coats' stitched with images inspired from stories; Alice Kettle, whose large-scale stitched work uses colour and line; Faith Ringgold's quilts; Anni Albers's weaving; and Sarah Corbett, whose craftivist work often includes the use of textiles to gently protest. You might also look up 'yarnbombing' or 'guerrilla knitting', adding knitting to public places, another form of using textile art to change the world.

Link: www.jjgallery.com/coats.html

Link: https://alicekettle.co.uk/

Link: https://craftivist-collective.com/

Link: www.whodunnknit.com/

Teaching collage and textiles

Collage and textiles techniques allow children to explore and make choices leading to personal creative outcomes. Within each larger area you are likely to be focusing on a specific technique and these are explored in more detail below. Each of these will have implications for your teaching.

Collage techniques

There are many different collage techniques that are suitable to explore in the classroom with primary aged children. The word collage is taken from the French word *coller*, which means 'to glue'. The chart below summarises those commonly used in schools, along with basic information about each.

A summary of basic collage techniques		
Technique	**Definition**	**Example in school context**
Collage	An image made from gluing a selection of materials onto a flat surface.	Children tear and glue coloured tissue paper onto a plastic surface using a lot of PVA glue. When the glue is dry the collage is peeled off the surface to create a translucent image. Each side is decorated with glitter / sequins to decorate.
Decoupage	Cut out images / photos are pasted onto a surface so that it appears they are painted directly onto it when varnished over.	Children collect images and text from magazines and newspapers around a theme identified by an adult or chosen themselves. They glue down their chosen images after arranging and rearranging to find the composition they find most attractive.
Assemblage	Constructed from collected and found elements, including three-dimensional items.	Children collect ten items (both natural and manmade) on a walk around a local wood. They use these as a basis for an assemblage representing their experience. They link to English by writing short impressions and including this text as part of their assemblage.
Photo montage	Collages made from photos or parts of photos, made by hand on paper or digitally onscreen.	Children create an imaginary scene using a mixture of found and created images. They use the photocopier to resize some of these to change the usual scale. They use the scanner to scan the finished scene and show each on the IWB. Some children use the IWB pens to draw into the scene and add handwritten and typed text.
Digital collage	Collage constructed entirely using digital technology and displayed onscreen.	Children choose a place of personal significance or interest and take some photos of it digitally. They manipulate these onscreen, cutting them, rearranging them, resizing them to create a semi-abstract representation of the place that conveys its essence rather than representing it figuratively.

You may have noticed that one technique has not been listed: the screwing up of small pieces of coloured tissue paper to fill in pre-drawn shapes. Perhaps you spent time screwing up tissue when you were at school – think about what the learning in art could have been when you were doing this. Whilst this activity could be part of creating scenery for a play or large-scale display for the school, the opportunities for individual learning in art tend to be limited.

At the early stages of a collage unit of work, when children are choosing from materials, it will be necessary to consider where they will do this and how they will store their collections. It can be useful to have a named bag for each child into which they can put their choices – the size of this will depend on the materials available to choose from. This will allow each child to feel that their materials are safe and ready for the next stage and allow you to put most of the remainder away, perhaps keeping a smaller selection for further choices later.

The nature of the materials being used will also influence your organisation of resources. If natural materials are being used, for example, they might deteriorate quite quickly so pressing them or drying them could be appropriate. Alternatively, you might compress the sequence of work so that the materials are chosen and used quickly before they are spoiled.

At the sticking stage the glue being used should be considered. Glues used in schools are washable but it is sensible to plan to avoid getting glue onto children, their clothes and the classroom. Teaching children how to use glue efficiently by firstly providing them with the right type of glue and tools to apply it and secondly covering them with aprons and the tables with paper will go a long way towards achieving this. Ensuring that collages can dry without sticking to each other and be available for further work where necessary is also important to work out in advance.

The elements of the process

When you are planning art involving collage techniques it is important to consider the various parts of the technique, so that you can identify how best to plan for and support children's learning. These include: collecting, selecting and discarding; cutting / tearing; placing and arranging; joining or attaching; and developing. Depending on your plans, these stages might be spread out in a series of lessons over half a term or combined within a shorter period of time. Each one will be explored more fully below:

- Collecting, selecting and discarding – it will be important to plan for children to make some choices about what they will include in their collage and what they will choose not to include. This will be related to the overall unit of work. You could plan a limited choice – natural materials collected from a walk in the local area; pictures focused on a theme from magazines; materials with interesting textures, reflective and shiny properties or within one colour; or you could plan for a freer choice. The plans you make for this stage will relate to the resources available to you and the ideas you have for the outcome of the unit of work. Bear in mind that allowing choice at this stage could result in a more varied outcome and more opportunities for children to follow their own ideas rather than conform to a predetermined outcome. Providing children with a named envelope in which to keep their chosen material is a useful way of organising at this stage.

- Cutting / tearing – when using some materials children will have to reshape them to use them effectively in their collage work. Tearing papers of different types can result in varied and accidental edges that are more interesting than cut edges. When cutting you might need to plan for adults to support in this area in order to help children avoid frustration. If the developing of cutting skills is not the main learning objective there is no reason why adults could not cut along lines drawn by children. Another factor to consider is the size – often children will draw shapes too small and intricate to realistically cut out. This can be addressed by encouraging them to cut freehand without drawing or to think about the size of the shape being cut out and tear and using the photocopier to expand small outlines into larger and more manageable ones.

- Placing and arranging – this is a crucial stage in designing and making a collage and should not be hurried through. The presence of glue will tend to short circuit the careful consideration and trying out needed for success at this stage. You can model the arranging and rearranging to try out different compositions so that children begin to understand that they can achieve different effects by placing next to, further away, overlapping and discarding altogether. At this stage it may also be necessary to select more or different things to use in the composition. The interplay between the background and what is being stuck to it should also be considered.

- Joining or attaching – how you plan for children to join their collage together will depend on the materials used and the planned outcome. In some instances, the outcome could be temporary and recorded by a photograph before being dismantled. When glue is used the type of glue and application technique should be right for the collage. When gluing flat onto large areas PVA or PVA diluted with water can be painted onto the surface with a large brush or sponge paddle and then items placed onto it and pressed down. When gluing smaller items or aiming for some parts to stick up or remain unattached use a glue spreader, a small brush or a glue stick. Sellotape, masking tape, double-sided sticky tape and other types of attachment could also be considered.

- Developing – it may be that the collage will be worked on in several lessons, developing and refining it. This is especially true when using collage techniques with older children, who will make more complex designs and be able to sustain attention on the same piece of work over a longer period of time. Collage is a particularly good opportunity to allow children to review and evaluate their work and suggest and make changes to improve and develop along the way.

It is advisable to make the teaching decisions about each of these stages at the planning stage so that you can build in choice, independence and time to make an individual response.

Find out more

Look up the article 'How to make art when we're working apart' on the British Library website. Explore how curator and artist Hannah Nagle uses the British Library collection to collect and combine digital images to make collages.

Connect this to using and editing screenshots; cutting, copying and pasting; and using specific tools on apps and devices to work in this way.

Also consider the implications for digital integrity and the protection of intellectual property.

Fabric and textile techniques

There are many techniques and processes that you might use singly or in combinations. The chart below summarises some that are commonly used in primary schools.

Technique	Definition	Example in school context
Using threads to wrap, knot, tie, plait, knit, crochet	Textiles can be made by combining threads in a variety of ways: both unstructured (wrapping, tying, knotting) and more structured using tools and specific stitches and patterns (knitting and crochet).	Children choose from a range of found and recycled items and thread and tie them onto a single thread at random or in a pattern.
Weaving	A way of constructing fabric using a framework (loom) threaded with threads that remain in place (warp) and thread that is passed back and forth and in and out (weft). Weaving can be done by hand or by machine.	Children make a simple loom from twigs tied together and threaded with warp threads of gardening twine. They weave with weft threads of natural colours including wool, string and dried grasses.

Technique	Definition	Example in school context
Patchwork and quilting	Fabrics can also be made by joining smaller pieces together as a patchwork. Traditionally patchwork tends to be made from geometrical shapes that tessellate. This is part of quilt making where the patchwork is sewn onto a backing with padding between. Quilts and other items can be made from patchwork. Padding could lead into stuffing when making 3D fabric items.	Children explore fabrics and choose one that evokes a memory. They each make a patch with a pocket into which they slide a short piece of writing describing the memory. An adult machine sews the patches together to make a class memory quilt.
Appliqué	Appliqué means 'to put on' and is the technique of cutting and joining pieces of fabric onto a base piece of fabric to decorate it. These might form a picture, a pattern or be more abstract. When the fabric shapes are cut to reveal what is below this is called 'reverse appliqué'. Appliqué may be used along with stitching and embroidery as well as stitching to attach other decorative items as above.	Children make an appliqué of the first letter of their name, decorating it with stitching and attaching beads, sequins and buttons.
Dyeing	Textiles can be dyed as whole pieces; tied to keep dye from colouring the whole surface (tie-dying); or painted with wax or paste to provide a resist to the dye (batik). Dyes have been made from natural materials (plants, insects, minerals) or more recently have been manmade, using chemicals. This has changed the range of colours available.	Children experiment with dyeing a large piece of cotton several times, adding more tying each time they dye, moving from yellow, to orange to red.

Technique	Definition	Example in school context
Sewing, stitching, embroidery	Sewing can be used to join fabric or add decoration to fabric by stitching in different ways or by using stitches to attach beads, buttons, sequins, mirrors or other decorative materials. Stitches such as running stitch, cross stitch, chain stitch, back stitch and many others can be used as well as stitching more freely to add decorative detail to fabric.	Children use simple stitches to decorate the print of the fish they each made above. These are arranged by the children (and sewn on by an adult) onto a large piece of fabric, made using tie dyeing in blues and greens.

Surface decoration using drawing, painting and printmaking techniques can also be applied to fabrics – for example, drawing with fabric crayons; painting with fabric paint; printing with objects or blocks onto fabric; and stencilling using simple cut shapes. Techniques such as screen printing, tapestry, felt-making, macramé and spinning thread from wool before using it to weave might be introduced, depending on the resources and expertise available to you.

LEARNING IN ACTION

Year 6 have been introduced to Sujuni embroidery. This is a technique from Bihar, in Northeast India. The large-scale fabric work involves creating shapes with a running stitch outline on a plain coloured background, often slightly padded underneath, and filling the shape with small, straight running stitches in a different colour. The fabrics are traditionally made by groups of women working together on the same piece and are given to family members. These usually depict the natural environment and daily life.

The class have seen a very large example in their local museum, based on a rural Indian landscape and including fish, birds, animals, rivers, trees and other images from the natural world. It was hanging on a wall and easy for the class to sit in front of and observe. They first looked at the figurative images, identifying and listing what they could see. They then considered the layout of the individual images in relation to each other and the scale and overall effect of the whole fabric.

After that they take a closer look at how the textile has been made: the outline of each image has been sewn around and the inside has been filled with straight running stitches, filling the outline completely. The colour of the fabric below the embroidery thread used for the outline and for the inside of the image is considered. They also think about how a group of people working together could organise the making of such a large piece of art.

In the case study above children have explored a specific traditional Indian craft in terms of the overall imagery and the technique used to make it. This was chosen by their teacher because it is available locally to look at as well as giving children the opportunity to consider textile art from another country and culture. There is much potential for using this experience to inspire art work as well as speaking and listening and research about the context of the place, culture and tradition.

Connecting to other aspects of the art curriculum

Using collage and textiles provides opportunities to make connections between a wide range of techniques that children have experienced in the art curriculum and give them some choice and independence. Indeed, this may be a way of allowing children to draw upon earlier learning from several areas of art, pulling them together to make artwork that combines knowledge, skills and understanding across the art curriculum. This could be by using another technique such as drawing, painting or printmaking to create papers or backgrounds to use in making collages or it might be by adding collage detail onto a drawing, painting, print or sculpture. Photographing or scanning their work and continuing to develop it onscreen could also be part of this process.

Creating the papers which children will then go on to use to make collages can be a wonderful opportunity for them to freely experiment with techniques such as colour mixing in painting; printing using rollers with string and textured materials tied around them; marbling and many more. Experimenting with mark making and then photocopying the sheets, reducing and expanding them, can result in some interesting papers to use in collage. When children work in this way they are collectively making the raw materials that the class will go on to use for their art. There are several ways of organising this:

- materials could be saved from a unit of work on printmaking, drawing or painting

- materials could be deliberately made during such a unit then kept to use in a later collage unit of work

- creating the materials could be planned for the initial stage of the collage unit of work

Having more varied materials to use to make collages can enhance the quality of the experience and help children make connections between different parts of the art curriculum and understand that techniques and processes can be

combined to great effect. When combining two or more art techniques or processes in this way children can make work over several stages, thinking about
how they are going to develop their work rather than making a one-off. This connects us back to the need to support children in reviewing, evaluating and then
developing their art work over the unit of work.

Working with form using threads and textiles could include creating three-
dimensional forms by making several two-dimensional forms and joining them,
such as when children make faces or panels that will be sewn together and
stuffed. This could at its most simple be two identical shapes, each decorated and
sewn around the edges then stuffed, or it could challenge children to consider
using more than two faces, which will fit together to allow the finished form to be
free-standing (with a flat base perhaps or by weighting down).

When making art in three dimensions, weaving and textiles can be used to create
new spaces such as cylinders, wigwams and cubes by draping over and from
frameworks. This can allow children to consider the inside and outside of what
they make. Weaving and decorating fabrics can also be used to explore changing
and enhancing existing spaces using mobiles, hangings, flags and banners.

Individual pieces of work by a class or year group of children can be planned
and made with the aim of joining them together to make a much larger finished
outcome. In order to create a sense of unity a theme, a limited range of colours
or a coherent way of joining might be planned from the outset so that the finished
pieces work together as a completed whole. When working in this way each child
can still identify their own work in the larger piece.

Planning to make a genuinely collaborative large-scale outcome will allow
children the opportunity to talk about their ideas, sharing and justifying them and
eventually agreeing on an approach that satisfies everyone. This can give them
a meaningful opportunity to discuss their art and cooperate in order to meet an
outcome. As an adult it is important to consider the points at which children will
make choices and how you will support them in coming to an agreement that
allows all to be satisfied, as well as helping them divide up the tasks and record
everyone's contribution to the whole. In this context, it is important that children
are not guided so completely that they are merely following instructions to produce an outcome that is largely directed by an adult's vision.

Find out more

Look up Collage Gardens on social media.

You will see that a collage garden is a collaborative project where individuals make free-standing three-dimensional collages which are mailed to one location and assembled outdoors to make a temporary sculptural installation. It is a wonderful way to connect with others and could be a strategy for mail art swaps with other schools.

Connecting to other curriculum areas

There is also scope to connect collage in art to learning within another subject area. Care should be taken when planning to do this. It is important for you to be clear about the art learning objectives and the learning objectives relating to the other subject (see chapter 5). Clearly, the success of a link like this is dependent on the clarity of the planning and the ability to be flexible with the use of time. It is important to consider the strength of the links and whether they support learning sufficiently within in each subject area to make the additional organisation worthwhile.

When making connections between collage in art and other curriculum areas it is important to keep a clear grasp on the learning in art or the activity, or the art could become too illustrative of the other subject. An example of this might be collecting images of a variety of landscapes or weather in geography. If the images are collected, sorted and discussed to develop geographical knowledge, skills and understanding, children are learning in geography and the mere collection of the pictures does not necessarily contribute to their learning in art. If, however, children go on to make a collage landscape of their own, based on an observed, researched or imaginary place, they will be using materials to create something more personal and will be exploring colour, texture and space. We can see in the work of textiles artists that knitting and crochet are being used to record daily rainfall and temperature in colour, such as Josie George, connecting to science and the environment, and artists like Victoria Rose Richards, whose embroideries represent aerial views and the landscape.

In English, connections can be made with stories where making fabrics, items made of fabric and fabric techniques themselves play a role. Spinning and weaving feature in some Greek myths, including that of Arachne and Athena, and in fairy tales such as 'Sleeping Beauty' and 'Rumpelstiltskin'. Fabrics and fabric techniques are used to illustrate stories such as those by Salley Mavor or Janet Bolton. Making an appliqué that brings to life a scene from a known story or is part of a new story that the maker will go on to write could be a link between reading and writing and art.

LEARNING IN ACTION

A Year 3 class have created a class story in English. Working together in groups in art lessons they create small-scale collage environments for each scene in the story. They use some of the figures from the Tim Holtz Idea-ology paper dolls collection as their characters. Having made the settings and props they use iPads and a stop motion animation app to film each part of the group story. The story is connected together and dialogue, sound effects and music are added, using the iMovie app.

Working together to use their art and their computing skills to bring to life some learning from English leads to meaningful learning in both subjects. There are smaller-scale links to other areas of the curriculum, such as music and design technology. There is potential for linking this type of activity to history if the story was set in a historical context or geography if the story was set in a specific place.

In mathematics there is scope to explore pattern making and tessellation in two dimensions and the use of shaped panels to construct three-dimensional textile objects. Children may have considered the properties of materials such as strength, density, transparency, resistance to water and many more in science and then designed functional items using these properties in design technology. They may have explored how fabrics are constructed by looking closely at them, taking them apart and considering the tools and equipment involved in making them either by hand or by manufacturing processes. This knowledge and understanding can be used to underpin work in art related to the visual and sensory impact of the making and decorating, rather than the purpose and function.

There is much scope for making connections between history, geography and RE when choosing examples made by artists, craftspeople and designers. This might include looking at and talking about what can be learned about the culture, geography, history and worship of an area or people after looking at their textile art. Children could also focus on learning a new technique exemplified by work from another time, place or religion and apply it themselves in another context or in response to a different starting point.

Excitingly, when we consider connections to the computing curriculum we can begin to think about adding elements of digital technology such as programmable lights to textiles and creating images, animations and GIFs that can be triggered by markers and QR codes on the fabric. Sewing onto fabrics using conductive thread and using coin cell batteries and LED lights can make a circuit to light up parts of a design. Caldwell *et al.* (2019) explore the use of LED lights in art projects in the context of STEAM activities.

Reflect and extend

Read the article 'Sensitising Children to Ecological Issues through Textile Eco-design' by Taieb *et al.*, published in 2010 in the *International Journal of Art and Design Education* (Volume 29, Number 3, pp.313–320).

Thinking about your choice of materials and what we do with them in the classroom can give children the opportunity to explore sustainable development and environmental issues.

Conclusion

Collage, textiles and mixed media can provide a range of opportunities for creating art work. These can build on the enjoyment that younger children gain from choosing, manipulating and making, using tactile materials. As well as working within the collage art form, collage techniques can enhance art work in other media such as drawing, painting, printmaking or sculpture. There are strong links to other curriculum subjects and there is also scope for using computing and moving into using digital media to create moving images by making simple animations.

Next steps

- Investigate your school library for examples of where illustrators use collage in their work.

- Find out how to make simple stop motion animations – children can make collage backgrounds and characters to use in this process. Start by talking with the computing coordinator.

References

Baker, J. (1987) *Where the forest meets the sea*. London: Walker Books.

Baker, J. (1991) *Window*. London: Random House.

Caldwell, H., Edwards, J. and Grantham, S. (2019) The arts in STEM: STEAM. In: Caldwell, H. and Pope, S. (eds). *STEM in the primary curriculum.* London: Learning Matters. Pp.153–168.

Child, L. and Borland, P. (2005) *The Princess and the Pea*. London: Puffin.

Cox, S. And Watts, R. (eds). (2007) *Teaching Art and Design 3–11*. London: Continuum.

Kapp, E. (2010) Warp and weft: language and literature. *START*. **Vol 37**, poster.

Further resources

Chastain, H. (2018) *If you can cut you can collage*. Beverley, MA: Quarry Publishing.

Manie, A. (2008) *Collage in the Classroom*. London: A&C Black.

Meager, N. (2006) Dream Collages. In: Meager, N. (2006). *Creativity and Culture.*

Art Projects for Primary Schools. Corsham: NSEAD. Pp.104–107.

Plowman, R. (2012) *The collage workbook*. New York: Stirling Publishing.

Chapter Padlet:

https://padlet.com/Jeanne/Chapter10

11

Chapter Eleven

Working in three dimensions

Introduction

Making art in three dimensions is a rewarding sensory and tactile experience for children. It is vital that children have opportunities to create art in three dimensions using a range of materials and techniques throughout their primary years. The experience itself is very different to that of working on a flat surface and can offer children less confident with or less interested in drawing and painting a very different context within which to enjoy making art.

Opportunities for children to work in three dimensions in schools can be less frequent. Practical considerations such as space, time and cost of resources as well as lack of confidence or subject expertise on the part of teachers and teaching assistants can result in less exploration of and making of art in three dimensions being planned. This can result in children encountering fewer processes because of the limited range available. It is possible to use found and natural materials from the local environment to work in three dimensions and this can be a way of adding variety and considering our role in caring for the built and natural environment and sustainability. Choosing and putting materials together to make something new is a satisfying and worthwhile experience and it is well worth overcoming any perceived barriers or challenges to give children access to these opportunities (Briggs, 2016, p.18).

Tools and materials

Storage of three-dimensional materials may pose more of a challenge than two-dimensional materials. You may find that some materials must be ordered in advance: using the curriculum map can help you identify when materials are required. Some materials can be collected from children's homes or local environments and a certain amount of planning ahead may be needed to ensure that you collect sufficient materials in time for the unit of work. Using materials from a local scrap store can also be useful (see Appendix 2).

As well as the materials listed in the appendices, found natural materials can also be used to create sculpture. These include leaves, flowers, twigs, seed heads, grasses, shells, stones and many more. They can be collected by the children themselves and brought into school for a particular project or they may be collected on site and used immediately. Teaching children about collecting natural materials whilst showing care for the natural environment and habitats should be considered before setting up this task: using only what is already on the ground is a good principle to follow here. Found manmade materials can also be used: this might include reusing discarded materials before they are recycled or disposed of. More temporary materials might also be used: ice, snow, mud and light can all be used to make ephemeral art.

Digital technology can support adults and children in recording the progress of three-dimensional work, recording it from different viewpoints and preserving it long after it has been taken home or removed. It can also be used as part of making environments and installations by creating art that is projected onto the IWB, screens or walls or created in virtual reality environments.

Try for yourself – malleable materials and what they do

Exploring the qualities of malleable materials

In this practical activity you will use a malleable material to explore what you can do with it and how it can be used with children.

You will need: a fist-sized amount of a malleable material such as salt dough, plasticine, clay or play dough. If you have more than one of these it could be useful to try out the activity with each and compare the different qualities.

What to do:

1. Roll your lump around to make a rounded sphere shape. Stick both thumbs into it to make a thumb pot shape. Move your thumbs around the edges, making your pot larger and the sides thinner.
2. Roll your lump into some sausage shapes, rolling them thinner and thinner. Coil these around to make a cylinder shape on a round base.
3. Flatten your lump and roll it using a rolling pin or other cylindrical roller. Cut five square shapes from it and join them to make a cube with an open top.
4. Roll your lump out again into a round or square shape about 2cm thick. Mark make into it and press things into it to make marks and shapes. Reroll it and draw into it.

It can be a good idea to try each of these several times as you will get better at each attempt and as you do this you can begin to identify teaching tips and suggestions to help children when you teach them these techniques. Questions to consider:

• Thumb pot – you may have found that it requires a fair amount of fine motor control to stick your thumbs in far enough to make a good hole and not so far that you go through to the bottom of the lump and out the other side. Continuing to press just enough to enlarge the hole and make the sides of the form thinner can also be a challenge, especially for children.
• Coil pot – you may have found that making evenly sized coils to use got easier as you practised. Being able to pick them up and form them into a

three-dimensional form also takes some care. It can be useful to have a form to guide you, such as a box or a roll of card.

- Slab pot – you may have found that rolling the material so it is of an even depth all over can be hard and picking each piece up to join it as you make a form can test your fine motor control. Exploring the thickness of the material in relation to the size of the piece to be cut and joined can help here.

- Relief surface – you may have found yourself experimenting with how deep you press into the surface of the material before going through it.

- General questions – if you were able to try these activities out with several of the materials you will have been able to consider the differences between them and the implications for teaching and learning. It is easier to manipulate and control some materials, whereas others can be harder to manipulate but tougher and able to withstand rougher treatment. You might also consider having some of these materials around for children to play with freely, in order to develop their skills and allow them to practise, especially in the lead up to a unit of work where children will be using them as part of their art work. When making the three-dimensional forms you were aiming to make them solid so that they could stand up securely – perhaps the thickness of the material, the base you used and how you joined the materials affected the solidity and stability of the forms.

In the task above you tried a few basic ways of using malleable materials to make three-dimensional forms. These can be used in combinations to make more ambitious forms – joining two thumb posts could make a spherical or egg shape, which can be cut through to reveal the inside or have parts attached to make handles, legs or other features; coil and slab pots can be made around any base shape. If you are going to teach these techniques to children, they must have the chance to practise and improve their skills before making their final piece of art.

Since children might have fewer and less regular opportunities to work in three dimensions in art, it may take longer for them to recall the knowledge, skills and understanding from prior experience. Some materials and associated tools may only be used as one-offs or used very occasionally in the primary years, especially if they are part of a special project or unit of work with an artist in residence, for example.

At the planning stage, it is important to identify any knowledge, skills and understanding that children need to build on in order to be successful in the new learning experiences that you are planning. It may be that prior experiences took place so long ago that it would be unrealistic to expect children to have retained them. Building in additional time to play with and freely explore the material and associated tools will be important to the effectiveness of your planning and the success of the children's learning. Observing children working with the materials as they use them freely will give you an insight into their prior knowledge and inform your planning, teaching and support in the rest of the unit. With older children you might identify some of the prerequisite skills and challenge children to try these out as a lead-in to your planned new learning.

If it is possible within your classroom organisation and the organisation of the curriculum, planning regular opportunities to play with and create with three-dimensional materials will allow children to maintain and develop their skills. Having play dough or plasticine available, for example, will support children's use of clay. Whilst a range of materials are often more readily and frequently available in Early Years classrooms and may continue into Key Stage 1, there are fewer opportunities for older children who have the fine motor skills to make the more varied and intricate models that would lead to making stop motion animation using digital technology.

Another aspect of working with the variety of materials that can be used to make three-dimensional art is the consideration you must give to health and safety. When using materials such as clay, plaster of Paris, withies or found materials, for example, it is vital that all the adults working with the children, and the children themselves, use the associated tools and materials with care for their own and others' safety. It is good practice to note the steps you are taking on the plans and it is essential that all staff know about these when teaching or supporting children. Advice is often present on the packaging of materials as well as on the NSEAD website.

Subject knowledge

There is a list of suggested tools and resources to explore in Appendix 2, along with additional detail about some of the more specialist tools, equipment and resources used in making art in three dimensions.

Teaching visual elements through working in three dimensions

The chart below makes suggestions in relation to each of the eight visual elements when using a range of materials: some of these are applicable to many materials and others are more focused on one particular material: these materials are indicated in brackets. The elements that will be most readily explored will depend upon the materials you are using for the experiences that you plan.

Line	Tone
Mark making and drawing into the material with tools	Using lighter / darker or contrasting tone (buff / red clay)
Using coils and strips of the material	Using various tones of the material
Using linear materials that can be shaped	Decorating the form with tones of the same / different colours
Using straight linear materials to create a framework (sticks)	Using light and shadow to make ephemeral art in the environment
Colour	**Pattern**
Using various colours of the material	Applying surface decoration onto the material before or after construction
Using glazes (clay)	
Painting onto the material	Constructing the material in a patterned structure
Using colours of paper, card, fabric over a framework or on a mould	Placing materials / objects to create a pattern in space
Using projections onto surfaces via mobile digital projectors	Using repeating patterns in creating video, animation or GIFs to be projected or triggered in space or form
Texture	**Shape**
Pressing into soft materials to create surface texture	Creating 3D shapes (regular / irregular; solid / hollow; using frameworks; wrapping or draping)
Choosing materials for their texture – contrasting or complementary	Using 2D shapes to decorate surface
Space	**Form**
Cutting away to reveal inside space, see through the form	Building up forms from coils, slabs or hollowing out
Placing several forms together	Constructing forms from sticks, withies
Making forms which define / contain space	Building up forms by using a mould
Using space to arrange within – installation	Draping and wrapping forms to change them
Changing how natural materials are distributed in a space	Placing 3D objects in an environment
Placing objects of made forms in order to change the way we see them	Creating an installation that can be entered and experienced
Using apps and tools to create digital space	Creating an installation or environment that has digital as well as real elements
Using apps and tools to place real objects into virtual digital space (green screen)	

Form and space are the key visual elements that are intrinsic to working in three dimensions. The potential for learning about and exploring these will depend on the materials and outcome that you are planning on: clay will provide a very different experience to that of using withies, for example. Children should encounter a variety of materials in order to explore these elements during the primary years. It is likely that other visual elements will be part of the experience, especially when decoration is part of the creation of the outcome. Material can be created digitally to be projected onto three-dimensional forms or triggered from patterns or markers on them, as well as changed in scale and setting by the use of apps and tools.

Key vocabulary

When you plan a unit of work using three-dimensional materials, it is important to identify any words that will be used: these might be entirely new words or familiar words used in a different context. It might also be an opportunity to consolidate and re-enforce words. Vocabulary could be considered in relation to the visual elements that underlie the planned learning (see chapter 2 for discussion of vocabulary relating to form and space) and also in relation to the materials being used and their properties or qualities.

Try for yourself – talking and making

Exploring the vocabulary relating to some three-dimensional materials

In this practical task you will consider some of the most commonly used materials and identify some of the relevant vocabulary you might expect to plan for children to develop and use. You may wish to reread the section about visual elements in chapter 2 before completing this exercise. Looking at a unit of work where you have used the materials or thinking back to activities you have supported or taught could also be helpful.

You will need: the pro forma below and any plans relating to working in three dimensions that are available

What to do:

Consider each material / activity and identify some key vocabulary that you think you would be able to introduce or consolidate. Note down the words into the following sections: visual element, material, activity.

Activity – Exploring the vocabulary relating to some three-dimensional materials

Material / activity	Vocabulary		
	Visual element	Material / qualities	Activity
1. A malleable material such as clay, play dough, salt dough or plasticine being used to make an animal.			
2. Sheet materials being placed over a mould, such as paper and paste around a jar to create a cylindrical-shaped container.			
3. A collection of natural materials from the immediate environment, such as stones and sticks being arranged on grass.			

In activity 1 it is likely that you have identified exploring the form that can be created by manipulating the clay. In addition to this, children could also be exploring how to make regular and irregular shapes as well as adding texture or pattern to the surface of the clay. When talking about the qualities of the material, younger children could be using words such as soft and squashy, whilst older children could be using words such as flexible or malleable to describe the way the material can be manipulated. When using the material to make an animal they could focus on words related to the animal, including describing its form and how this could be made by rolling, hollowing out and joining, as well as how it can be decorated by mark making to create textures or patterns or by smoothing the surface.

In activity 2 it is likely that you have identified form where the child is creating a new form by applying paper and glue to the chosen container. Texture may also be discussed, especially where the aim is to make a smooth surface to decorate later, when colour and pattern might also be relevant. When talking about the qualities of the materials, words such as slimy, wet, thick and slippery can be used to describe the paste. The contrast between the paste and the smooth, hard surface of the container might be described. The flexibility of the gluey paper can be explored, as well as the changes that occur when the paste dries, leaving a hard surface. Within this activity vocabulary relating to creating a smooth surface, overlapping strips and pieces of paper, can be explored as well as words relating to any decoration that will be added later.

In activity 3 it is likely that you have identified space as children arrange and rearrange their chosen items, as well as one or more of form, shape, colour and texture as children collect, evaluate and choose natural materials based on their visual and tactile qualities. When arranging their chosen materials space and pattern may also be important, depending on what criteria they choose to base their arrangements on. Given the openness of this activity there may be a greater range of individual responses that each relate to different visual elements. Talking to children about their choices and arrangements will be crucial to understanding what has inspired and influenced their response and outcome. Positional vocabulary will also be used to identify and describe where items are in relation to each other and how space has been used.

When working with three-dimensional materials there are many opportunities to develop a range of vocabulary in practical situations and this can be especially supportive for children learning English as an Additional Language and children with a need to develop language.

Find out more

What is sculpture?

Explore the term sculpture in the 'art terms' section of the Tate website.

Link: www.tate.org.uk/art/art-terms/s/sculpture

Artists, designers and craftspeople

There are usually a few, sometimes many, examples of sculpture or three-dimensional art available to look at in the local environment. Public sculptures have been placed for different purposes over time and more recently this has become even more common. You may find a sculpture park nearby or a sculpture trail that has been set up temporarily or permanently. If there are several sculptures nearby you could create your own sculpture trail, identifying some background information, questions and starting points to support learning in relation to each sculpture or, with older children, help them to do this. It is vital that children can see and explore original sculptures at first hand: given the sensory and tactile nature of sculpture as well as the significance of the scale of a sculpture and the space around it, looking at a photograph or image on a screen can rarely convey the qualities and impact effectively.

LEARNING IN ACTION

A group of initial teacher training students are organised into threes and allocated a sculpture from the campus to use as a focus for talking about art and inspiring the making of art in the primary age range. Before they consider their sculpture they discuss, as a group, the essential areas to include. They identify the following areas:

- Who made the sculpture? Information about the sculptor and his / her work.
- How was the sculpture made? The materials, tools and techniques used by the sculptor.
- What do you notice, think and feel about the sculpture? A personal response to the sculpture after looking at it from all viewpoints, feeling and talking about it.
- How might this inspire your own making of sculpture? A connection to the children's own ideas and practical art work.

Having this framework allows the groups of students to work independently but develop a consistent approach to use as a sculpture trail. They are also challenged to include two levels, so that their material can be used by younger and older children within the primary age group.

Although their trail is focused on some specific sculpture their learning and the approach can be applied to sculptures near their placement schools or first jobs.

When you are researching sculptures or sculptors that you can use to inspire and support learning, you will need to know more about the types of materials sculptors use: some of these would not be available to use in school. The list below identifies some materials you could encounter when looking at sculptures outdoors and in galleries and museums: you can look for examples of each and add them below.

Material	Notes	Examples
Metal	Bronze sculptures are often cast from a mould, or sometimes made from pieces of metal welded together. Other types of metal can also be used to make sculpture.	
Marble	Marble is a type of limestone rock that is carved into a sculpture. Other types of stone can also be carved.	

Material	Notes	Examples
Wood	Wood can be carved into a sculpture and / or pieces of wood can joined.	
Terracotta	Terracotta can be made into relief or sculptural forms and then fired without glazing.	
Ivory	In the past ivory from animals' tusks and horns has been carved to make sculpture. More recently, attitudes towards the use of ivory have changed.	
Concrete	Concrete can be cast and / or carved into.	
Fibreglass	Fibreglass can be cast into forms then decorated and is hardwearing and light.	

Whilst it is unlikely that primary aged children will make sculptures using these materials they can see them and learn about them when exploring sculpture and sculptors. Recently, some sculptors have worked in materials that make their work ephemeral, available to the viewer temporarily until weather and human activity cause it to be lost. Digital technology can be crucial here: photographing and filming the artwork as it is created and on completion might be the only record of it for the future. Often the temporary nature of the work and the changes that follow from its nature are a powerful aspect of it and the participation of the viewer can be crucial.

Material	Notes	Examples
Ice	Ice from nature or made in moulds melting	Nele Azevedo, Olafur Eliasson
Snow	Making patterns onto a snow surface	Simon Beck
Sand	Making patterns onto a sand surface	Jon Foreman
Stone	Placing and arranging stones	Richard Long
Leaves / sticks	Placing and arranging natural materials, often using nothing other than what is available on site	James Brunt, Andy Goldsworthy,
Found manmade materials	Collecting, placing and arranging arrays of manmade materials	Tony Cragg, Romuald Hazoumè, James Alderton

Material	Notes	Examples
Light	Drawing in space with light, arranging lights into installations and environments	Yayoi Kusama, Greyworld
Movement in space (walking artists)	Creating movement and interaction in space, sometimes moving objects	Richard Long, Hamish Fulton (Slowalk)

It can be interesting to give children a sense of how sculptors work. It is important to convey that sculptures do not spring to life fully formed but are the result of research, inspiration and hard, often very physical, work. When an artist makes a sculpture, especially if it is going to be large-scale, they often make a 'maquette' – a small-scale model to show what the sculpture will be like, before the full-size sculpture is made, which is often produced by other specialists in the material and technique. Looking up Henry Moore's Maquette Studio at Perry Green on the internet can allow children to have an insight into the work that goes on before the finished sculpture is completed.

Link: www.henry-moore.org/visit/henry-moore-studios-gardens/studios-and-tapestries/bourne-maquette-studio

Exploring the work of Rachel Whiteread can give you a sense of the scale involved in making sculptures.

Link: www.luhringaugustine.com/artists/rachel-whiteread/artworks/sculptures4

Watching artists who make temporary sculptures and installations can emphasise to children that there is more to this than simply gathering and arranging – considering pattern, space, form and colour is part of the thinking behind these works, as is drawing attention to environmental concerns and having an impact on the viewer, causing them to look again at what seem initially to be ordinary materials and spaces.

You can also consider the inspiration or purpose for the sculpture. Perhaps it was to commemorate a local or national figure, event or occupation; it may have been to provide a focal point or enhance a public space; or it could have been to provoke or please viewers. People's feelings about a piece of sculpture in their locality change over time and it can be interesting to consider the range of responses a piece of public art can inspire.

Over time it is important to introduce children to different types of sculpture made from a variety of materials and in different styles. Think about looking at both figurative and more abstract sculptures so that children can learn about the changes in approach to sculpture and the range of possibilities there are for making three-dimensional forms and using space. Sometimes a more abstract piece of sculpture will inspire more open discussion and speculation about the artists' intentions and the response from the viewer.

Reflect and extend

Find Marie Huard's article 'The Case for Class Discussion: Sixth-Grade's Exploration of El Anatsui's Contemporary Sculpture', published in *Art Education* (Volume 70, Number 6, pp.14–19) in 2017.

Read about how she used the sculptures of El Anatsui to explore making and talking about art.

Teaching and learning

The media and processes you might use when exploring art made in three dimensions are varied and dependent on the material being used. As with any art technique or material it is vital that the adults teaching and supporting learning know enough about the material and how to use it to explore and make in art. This may appear more daunting because of the range of materials available and the factors such as the cost of resources, the need for specialist equipment or tools and the space required for storage of materials, work in progress and finished work. It is vital to overcome any anxieties and allow children to have these opportunities for learning rather than restrict them mainly to two-dimensional materials. There are some children who can enjoy the making process; they can achieve more and feel happier and more confident in these areas than they are when holding a pencil or a paintbrush.

The chart below suggests some techniques that children can be taught and how these might be explored in making finished outcomes.

Materials	Techniques	Ideas
Materials that can be manipulated and moulded (clay, plasticine, salt dough, play dough, Fimo, etc.)	Rolling out to make a flat surface to work into / onto Rolling out flat and constructing slabs into forms Hollowing out (thumb pot) Constructing from coils Shaping into forms (small scale)	Make clay tiles, shapes or hanging plaques Make cylinders, box shapes, buildings, wrap round card to make a hollow body for a creature Make pots, bowls, bodies of creatures, rounded hollow forms including spheres

Materials	Techniques	Ideas
Pouring and casting (plaster of Paris, papier-mâché)	Creating or finding a surface / mould to take a cast from Pouring into the mould Pressing papier-mâché onto the surface	Find interesting textures in the environment to take casts from Make a surface to mould from by collecting and sticking material onto a surface (2D / 3D) Use a mould (bowl, plate, jar) as a basis for the shape
Linear materials (wire, sticks, straws, withies, rolled paper)	Bending, twisting, shaping wire Rolled newspaper tubes and cylinders joined to make forms Flexing withies and joining them into the chosen form with tape, string Placing and joining sticks and straws with wire or tape to hold their form	Make a figurative form (fish, leaf) and extend from there Make an abstract form exploring the shapes that can be made (curved / linear) Make a framework with an inside and outside or views through Make a curved framework from card strips to form the basis of a mask or face
Sheet materials (paper, paper lamination, modroc, fabric)	Drape over linear forms (wire / withies / sticks / rolled newspaper) Wrap around hollow forms (boxes) Stretch between (poles, sticks, fences, floor to ceiling) Create holes by tearing, cutting	Build on the ideas above Fully enclose or cover the shapes and forms Leave spaces to look through so both inside and outside can be seen or entered
Natural / manmade found materials	Collect and rearrange within the existing environment Place found or made objects together in groups	Make subtle alterations to the landscape by collecting and placing Collect and arrange manmade and familiar objects for a personal purpose or to suggest an idea or feeling

Exploring and making with the materials before you plan, teach and support is vital as this first-hand experience will allow you to identify how you can plan for learning, suggest ways of overcoming any challenges and plan effective and worthwhile experiences. In addition to this there are resources available to support the development of your subject knowledge and confidence when using three-dimensional materials and some of the most readily accessible are online. Look at Darrell Wakelam's website to explore sculpture making with cardboard and tape, for example.

Organisation of space and resources

Three-dimensional art works may present challenges when you are organising space and resources in the primary classroom. This will depend on the size of the space available to you. It is important to consider how work in progress will be stored, how finished work will be shared and / or displayed and how time can be organised effectively.

When you are considering how to store incomplete artwork any special requirements of the material will be vital: half-finished clay work, for example, will need to be stored damp in an airtight container so that it is still malleable enough to continue using. Other materials, especially fragile materials, may need a space where they will not be squashed or knocked over. Some materials will have characteristics that mean that they need to be used to make the work in one session without stopping and others allow work over several sessions with no detrimental effects.

Being flexible about your use of time can be helpful in addressing the considerations outlined above. If you are planning to work with a material where the making experience will be most successful when accomplished in one session, perhaps where you might usually have an art lesson a week you can bring forward the time from the next week, so that the class has all morning or all afternoon to work continuously. Identifying the most effective use of time at the planning stage can help you allocate it to support learning throughout your unit – an equal amount of time each week may not be the most supportive for learning when working in three dimensions. When working with older children, building in short periods in which to stop, reflect and evaluate is also important to plan for. For some types of three-dimensional work working outside might be the best choice, or perhaps working offsite. The weather and the temporary nature of the outcomes will then need to be considered.

It is also important to plan ahead for how the finished outcomes will be shared, displayed and recorded. A different kind of space is needed to display three-dimensional art: small individual pieces can be arranged on shelves or cupboard tops at different heights. It can give a sense of completion if each child makes a label identifying the name, title and material used to display with their art, as in an art gallery. Large-scale, collaborative and installation art could be displayed temporarily inside or outside whilst children and parents look at it, or more permanently if space of the appropriate kind is available. Recording the art work, perhaps by taking several photos from different angles or taking a short video moving all around the sculpture, can document the finished work without having to store it indefinitely.

Work in relief

As well as creating art work that is standing in space and can be seen from all around, art work can also be created in relief: creating texture or images that cut into or stick up from a flat surface. Making relief forms can be similar to, and a development from, some of the collage techniques discussed in the previous chapter. When a sculptor creates a relief this could be through adding to the flat surface to lift up parts of the surface or it could be by taking away from the flat surface to leave some parts higher, depending on the material being used. Reliefs can be explorations of texture, decorative patterns, figurative designs telling a story or depicting a person or entirely abstract.

When adding to a flat surface, children might be using collage bits and pieces or card and paper to create some raised elements, before layering paper and paste over and pressing this in around the raised areas so that they are covered smoothly. A similar approach can be employed using sheets of modroc over a surface which has been prepared. Rolling out thin layers of salt dough or clay and cutting shapes from them and then placing them on or fixing them to a flat surface can be another approach.

LEARNING IN ACTION

A class of Year 6 children have been making careful observations of the surface of shells, rocks and stones using magnifying glasses and micro-scopes. They have made drawings and collected close-up photographs and have focused on the textures and patterns. It is clear from their sketches and notes that some surfaces exhibit more random features and others have more patterned elements. All of the surfaces they investigate in depth are more interesting and varied than they first appeared.

Following their research, each child makes a relief plaque based on the tex-ture and pattern they have observed, aiming to expand and exaggerate the texture so it can be felt more readily than when part of a very small object. The children are shown two techniques for making their relief: applying plaster and casting and using paper lamination to cover the surface with flat sheets of tissue soaked in wallpaper paste. They can choose which they want to use depending on the effect they would like to achieve.

Children who have chosen to cast with plaster work onto shallow card / plastic trays using thread and different thicknesses of string, seeds and pulses, paper and card and other found and collected materials to create a raised surface. Children who have chosen paper lamination work onto a thick card base that they have cut to the shape they chose.

When the relief plaques have been cast or covered and left to dry they are all varnished and mounted onto a wall inside the school, so that children and adults can enjoy the sensory experience of feeling them as well as looking at them.

In the case study above the emphasis is on creating a textural form in relief that can be touched as well as looked at. Each child has designed and made their relief shape and these have been combined in a display to make a collection. Another approach might have been to challenge children to work on a large-scale collaborative piece which would have required them to plan, explain and negotiate how to use the larger space.

Reliefs can also be figurative, perhaps representing single, simple shapes (fish, leaves); a scene from a story; a real or imagined person or creature; or a building from observation or research. Tiles or shaped plaques can be created and holes can be cut through them. When working with older pupils, more control over tools and materials is likely to result in more detailed and complex results than when younger pupils are using this technique.

Organising a class, a year group or even the whole school to each make a small piece which becomes part of a greater whole can be a great way of creating something long-lasting to display in the school. Alternatively, building in this kind of activity for each Year 6 class to do and then adding the finished art work to those made by previous Year 6s can be a pleasing commemorative activity to mark their time at the school. It is important to ensure that although there may be a unifying theme such as a technique, a process, a colour range or a shape, there is still some opportunity for individual creative response.

Work in relief and three dimensions

Art that is created in relief can also be transformed into something more three-dimensional by changing it into something that can either be hung or stood up. Curling a rectangular relief around into a cylindrical form or creating two pieces of identical size and shape then hanging them so viewers can look at each side, for example. When this is part of the outcome it gives children the opportunity to consider what the viewer of the sculpture will see from a variety of viewpoints rather than just looking at the one view of the relief surface.

LEARNING IN ACTION

Year 2 children have previously explored mark making into a malleable surface. They are familiar with using play dough and plasticine and early in the unit of work they have been given the opportunity to use wooden tools to make marks into the surface so they can practise the sorts of possible marks they might use when working with the clay. They have also collected some found items from around the classroom that make interesting textures and patterns when pressed into the surface. The children have been taught how to use wooden guides and a roller to make a smooth surface of an even depth to make marks into.

In the middle of the unit of work the children have developed a design by working a rectangular piece of paper of the same size as the clay that they will use for the finished piece. They can also pick up and reshape the paper into a cylinder so that they can have a look at the design in three dimensions, as well as when working in relief. Their teacher has encouraged them to think about the marks made at the right and left edges of the rectangle so that the place where it curls round and joins might be disguised.

When the children make their rectangular reliefs some designs are random explorations of marks and textures; some are repeating patterns; and some have figurative elements created from the combinations of marks and textures. Some children have deliberately planned for continuous marks that join when the relief is rolled into a cylinder and others are more interested in the free mark making experience.

They are supported in changing their reliefs into cylindrical shapes, using card shapes to reinforce them and give them stability at first. Help is also needed to make sure that the marks and textures do not get smoothed over or squashed during this process. Later, the clay cylinders are fired and the children can consider the change from malleable material to hard surface.

If this unit of work was carried out with older children, more could be expected of them in terms of designing a pattern or image that 'joins up' when the left and right edges are joined. As well as mark making and pressing into the clay surface they might also draw and cut additional thin layers of clay in shapes to attach to the surface. These activities would work with air drying clay which would not need firing but would be more fragile and have a somewhat different finished result when dry.

Work in three dimensions

When we plan for children to make sculpture and three-dimensional forms in art, we must ensure that we teach the necessary techniques so that children can use these to create their own outcome. At the early stages of a unit of work some time must be spent on learning or developing the required skills. It may be possible to build on prior experience of the material and related techniques or these could be entirely new. Connections could be made to the experience of using materials, tools and techniques in design technology and science perhaps.

At these early stages it is important to demonstrate techniques and skills clearly and give children opportunities to try these out, practise and improve. Working on a smaller scale, in pairs or with more 'throwaway' materials can be useful as children will feel under less pressure to achieve their final outcome immediately.

Working in a range of scales

When working in three dimensions children should also have the opportunity to create three-dimensional forms in space, not just on a small scale but in a range of scales and situations. Although small individual pieces can be combined to make a greater whole, such as when making tiles, making one very large sculpture or installation is an exciting experience with different learning opportunities. Planning for the large-scale experience to be temporary and perhaps outside, either on or off site, can be a useful way of addressing concerns about space in the classroom.

It may be that younger children have the opportunity to move and change forms in space more often than older pupils, because they are likely to have access to role play indoors and outdoor play. In the outdoor context, children will spontaneously make collections of natural materials such as leaves, flowers, seed heads and sticks, arranging them in space in random and decorative arrangements. Older children can also be given this opportunity, but with teaching and time to think and experiment they can work with more intention and subtlety. When this kind of activity is planned as part of the art curriculum, it is important for developing learning that it is extended beyond simply finding and placing and challenges children to articulate why they have made the choices they have made; and how this relates to form, space and other visual elements such as shape, colour, texture and pattern. Recording this in photography or video can be a useful record and using time lapse to capture the making and deterioration of the art can also become an outcome in itself.

A next step for older children can be to make installations leading to a bigger and more purposeful investigation of form, space and viewpoints. In the context of a unit of work this might include learning about what an installation is; researching some outdoor / indoor installations and information about the artists who created them; and making some mini-installations with junk materials, found objects and small world toys. They can then go on to designing a large-scale, collaborative and temporary installation in the school grounds. This can lead to an event where other children and parents come and experience the installation before it is removed, giving a sense of creating for an audience and getting feedback from them. In chapter 4 the construction of a multisensory environment incorporating elements of art made and displayed using digital technology was explored and this is an example of a large-scale, collaborative, temporary installation of this kind.

Another approach to scale might be to trick the viewer by first making a relatively small form or maquette and then placing model people /or animals near it and photographing or filming it. In chapter 1 the idea of creating a sculpture and using green screen technology to place it in locations around the world was explored.

LEARNING IN ACTION

Children in Years 5 and 6 are exploring three-dimensional environments and they use boxes, card and paper to create mini-installations. Some of the children work alone and some in pairs and small groups. Throughout the making they have a small figure to give them a sense of scale, reminding them that the viewer will see the space differently to the way they see it themselves. They also design a path through the installation for their viewer, using a grid of squares that is stuck on the 'floor' of their box and connects to the tiled floor in the school hall. Alongside this practical making they use green screen technology and photos / video of themselves to create a film or series of photos that shows them inside their installations, looking at the world they have created.

In the example above children use the tools of digital technology along with real materials to create and manipulate space and form, allowing them to work on a small scale but experience the challenges of creating an installation.

Connecting to other types of art

When planning opportunities to work in three dimensions, connections can be made to other areas of learning in art. Painting can be used to decorate; drawings, paintings and prints can be cut, folded and reformed into three-dimensional objects; and collage can easily move into work in three dimensions, depending on the materials chosen and how they are attached. Digital technology can be used to support learning effectively here, especially when seeking to record temporary art work; the stages of development of a three-dimensional work and the outcomes which are unlikely to be able to be stored effectively. Although art created in a virtual environment using tools such as Tilt Brush seems and feels like painting, because the colour hangs in the air the maker can create paintings in three dimensions for the viewer to explore.

Reflect and extend

Read Victoria Pavlou's article 'Understanding Young Children's Three-Dimensional Creative Potential in Art Making', published in the *International Journal of Art and Design Education* in 2009 (Volume 28, Number 2, pp.139–150).

Think about how the learning experiences of the five- and six-year-olds outlined could help you in your practice – especially when planning for older children.

Connecting across the curriculum

There are many starting points that can inspire the making of three-dimensional forms and the use of space in art and planning should ensure that children encounter a variety of these. Productive and meaningful links can be made with other areas of the curriculum, such as looking at artefacts made in the past (history and RE); exploring and using the environment (geography); exploring the properties of materials (science); and using stories and poetry (English).

There is, of course, a strong connection to design technology, although when working in three dimensions in art there may be less focus on making a useful finished object and more significance placed on making to satisfy a creative urge. In design technology the focus will be on creating with a purpose or function in mind. Many of the skills children use in making in digital technology can be applied in working in three dimensions in art. Making the backgrounds and props for stop motion animation is one example of this.

LEARNING IN ACTION

Teaching assistant students are working with the organisation Into Film to learn how to make simple stop motion animations and consider how this can be used to support learning with primary children. They learn about how to set up the learning environment and use an app (iMotion) to record their animations. They use a range of art materials to create environments, characters and props to use. As they work it is clear that the activity draws upon skills from a range of curriculum areas, including art, design technology, science, English and computing, as well as problem-solving and team work. Thinking about scale and colour and how to make three-dimensional objects stand up stably and tell an engaging story are challenges they solve together. Some of the students use plasticine to create their films or include line drawing, whilst others use plastic and cellophane on a light box or paper and card.

Link: www.intofilm.org/

Figure 11.1 A suggested set-up for stop motion animation

In the example above a creative challenge drawing upon skills, knowledge and understanding from several subjects is brought together with digital technology as a vehicle for creating something from them. Setting this in an art context or with specified art materials can focus the connection more fully on the subject; set in a science context it can be an opportunity to express science concepts using visual tools, or it can be an opportunity to allow children to freely engage in creating, whilst demonstrating to you their strengths and ideas. Fleer and Hoban (2012) discuss the ready availability of art materials and small toys that lend themselves to making what they call "slowmations" (slow animations) in the context of science. This utilisation of existing resources in new and creative ways in a variety of subjects and contexts has great potential for learning across the curriculum. Fleer (2018, p. 956) goes on to explore this in the context of imaginative storytelling, where making animations allows young children to "reproduce their imaginary role play in digital form".

Sculpture can often be a form of art that draws our attention to issues of social justice, protest and activism in the world. When children encounter or make sculpture of this kind it can be an opportunity to discuss spiritual, moral, social and cultural ideas. Artists have drawn attention to climate change, an example being Eliasson's *Ice Watch* and his chronological sequence of photographs of the same glacier as it changes over time.

Link: https://olafureliasson.net/archive/artwork/WEK109190/ice-watch

We can increasingly make connections to the computing curriculum as the devices, apps and tools that are becoming more readily accessible in schools and day-to-day life, including children's play, allow us to be in virtual digital spaces as participants and makers. The virtual world of Minecraft and the making space in CoSpaces can be a vehicle for making and exploring art as Flint *et al.* (2018) discussed in their research about recreating a sculpture park in the digital world of Minecraft.

Conclusion

Working in three dimensions in art is an exciting experience for children and as such must be included in any sequence or unit of work. It offers scope for creativity and sensory experience and may engage some children who are less attracted to working in two dimensions. Although it might pose challenges to us in relation to our subject knowledge and organisational skills, the enjoyment and learning opportunities should give us the impetus to overcome these challenges and ensure that children have a varied and inspiring experience.

Next steps

Find out more about the three-dimensional art available to you locally by:

- looking around your immediate school and local environment

- researching on the internet

Learn a new three-dimensional art technique by finding a local workshop or event.

References

Briggs, P. (2016) *Make Build Create*. London: Black Dog Publishing.

Fleer, M. (2018) Digital animation: New conditions for children's development in play-based setting. *British Journal of Educational Technology*. **Vol 49**, No 5, pp.943–958.

Fleer, M. and Hoban, G. (2012) Using 'Slowmation' for intentional teaching in early childhood centres: Possibilities and imaginings. *Australasian Journal of Early Childhood*. **Vol 37**, No 3, pp.61–70.

Flint, T., Hall, L., Stewart, F. and Hagan, D. (2018) Virtualizing the Real: A Virtual Reality Contemporary Sculpture Park for Children. *Digital Creativity*. **Vol 29**, No 2–3, pp.191–207.

Further resources

Clough, P. (2007) *Clay in the Primary School*. London: Bloomsbury.

Clough, P. (2007) *Sculptural Materials in the Classroom*. London: Bloomsbury.

Huard, M. (2017) The Case for Class Discussion: Sixth-Grade's Exploration of El Anatsui's Contemporary Sculpture. *Art Education*. **Vol 70**, No 6, pp.14–19.

Krumbach, M. (2007) *Clay Projects for Children*. London: Bloomsbury.

Utley, C. and Magson, M. (2007) *Exploring Clay with Children*. London: Bloomsbury.

Wenzel, A. (2010) *13 Sculptures Children Should Know*. London: Prestel.

Chapter Padlet:

https://padlet.com/Jeanne/Chapter11

12

Chapter Twelve

Making digital art

Introduction

Making art that exists wholly in the digital world is a relatively new technique in the world of art as well as in education and it provides us with some interesting opportunities. Over the last ten years many of the tools available to explore this way of making art have become increasingly common in primary schools, including those that seemed unlikely to arrive in primary schools when they were first unveiled to the world. Using digital tools and techniques as part of the art curriculum can provide inspiring and inclusive opportunities for individual and collaborative making of art as well as being a way to use the devices that are available in schools, and increasingly in homes, in creative and active ways to make, rather than passive ways merely as consumers. Seeing themselves as inventors, creators and makers with technologies can be powerful and motivating for pupils.

There are many digital tools available to use in schools, some of which may be part of the commonly available equipment such as interactive whiteboards, tablets and laptops, but used for art making, and others which may be more art specific. One important aspect of embedding making art with digital tools and devices into the curriculum is equipping pupils to be creative users and makers who use a range of tools and devices and in this, as in the other areas of art explored, experimenting and exploring is vital. In some ways in this area it could be easier, as it is possible to make and remake, do and undo, saving outcomes as we go. There is less fear of 'spoiling' and 'wasting' and therefore more likelihood of risk-taking and productive use of trial and error. In addition to this, digital tools give pupils access to a range of different ways of making art, including manipulating and combining images, light and sound and exploring augmented and virtual reality – experiences they are increasingly familiar with in the context of entertainment.

Tools and materials

There is a list of suggested tools and resources to explore in Appendix 2, along with additional detail about some of the more specialist tools, equipment and resources used in working with digital devices and tools.

Devices

You are likely to have access to some or all of the following devices: PCs or laptops; tablets and other mobile devices; interactive whiteboards and / or large screens; fixed and / or mobile projectors; visualisers and combined or individual photocopiers / printers / scanners. You might have other equipment that supports some of the above such as: tripods or stands; lightboxes; green screens; robots or other programmable toys; 360 cameras; styluses or pens to use on tablets and screens; drones and attachable lenses for mobile devices. All of these have the potential to be used to make digital art.

Software, apps and tools to use on PCs, laptops and tablets

Alongside the computers or tablets that you use in day-to-day teaching and learning, the software and apps that are available on these can be used to make art, along with those that are more specifically focused on art. The chart below summarises some of the main software and tools you might have available to use. You could use this as a checklist to begin to evaluate what is available to you.

	Notes
Camera (still and video)	Most mobile devices have a built-in camera that will take still images and video. This can be used to take a series of photos or videos that can then be edited and manipulated to make digital art.
Photo editor	Along with the camera, devices will have editing tools to allow images to be cropped and resized, to manipulate the orientation, colour and light as well as draw onto (mark-up) and open in other tools to go further.
Photo collage maker	There are many free photo collage makers that can be used to combine and position images together to create new images. Options include creating grids, choosing positions (freestyle) and using pre-made templates. Having made a photo collage there are often tools that allow for the addition of frames, colour and patterned backgrounds, text and free drawing,
Slide presentation maker	Slide and slideshow makers such as PowerPoint (Windows), Keynote (IOS) and Google Slides all contain tools that can be used to make art. They can also be combined with other digital material such as photos and video, sound and music. It is also possible to make simple digital animations using the tools in slide makers.
Screenshot tool	It is possible to take a screenshot on most devices. This might be by using the 'snipping tool' on a PC or laptop or by using a shortcut on a tablet. Capturing what is on the screen in the moment can be useful when making art. Many apps and tools also allow for what is being created to be saved to photos or camera roll.
Screen recording tool	Being able to record what is happening on the screen can allow for the capture of change and movement. The addition of narration, sound or music can also be captured in this way, allowing for the finished art to be multisensory. This might be part of the software or it could be available within slide-making tools.

These tools are useful across the curriculum in day-to-day teaching and learning and the creation of resources and can be used creatively, singly and in combinations, to make art as well as to capture and share what pupils are making. In addition, there are tools and apps on devices as well as tools available online that are specifically focused on making art and it is useful to have access to some of these. They might also be used in the subjects of computing and design technology. You could annotate this chart with the specific names of the tools you have access to.

	Notes	Examples
On screen painting	Apps and tools that are focused on drawing or painting on the screen using a finger or stylus as a tool to create marks and lines.	Sketches Brushes Tagtool
Video editing tools	Apps and tools that allow video to be edited and developed.	iMovie
Stop motion animation	Apps that support the creation of stop motion animation using a series of still images combined in a sequence to make a film. Many of these have additional useful tools such as a grid and / or onion skin to help position objects.	Stop Motion Studio iMotion I can animate Animate It Lite Puppet EDU Draw and Talk series of photos in PowerPoint
Green screen	Apps that use a photo / video taken against a green screen to allow for manipulation and a combination of foreground images and backgrounds.	Do Ink Green Screen (IOS)
Sounds and sound recording	Apps that allow sounds, sound effects and music to be created, recorded and added to images and video, making the finished art multisensory in nature.	Keezy GarageBand Voice Recorder
Augmented reality (AR) and virtual reality (VR)	Apps and tools that allow us to create and interact with digital material in the physical world.	HP Reveal EyeJack CoSpaces AR Makr Reality Composer CoSpaces / Blocks Tilt Brush

The apps and tools listed above are quite open in nature, leaving the pupils the opportunity to create and manipulate the artistic content for themselves. In addition to these there are some specific apps and tools, including some available online, that have interesting but often limited or specific functions and can be used creatively, especially when combined with the tools listed above. Some of these will be explored as examples in the rest of this chapter.

Other useful resources

You will have seen from the list in Appendix 2 that there are other apps, tools and resources that can be harnessed in making digital art. Some of these might be used in science (microscopes, lenses and other viewers) and computing (robots and other programmable toys and coding apps such as Scratch). There also many physical resources that can be used alongside digital devices and tools as part of the making process. Those used in multisensory play activities with EYFS pupils, such as lightboxes and other ways of playing with light such as torches, fairy lights, LEDs and glowsticks, can be used to make art. You will have seen in previous chapters how physical materials and resources can be combined with digital ones to make art.

Alongside some of the resources explored above there will be supporting resources that make them easier for pupils to use. When using a mobile device, it is often helpful for children to have a stand or tripod to help keep the device steady and in the position needed. These can range from home-made using sturdy card to expensive specialist equipment, depending on the situation you are in. When animating or using green screen it is possible to buy backdrops and screens but also green card, fabric or simply painting a wall green can be just as effective and user-friendly. Searching online can allow you to see how teachers and other creative users of technology improvise and solve problems, so it is not always vital to buy all the most expensive equipment. An example of this is these user-friendly and easy to make tablet stands, to use when you are making stop motion animation.

Link: www.instructables.com/id/Cardboard-iPad-Stand/

Subject knowledge

When you are planning to teach digital art making, identifying the relevant visual elements can help you be clear about the learning that will take place. As with any aspect of art there will be subject-specific vocabulary as well as words used with a specific meaning in this context. There are specialist techniques and processes in this area that you will need to know about, just as in any area of art making.

The chart below makes some suggestions in relation to each of the eight visual elements. When you are planning and teaching a unit of work that involves making digital art it is important to identify one or two visual elements that you will focus on with the children. It is likely that this will have been done at the long-term planning stage.

Line	Tone
Drawing with light (slow shutter apps) Drawing on screen (drawing / painting apps) Screen recording of drawing on screen Programming an object or toy to move and draw Drawing GPS using running / walking / mapping apps	Experimenting with the effect of light on surfaces (light / dark / fluorescent) Adjusting the tone of a colour in a painting app Adjusting the tone of a photo in colour and / or black and white in photo editing
Colour	**Pattern**
Experimenting with changing colours using drawing and painting tools on screen Projecting colours onto surfaces to explore effects Deconstructing images and photos using colour sorters	Using tools and apps to manipulate images using pattern effects (photo manipulation apps) Creating repeating patterns (time lapse app, GIFs, stop motion animation, copy and paste)
Texture	**Shape**
Photographing and looking more closely at textures (magnification tools and apps)	Choosing shapes (photo manipulation apps) Changing shapes (cropping tools, shape apps) Layering shapes next to and over each other (copying, pasting, moving)
Space	**Form**
Placing and moving objects in space and changing their scale using green screen tools Placing and moving objects in augmented or virtual reality exploring scale and space. Creating installations and changing the environment	Manipulating size, orientation and scale of forms Creating and / or manipulating objects in virtual or augmented reality Manipulating 2D images into 3D (tinyplanet apps)

As you read the suggestions in the chart above you might have noticed that they have strong connections to the visual elements charts in the previous chapters. In some instances, the use of digital tools can be a substitute or alternative or one of several tools used together. In this chapter the focus will be on the additional and different ways of working that digital approaches provide.

Artists and makers in digital technology

There are many artists who use digital technology as part or all of their tools for making art. In chapter 4 you were introduced to some of these. Established artists whose names you may already know, such as Yayoi Kusama, Olafur Eliasson and David Hockney, who began working in other media, have absorbed digital making into their repertoire as tools and approaches have become available. One way into children's making of digital art is to show them what an artist they have already encountered does with digital media. This reinforces the idea that digital tools can be used alongside physical materials as a way of being creative and expressing oneself. Other digital artists may be less familiar and this might affect your confidence in choosing them to share with your pupils. In some ways, though, this is a positive, as it allows you to make more exciting choices led by your personal and your school and pupils' interests, rather than relying on known 'famous' artists. It also may lead you to expand both your own and the children's ideas of who an artist is and what they do and make connections to STEAM approaches. When you are making choices, it is worth considering whether the art and artists are doing something with digital media that could not be done in any other way. Using and manipulating light to make art is one example of this.

Painting with light

You may have noticed the increasing prevalence of outdoor digital art projections and installations in towns and cities during the winter. Some of these are digital art projected onto large buildings, sometimes to commemorate historical events, such as those by Luxmuralis, whose work is usually projected onto cathedrals. Others are more immersive and interactive pieces of art around a trail outdoors or in the streets, in woods or around the grounds of stately homes such as Lumiere London, Light Up Leicester and the annual interactive light festival at Compton Verney. All of these are created by artists using digital tools and some of them include opportunities for the viewer to take part and contribute to or control the art.

Many digital artists make use of images projected onto a wall from a tablet. Often a feature of this art is that the viewer's interaction is a part of the art itself. For example, the CROSSROADS exhibition in Amsterdam featured a projected time-line controlled by visitors using an iPad, enabling them to explore connections between diverse museum objects. A group of designers in Seattle experimented with a simple iPad drawing app and a black background to project live murals drawn by themselves and their audience onto surrounding buildings as digital graffiti. At the Ars Electronica Festival 2018 in Austria the app Tagtool was used to project live art, animation and sound onto walls. Some of these became immersive spaces for children to explore and others were the backdrop for dance performances.

Link: https://cemec-eu.net/cms/

Link: www.seattledesignnerds.org/news/2016/11/4/lights-and-projection

Link: www.omai.at/tagtool-convention-ars-electronica/

Try for yourself

In this practical activity you will try out an app that allows you to paint, animate what you have painted and then project your image onto a surface.

You will need:

An iPad

The free app Tagtool

Access to a digital projector, preferably mobile, but if not, use a fixed one

What to do:

Watch the Tagtool tutorial available here: www.youtube.com/watch?v=hi-BjLz5-ul

This shows you how to add and animate layers that combine to create a colourful, moving figure. Either follow along and make what this artist, Josef Dorninger, makes or make something of your own, following the steps. It could be applied to anything you would like to create: a bunch of flowers, fireworks, buildings, for example.

When you have finished, try projecting it. If you have a small, mobile projector think creatively about where your projection could have most impact. Perhaps it could appear somewhere unexpected in school or outside in the grounds or it could be a digital addition to a part of the building or an existing piece of art. It could be timed to appear and disappear at random or with regularity.

You can experiment with this medium of projected live painting for yourself using a tablet connected to a small portable projector via AirPlay or using an AV adapter. It is particularly effective when projected in a darkened space. There is a free version of the live painting and animation app Tagtool mentioned above that has a simple paint tool for creating and animating coloured layers within an image using different sizes of brushes. The idea is that you paint and animate each layer as you go and then reorder the layers to bring objects forwards or backwards and group them. Each layer can be animated separately and the animations recorded and projected. Other people can be invited to join in your Tagtool session and paint alongside you in multiplayer mode as long as they are all on the same wireless network.

Other apps worth considering for live painting are those that enable you to draw with neon colours on a black background, such as Art of Glow, Glow Colouring or Forge of Neon, or that create colourful patterns and tessellations, such as Amaziograph or Kaleidoscope Drawing Pad. These can create inspiring sensory spaces when projected onto the walls of a white tent or mosquito net and combined with music. You might also look at the app Mega Photo, which has hundreds of photo effects and filters to choose from and can be used with imported drawings or photos. Effects such as mosaics, light tunnels or spinning globes can be combined into a video to be projected onto walls or white objects. Or you can project live interactions with the effects which move and distort as you tap, pinch or rotate them, perhaps in response to music.

There are many possibilities for creating a multimedia performance based on a combination of live painting, dance and music. *Wood Wide Web* from the Czech company Tineola Theatre is based on the invisible life below a forest floor and would make an excellent provocation for a class project. This approach also relates back to the Learning in Action story discussed in chapter 4, based around creating multisensory environments.

Link: www.drawinginmotion.com/

Reflect and extend

Explore the case study in Chapter 10, 'The Arts in STEM: STEAM', by Caldwell *et al.* (In: Caldwell *et al.* (eds), STEM in the primary curriculum, 2019, pp.158–161).

This explores a simple way into drawing or painting with light using everyday materials and a slow shutter app on a tablet. It is a good starting point if you have not worked in this way before.

Teaching and learning

Using digital approaches to make art will include the same learning opportunities as if physical materials were being used. A combination of opportunities to explore and experiment with new devices and tools, along with teaching specific ways to use them, will be important if children are to learn and be creative. Using the readily available devices and tools to create art, along with using more specifically art and digital technology focused ones, can enrich the range of experiences offered in the art curriculum. If you are just beginning to incorporate digital approaches into the art curriculum, using the devices, apps and tools that you have to hand is a good starting point.

Starting with a mobile device:

LEARNING IN ACTION

A group of undergraduate students are exploring how to use mobile devices to explore and make art. They work in pairs and each have a tablet or phone and access to the free app PicCollage. They are given an art word to explore at random through a lucky dip. These words are based within the vocabulary of the visual elements. They are asked to move around their immediate environment to take a set of photos that visually exemplify their word. They have access to a building and some outdoor space. They are asked to take about twenty photos and when they have done this they stop and return to the classroom. At this point they are asked to evaluate their set of photos by considering the following questions:

- Is it clear in each image what your chosen word is? If not, take a few more photos that really feature an aspect of the word and / or edit the photos you have taken to make that the main feature.
- Do you have a range of examples of your chosen word (e.g. a range of shades of red, thin to thick lines, different curves or patterns)? If not, take a few more photos that add some variety to the collection.

When they are happy that they have captured a coherent and representative set of images the students move to the collage making tool. They are asked to make a 4 x 4 grid of images and add the photos they feel best represent the range of the chosen word. Then they are asked to evaluate how this looks in the grid. At this point they can choose to move the photos around to make a pleasing array. They can also choose whether to have a coloured frame around the photos or shrink this away so that all the photos appear next to each other with no gaps.

When they are satisfied with the photo collage they are asked to save it to the camera roll, delete all the other photos used to make it and then AirDrop or email it to their tutor. The photo collages are shared as a slide sequence and the group are asked to supply the word each suggests. They discuss the challenges of representing the words visually and how focusing on the word supports understanding of the nuances of it in the context of the subject.

Questions to consider:

Taking photos: It is easy to assume that everyone knows how to take a photo. We are surrounded by people with devices that take photos and the sheer amount of taking, sharing and discarding of photos can lead us away from thinking about determined purpose and composition. In this activity the group were asked to take photos for a specific purpose (to visually exemplify a word) and demonstrating this can support making more effective choices. Perhaps taking some images that model what you are looking for and some that do not and sharing this set with the class for them to evaluate and give advice about is a productive way in. Another way in is to share some examples – look for the work of Liz Atkin, Phil Barnett and Jane Hewitt for examples of collecting groups of images in photo collages. Showing the children how to use the viewfinder and zoom in and focus is also useful, as well as how to crop photos after they have been taken, to retain the chosen part of the photo and eliminate the irrelevant.

Evaluating and developing: You will have noticed that threaded through the activity were stopping points where the students were asked to evaluate the set of photos against the purpose of the activity. It is all too easy to take many, many photos and lose sight of the purpose and focus. Building in these evaluative steps is important to allow children to act as artists, selecting and discarding visual material. You can set a rule or convention that only twenty photos can be taken and after that for each extra photo added one must be deleted. This again will build in a sense of discrimination and judgement.

Composition: Having collected the raw material for making (the photos), the way that this material is used allows us to be creative. In the activity students were asked to choose a grid and working within this constriction they were allowed freedom to place the photos. More freedom can be built in by choosing the 'freestyle' option, where photos can be moved around freely. Again, evaluation is important here; trying out different placements until the one that the maker is happy with is essential in the creative process.

Sharing the art: If every child in the class completes an activity like this you will have thirty photo collages to share. These could be added one to each slide in a slide sequence and projected in a carousel of images in the classroom, in assembly or on the school website. They could be put back into PicCollage and made into one large final image, like a digital quilt, and then shared through projection. When making digital art it is important for the creators to see it complete and shared in its digital form, as the quality of the colours and the light is much more evident to the viewer in this form than if it were to be printed out. Seeing your art shared like this is a powerful moment for the artist.

Planning for learning: In the activity above students were asked to focus on a key word chosen at random from the visual elements, but of course there are many focuses that could be chosen, depending on the learning you are planning for. You might take a specific visual element (colour, line, tone, texture, pattern, shape, space, form) and develop words from the one you have chosen in order to explore it more fully. You might choose from natural or manmade environments or seek to explore abstracts by using close-ups, using the magnifier tool or using attachable lenses if you have them. This could be a starter activity to activate observation and understanding before developing it in another direction or it might be a full project in itself.

Organisation and practicalities: You might be fortunate enough to have a mobile device for each pupil, or it might be necessary to work in pairs, either to make a shared product or to work individually by pairing this activity with another one. Sharing devices and tools will often be a feature of working with technology and this can be harnessed as a strength, developing collaboration and giving children access to a larger pool of ideas. Some artists do work in pairs and groups, collaborating to make a shared end product, so this approach should not be seen as a deficit model.

In this example, a commonly used app on a mobile device is used to create a digital artefact that can be shared or used as the basis for further digital or physical making. There are other opportunities to use the software or apps available on devices to create images, both static and moving. Making digital animations on the screen is accessible through most mobile devices and laptops / PCs. When making digital art the artist can make and save many versions of their work, later making choices about what to keep and what to discard. This aspect of making art can be attractive to the child who fears to 'spoil' their work. A change could be positive or negative and if it is unwanted it can be undone or deleted.

Try for yourself

Changing images with apps

In this practical activity you will try out some apps that can be used to change images. The purpose is to get a sense of what is possible in terms of manipulating images to make new art.

You will need:

A tablet or laptop / PC

The apps listed below (all, or some, of these and some that you have used and like)

The pro forma below

What to do:

Choose one image from your camera roll.

Choose five of the apps, either from the list below or some from the list and some of your own.

Use the image that you have chosen and manipulate it in each of your chosen apps to explore the tools available.

Make some notes about what each of your chosen apps can do. Some will have features in common and a few that are distinct to the app.

Activity – Changing images with apps

App or tool (IOS)		Function	Your notes
Be Funky	IOS Google Play Online tool	A free photo manipulation app that applies edits, effects and frames to a photo. Each of these can be changed in intensity using a slider.	
Color Viewfinder	IOS (Colrd online tool)	A free app that takes a photo and analyses the colour then produces a colour palette of the key colours in different formats.	
Cut Paste Photos	IOS Google Play	A free app that allows parts of photos to be cut out, manipulated and effects added, including animated effects.	
Distressed FX	IOS	A free app that applies a very wide range of effects to a photo. Each effect can be changed using sliders to make them lighter / darker or more / less coloured.	
Fragment	IOS Google Play	An app that allows photos to be manipulated in a variety of ways at random or purposefully moving towards abstraction.	
KaleidaCam	IOS Android	A free app that applies various kaleidoscope effects to a photo or what can be seen through the viewfinder. This can be further changed by the user.	

App or tool (IOS)		Function	Your notes
PixelWakker	IOS	A free app that changes a photo into pixels and allows the user to change the size and saturation of the images.	
Rollworld Tiny Planet	IOS Google Play	A free app that allows the photo to be 'rolled up' in a variety of ways. If the photo is a landscape this can create a tiny planet.	
Snapseed	IOS Google Play	A free app that adds a wide range of effects to a photo in combinations and gradations.	
StoryZ	IOS Google Play	A free app that allows the addition of some motion effects to a photo. When carefully planned this can add an element of animation and be useful for GIF making.	

Note: some of these free apps also contain opportunities to have a paid-for component but this is not necessary for most activities.

As a teacher or supporter of learning it is important that you know the possibilities of the tools available in any app, tool or site that you plan for children to use. Planning for them to freely explore to see what they can do and then share what they have found is a good way in. The approach of changing the same image over and over again can be useful here, as can stopping to remember how various effects were created and demonstrating them. This can be captured by the child using screen recording, so perhaps you could challenge them to make a one-minute demo video of their favourite tool and effect. After this free exploration, the user is much more likely to be able to work purposefully to create a piece of art.

Ways forward with using apps like this are for the user to work individually to manipulate their image and save it in a number of incarnations and then present these as a photo collage, showing the variations. Working more collaboratively, students can swap photos using AirDrop and work on each other's images in a 'pass the photo' activity. The images created could be used in further digital making such as backgrounds and projections, or used in combination with the physical making of art.

Reflect and extend

Explore 'Case study 1: swap and share', Heaton and Edwards (2017, pp.120–124) in Caldwell and Cullingford-Agnew's book *Technology for SEND in primary schools*.

This explores a teaching sequence based on the approach outlined above.

How could you adapt it to use in your teaching?

Making interactive digital art

Both mobile devices and laptops / PCs have apps or tools that support making images on the screen. A painting or drawing app or tool can be used to make an image using many choices, as explored earlier in this chapter. A next step can be creating an image that moves through digital animation. This can be saved as an animated GIF and shared in several ways, as well as be taken into augmented reality, as we will see later in this chapter. The chart below outlines two options for learning how to do this using the most commonly available tools.

Device	App or tool	
iPad or MacBook (IOS)	Keynote	It is possible to use the shapes and objects available in Keynote along with your own drawing onscreen to construct and animate digitally. When the digital animation is complete it can be saved as a GIF or a video. Useful starting points for learning to do this are Apple Teacher *Keynote for iPad Starter Guide*, available free from the iBook store. Educator Simon Pile's iBooks *Animating Keynote* and *Doodle-a-Day* are both user-friendly introductions to creating digital animation on the iPad, with many starting points that you can take further.
Laptop (Windows)	Microsoft PowerPoint and www.giphy.com	In PowerPoint there are many shapes and objects that can be found in 'Insert' that can be used along with your own drawings made in 'Draw'. In the 'Animations' menu movement can be added, ordered and timed, resulting in a digital animation that can be saved as a GIF or a video.

Although children pick up how to make and animate images quickly when using an iPad, similar options are available on a laptop / PC and ultimately the finished outcome can be the same: an animated GIF that can be shared onscreen, inserted into a slide sequence, added to the school website and shared on social media, or a short video that can be used in a similar way. In addition, it can be triggered in augmented reality by a marker or QR code, appearing as if in our own environment, like the Google AR animals explored in chapter 4. As when making a painting or drawing, choices about colour, shape, line, tone and pattern will play a part in the creation, with the addition of how part of the image can appear and disappear at different times and move into and out of place. When working with a class, if each child makes a small animation around a theme and they are combined together in sequences and groups this can produce an impressive result that includes both individual elements and shared outcome. They can be displayed on a padlet, where they will play simultaneously in a grid layout.

Another tool that can be readily used in the classroom to learn about and make art is the green screen. This is an example of technology that seemed light years away from day-to-day use in a primary classroom several years ago, but now provides great opportunities to place ourselves or our creations digitally in a range of real and imagined situations. Works of art can be chosen and interacted with, placing the child in front of them to give a guided tour or enabling them to become part of the scenery – choosing paintings of groups or crowds of people can work well here. The art that pupils make can be placed in a variety of locations, including as backdrops to interaction or new locations, as in the sculpture-based example discussed in chapter 1. When using the green screen, the images or videos that are combined can be photographs and video taken by you or the child or found online or created through using other physical and digital materials. Earlier in this chapter, the idea of using materials readily to hand with the green screen app was referred to. Here are some examples of my green screen collection.

Figure 12.1 A collection of readily available materials to use in green screen work

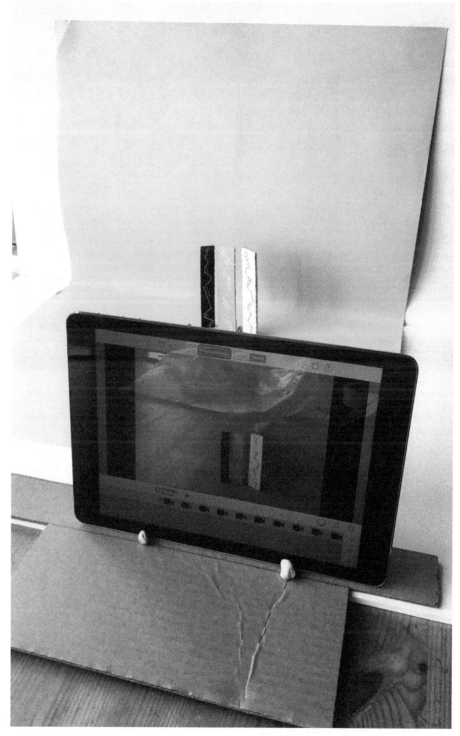

Figure 12.2 Steps in using green screen to make images

Figure 12.2 Continued

Recently, making digital environments using images and emojis found online, in combination with photographs and scenes with live links, has popped up as a tool for teaching. These 'bitmoji classrooms' are constructed in Google Slides or PowerPoint by teachers, to use in remote learning situations. Children can click on items within the larger image to be taken to activities and websites. There is great potential for using this approach to create their own imaginative scenes and environments in the context of art.

Link: https://mypad.northampton.ac.uk/fdlt2012/

Exploring and making augmented reality in art

When working digitally there are also opportunities to use more ambitious approaches. This includes exploring augmented and virtual reality. Over the last few years augmented and virtual reality in game-playing at home, in entertainment and in museums and galleries has developed enormously. Augmented reality can be defined as when we interact with digital objects in the real world using a digital device. Examples of this are the recent Google AR objects that can be viewed with mobile devices; the Merge Cube; the HP Reveal app (formerly Aurasma); the EyeJack app; Pokemon Go!; Google Street View and other Google AR explorers. Virtual reality is a much more immersive experience and includes using a headset and controls to feel as if we are immersed within the digital environment and able to interact to control and create within it. Examples of this are Google VR, Tilt Brush and CoSpaces.

Augmented reality provides new ways for audiences to interact with artworks. For example, the Take Festival in Vienna used AR to bring together fashion and art, as the audience interacted with the physical art using the app Artivive on their mobile phones:

Link: www.youtube.com/watch?v=Mb3OfHnFjqE

In this video a number of artists talk about building interactive environments that take people away from their everyday realities and explore our relationship with physical space by bringing experiences out of the screen through animation and sound:

Link: www.youtube.com/watch?v=F9-PMm6YdUU).

Audiences can use their phones to unlock the physical artwork and interact with its digital layer:

Link: www.youtube.com/watch?v=mdvVDXpZxqo).

Augmented reality experiences are triggered by something in the real world. You have probably used QR codes along with a mobile device. When you hold your phone or tablet over the QR code the QR code reader app causes a website to open or a video to play. You can download a QR code maker to make your own QR codes to attach to whatever material you would like to connect the viewer to. Some AR apps use symbols or images as the trigger for the action in your device. These include HP Reveal and EyeJack. Other ways of triggering AR are through markers or GPS tags. When we are using AR technology in art we need to have a digital product to link to the trigger. This could be a photo or a video of a piece of real or digital art, an animated GIF or a link to any of these online. The connection between the trigger and the digital product – whether it is obvious, through a QR code, or hidden, through the embedding of the trigger into a picture or text – can also be a creative opportunity.

Try for yourself – using augmented reality in art making

In this practical activity you will try out an app that allows you to connect a digital animation to a trigger in the real world – a symbol or a picture on paper for example.

You will need:

A laptop / PC and access to the website EyeJack Creator

Link: http://creator.eyejackapp.com/

An animated GIF (make one using the tools outlined earlier or download one from the internet, taking care to choose one that is available to use freely through commercial commons)

A trigger image: a picture or a symbol either made by you or in a book

A mobile device with the EyeJack app (free) loaded onto it

What to do:

Begin by selecting the artwork that will trigger your animation.

Upload this to the EyeJack Creator desktop app on your computer. The app then takes you through a short series of steps to add either a sequence of PNG images, a GIF, an animation or a film to your trigger image. GIFs and PNG sequences have the advantage that they can have transparent back-grounds. You can then add sound.

When you select 'create', EyeJack Creator generates a QR code for the viewer to scan within the EyeJack app on their phone. Once they have done this, they can hold their phone up to the trigger image on a screen or to the actual artwork on a wall and the animated layer will spring up and play on their device.

The trigger and the animated overlay can be created digitally using apps and tools such as Sketches, Brushes, Keynote, PowerPoint, iMotion, or iMovie.

Here is a tutorial on how to make your own GIFs with transparent backgrounds in Keynote. Link: www.youtube.com/watch?v=diXG192U8G8).

Using augmented reality tools to connect digital art with the real world can be magical for children to see, so the opportunity for them to create the magic is a motivating experience. It can be shared with other children in school and with parents, allowing the children, as the artists, to see how the viewer reacts to their art, another important aspect of being an artist. For more ideas about using this approach in art explore teacher Tricia Fuglestad's blog.

Link: https://drydenart.weebly.com/fugleblog/
book-covers-that-come-to-life-with-ar

To use augmented reality in a slightly different way, the app AR Makr enables a part of the room or a flat surface to become the space in which to create a scene. Images can be made or chosen from a library of images to overlay onto a set of 2D or 3D objects within the real-life setting, adding layers and depth. For this to work, images must have a transparent background. However, the tools within the app can enable this. Scenes can be populated with children's physical drawings or digital drawings created within the app, or images can be imported from the app library or the internet. Once they have been arranged, the images pop up in 3D as the viewer holds their phone over the designated space. The screen record option on an iPad or phone can be used to create a short, narrated video, or an iPad can be set up on a tripod so that the viewer can walk into your scene or so that you have a film of yourself interacting with it.

In addition to the tools and apps mentioned so far, there is a growing number of simple to use AR apps for mobile devices, many of which can stimulate artistic creativity. One of these is Reality Composer. Children can also experiment with 360 stills or video as creative mediums for making their own images and films. We have seen that the ability to paint and sculpt in 360, to collaborate on live paintings and to use augmented reality in combination with art all add new dimensions to digital art.

Reflect and extend

The introductory chapter to Liu *et al.*'s book *Virtual, Augmented and Mixed Realities in Education* (Dede *et al.*, 2017, pp.1–16) provides a useful introduction to some of the definitions, theories and themes that are relevant to the use of AR and VR in education.

Read this with a view to identifying its relevance to your classroom and school and any future plans for developing art making into this area.

Connecting to other types of art

Opportunities to use digital tools as part of the making process when using other media have been explored in previous chapters. When making art that is wholly digital it is possible to connect to each process or technique and explore it in a digital form. This is not to suggest that it should or could replace the physical process but it could further develop the scope and creative opportunities available. Matthews and Seow (2007, p.270) explored the implications of children using digital drawing and painting tools and noted that these tools have inherent features of their own that can support learning about aspects of art such as colour and tone. The chart below outlines some physical / digital art connections to explore when you are deciding where to include a wholly digital outcome in the art curriculum.

	Physical (see earlier chapters)	**Digital**
Drawing	With tools such as pencils and pens on surfaces such as paper and card.	Programming a robot or toy to move the drawing implement. Recording using GPS as the artist walks their drawing onto the virtual world of digital maps. Using a stylus or one's finger on the screen of a device. Drawing with light recorded with a slow shutter app.
Painting	With tools such as paintbrushes on surfaces such as paper.	Using a virtual reality painting tool such as Tilt Brush to paint in space. Painting with UV paint that can only be revealed to the viewer by a black light torch. Using a stylus or one's finger on the screen of a device. Creating an animated GIF or short video.

	Physical (see earlier chapters)	**Digital**
Printmaking	With objects and constructed tiles onto paper.	Creating a digital stamp or sticker to copy and paste.
Collage / textiles	Choosing items to arrange and / or attach to surfaces.	Collecting items by photographing or scanning them and arranging them on the screen. Sewing with conductive thread into fabrics. Adding programmable LED lights to textiles.
3D art sculpture / installation		Using a virtual reality painting tool such as Tilt Brush to paint in three-dimensional space. Creating digital sculptures viewed through EyeJack or HP Reveal. Creating stop motion animations. Creating multisensory environments using a combination of digital tools and approaches.

Often the tools of AR and VR require images, videos and objects to be made in order to be used in the digital environment, which leads to string connections back to art making using physical resources as well as combining a number of digital approaches. It is this mixed approach that can trigger new ideas and creativity, often when collaborating with others to make art. As cybernetics and AI increasingly transform our world, it becomes imperative that artists understand the intersections between technologies and the arts and that digital art becomes embedded in their studies alongside analogue art. Whether an artwork is made with paint or code, it could be argued that the critical thinking that lends it substance and makes it meaningful stays the same regardless of the tool.

Connecting across the curriculum

There is scope to connect making digital art to learning in other curriculum areas, especially when seeking to make meaningful cross-curricular links. It may be that the technology itself provides a connection. An example of this is in geography, where children will be exploring maps and mapping. Looking at the world from above using Google Maps allows children a new view of landscapes and zooming into the world using Google Earth and Street View allows them to explore distant locations. In the recent pandemic, at a time when many were confined to one location, artists used these tools to explore and respond to the environment, making virtual sketches of the places they explored. In the example below GPS is used to create art on the landscape that exists only in the digital world.

LEARNING IN ACTION

A group of teachers from four countries are exploring ideas for using digital technology when working outdoors (Edwards, 2017, p.17). They experiment with using a walking app (MapMyWalk) to record their movements, drawing virtually on the landscape as if they themselves are the drawing instrument. After learning how to use the app by making simple patterns they found that there were some useful teaching tips in terms of stopping and starting recording, planning ahead, getting a sense of scale and collaborating.

Sophisticated examples of this kind of art made by runners and cyclists can be found online. There is a more detailed outline of this example, with supporting resources, on the chapter padlet.

Figure 12.3 Virtual drawing by walking with GPS

The wholly digital nature of the outcome of the artmaking explored above, along with the collaborative nature of it, is made possible because of GPS and mobile devices. It provides another perspective on drawing as well as having potential for connecting to learning in geography as well as art.

As has been explored in chapter 4, there are strong connections to the computing curriculum when coding and designing generative art, as well as when using augmented reality with art. Including art, or more widely, the arts, in the science, technology, engineering and mathematics (STEM) approach, and developing it into STEAM instead, can bring together these areas of the curriculum.

Find out more

Explore the international project Digital Learning Across Boundaries (DLAB) project 'STEM to STEAM'. These materials share ideas and resources based around using the arts and digital technology with STEM subjects in an international collaboration.

Link: http://dlaberasmus.eu/courses/stem-steam-online-course/

Conclusion

In this chapter, some of the newest ways of creating art have been explored. Your opportunities to work in this way yourself and with children will depend on your working context, but most devices commonly used in school can give you access to some of the ideas explored in this chapter, as well as ways in to connecting to the newest area of the curriculum: computing. Starting out by using what is available to you creatively and building on this over time as you seek out resources, ideas and people who can help and inspire you is a good way forward. You might well find that the children you work with have expertise and enthusiasm that you can draw upon when using technologies creatively. Incorporating making art with digital tools alongside the media processes we have always used in schools can enrich what we offer to children and give them the inspiring art curriculum they deserve.

Next steps

Check the creative potential of the devices you own and use. Make sure that you know which apps and tools lend themselves to creative making and have a go at using them with thought to how they could fit into your teaching.

Look out for opportunities to experience and create with augmented and virtual reality.

References

Caldwell, H., Edwards, J. and Grantham, S. (2019) The arts in STEM: STEAM. In: Caldwell, H. and Pope, S. (eds). *STEM in the primary curriculum.* London: Learning Matters. Pp.153–168.

Dede, C., Jacobson, J. and Richards, J. Introduction: virtual, augmented and mixed realities in education. In: Liu, D., Dede, C., Huang, R. and Richards, J. (eds). (2017) Virtual, Augmented, and Mixed Realities in Education. Singapore: Springer.

Edwards, J. (2017) Crossing boundaries through digital learning. *AD.* **Issue 20**. Pp.16–17.

Heaton R. and Edwards, J. (2017) Art. In: Caldwell, H. and Cullingford-Agnew, S. *Technology for SEND in primary schools.* London: Learning Matters.

Matthews, J. and Seow, P. (2007) Electronic Paint: understanding children's representation through their interactions with digital paint. In: Herne, S., Cox, S. and Watts, R. (2009) *Readings in Primary Art Education.* London: Intellect Books. Pp.269–286.

Further resources

Cullen, J. and Evans, S. (2007) The friendship project – digital art meets PSGCE. *START.* No 25. Pp.26–27.

Edwards, J. (2014) Inspired by Digital. *AD the NSEAD magazine.* **Issue 11**, pp.24–25.

Sakr, M., Connelly, V. and Wild, M. (2018) Imitative or Iconoclastic? How Young Children use Ready-Made Images in Digital Art. *International Journal of Art & Design Education.* **Vol 37**, No 1, pp.41–52.

Wang, T.W. (2018) Empowering Art Teaching and Learning With iPads. *Art Education.* **Vol 71**, No 3, pp.51–55.

Chapter Padlet:

https://padlet.com/Jeanne/Chapter12

Going further

There is so much to learn about art and teaching art to children: this book should be seen as a place to start. Throughout this book indications of specific next steps have been made at the end of each chapter. As you complete your training as a teacher, move into teaching and develop your subject knowledge and pedagogical understanding, you will continue to learn in response to your own reflections on your practice and your evaluations of the needs and interests of the children you teach. Below are some suggestions of how you can continue to learn about art and the teaching of art in primary schools.

- Be observant when you are in schools whether as a visitor, on placement or as a member of staff. There is so much to learn from the ideas of other teachers and the learning experiences they plan for their children. Just walking around an unfamiliar school can serve as an injection of new ideas and different ways of approaching learning. Take notes (or photos, with permission) of things that catch your eye.

- Be prepared to learn about unfamiliar art processes and materials and seek help from your colleagues to develop your skills, knowledge and confidence. If you have an interest or skill in an area of art, craft or design share this with your peers, colleagues and children.

- Be prepared to keep up to date with the digital technology available to you and be prepared to find out what else is available. Maintain an attitude of determination to use what you have creatively and effectively and keep alert to what else is coming along.

- Look out for local art exhibitions and art in galleries, museums, parks and historic houses. As well as expanding your own knowledge of art this may lead you to possible visits for the children you teach, useful learning resources and contacts with artists and curators. Some exhibitions also have activities and workshops for adults and / or children to participate in. Pay attention to stories in the media about high profile exhibitions of the work of significant artists.

- If you are concerned about your own ability to draw and teach drawing seek out local classes and online workshops so that you can learn and build your confidence as a teacher.

- Join the National Society for Education in Art and Design. This will help you keep up to date with issues of art education, give you access to interesting teaching ideas and people with expertise and ideas.

- Get your school involved with art and digital technology events in your local area; join in national events as a school; and use social media effectively as a resource. Think about putting on a school exhibition online or in the real world or supporting and encouraging children to participate in local exhibitions.

- Make connections with people involved in art in the local area – artists, craftspeople and designers; curators and gallery staff; and art students at college and university.

Above all, enjoy teaching art and creating with technology and make sure that the children you work with enjoy and learn in art lessons.

A1

Vocabulary to use when discussing visual elements

Colour:

Names of colours (both identifying and descriptive)

Technical vocabulary – primary, secondary, complementary, hue, tint, shade

Words to describe the quality of the colour – bright, vibrant, intense, dull, pale, pastel, neutral

Comparative vocabulary to describe and compare the tone of the colour – light, lighter, lightest, dark, darker, darkest

Words to describe how colours affect each other – matching, clashing, contrasting

Words to describe the 'feel' created by colour – hot, warm, cool, cold

Tone:

Tone, tonal, contrast, light source, shade, shadow, gradual, distinct, reflection

Black, grey, white

Words to compare tones – light, lighter, lighter than, lightest, dark, darker, darker than, darkest (these can be attached to colour words)

Line:

Line, linear, outline

Words to describe continuous lines – straight, curved, flowing, zig-zag, wiggly, smooth, spiral, sweeping, looping, continuous, angular, rhythmic, boundary, corner, turn, joined, overlapping

Words to describe the quality of line – thick, wide, broad, narrow, thin, light, dark, soft, hard

Words to describe marks and broken lines – dot, dash, point, spot, broken, short

Words to describe the position / relationship of lines – diagonal, horizontal, vertical, parallel

Words to name and describe shapes when outlines are made with lines (see below)

Pattern:

Words to describe pattern – random, regular, irregular, decorative, rotation, transformation, translation, tessellation, linear, spiral, repeating, symmetrical, line symmetry, reflective symmetry, line of symmetry, axis of symmetry, geometric, natural, manmade, simple, complex, interlocking, overlapping

Words to identify parts of a pattern – border, motif, grid, surface

Words to describe the design of specific patterns – plaid, polka dot, stripes, gingham, basket weave, etc.

Words used to describe specific patterns from different times and cultures – Rangoli, Celtic, Greek

Words to identify two-dimensional shapes used to make patterns (see below)

Texture:

Feel, touch, surface quality, tactile

Words to describe textures – coarse, rough, bumpy, scratchy, smooth, silky, slimy, squashy, hairy, furry, feathery, wet, dry, soft, hard, cold, cool, warm, hot

Shape:

Words to name two-dimensional geometric shapes – circle, circular, semi-circle, triangle, square, rhombus, rectangle, pentagon, hexagon, heptagon, octagon, polygon, quadrilateral, kite, parallelogram, trapezium

Words to describe types of shape – geometrical, symmetrical, asymmetrical, simple, complex, regular, irregular, flat, negative

Words to describe qualities of shapes – edge, side, corner, outline, filled, surface

Words to describe relationships between shapes – tessellating, overlapping, intersecting, touching, background

Form:

Words to describe three-dimensional geometrical shapes – cube, cuboid, pyramid, sphere, hemisphere, spherical, cone, cylinder, prism, tetrahedron, polyhedron, octahedron, dodecahedron

Words to describe viewpoints of forms – inside, outside, through, next to, beyond, beside, behind, in front, above, below

Words to describe how forms are made – join, stick, twist, tie, squash, bend, fix, fasten, arrange

Words to talk about form – solid, hollow, surface, viewpoint, scale, volume, weight, mass, rigid, framework

Space:

Words to describe viewpoints, positions and relationships in space – near, far, next to, beside, under, below, above, inside, outside

Words to describe the quality of space – enclosed, airy, claustrophobic, high, low, open, large, small, narrow, wide, dark, light, busy, full, empty, crowded, quiet, noisy, peaceful, still

Words to describe space in a flat composition – background, foreground, perspective, distance, depth, middle

A2

Appendix Two

Tools and materials

There are a range of tools, resources and materials that are necessary for teaching the art curriculum effectively. It is important that you know what these are and how they can be used to support learning.

Try for yourself – exploring the resources and materials at your school

Finding out more about the tools and resources available for use in school

You will need:

The pro forma below to annotate onto. This could be a paper copy, photocopied from this book or downloaded and printed out from the website or it could be completed electronically.

What to do:

Use this checklist to look around the classroom and any central storage area for art resources in the school. If possible, talk with a class teacher or the school's art coordinator about the available resources.

Chapter 7 – Resources used in drawing

Look for	Location	Notes / questions to follow up
Graded drawing pencils 4H 2H H HB B 2B 4B 6B		
Charcoal and white chalk		
Coloured chalks		
Fine line black pens		
Pens of a range of thicknesses, e.g. fine / broad / brush / marker		
Oil pastels		
Soft pastels		
Biros / ballpoint pens		
Wax crayons		
Coloured pencils		
Watercolour pencils		
Charcoal / pastel pencils		
Sticks / stones		

Look for	Location	Notes / questions to follow up
Cartridge paper		
Sugar paper		
Newsprint		
Tissue / tracing paper		
Sand		
Clay / play dough / plasticine		
Cornflour		
Plastic / Perspex		
Viewfinders		
Rubbers (soft, putty)		
Fixative (for adult use)		

Points to consider:

Graded drawing pencils

Drawing pencils are graded with numbers and letters. H pencils are harder and make a lighter mark, with 9H the hardest. B pencils are softer and make a darker mark, with 9B the softest. HB pencils are in the middle and are commonly used for a range of general classroom purposes. A selection of B pencils should be available for children to use in art lessons – 4B is a good pencil to start with, although you will want older children to experience a greater range including 2B and 6B. They can be bought in boxes of twelve and will last a long time if cared for. These pencils should be stored separately and never mixed up with the pencils used in the class for general work. Children can be taught to identify their art pencils and look after them appropriately.

Black pens (fine, broad, brush, marker), felt pens and biros

Pens make a different sort of mark than pencils and children should have the opportunity to use pens of different qualities and thicknesses to draw with. Classroom felt pens often come in fine and broad as well as brush tip and marker pens tend to be bigger to hold and can have rounded or straight tips: all of these make different marks. The ink from most pens can now be washed off hands and clothes and so even the youngest children can use them. Using a black pen is also useful if you wish to copy, enlarge or reduce children's drawings on a photocopier.

Pastels

There are several different kinds of pastel available. Soft pastels have a chalky quality and can be blended, although the colours are more vibrant than chalks. Oil pastels have an oily feel and again can be blended and have very rich and vivid colours. Pastels tend to come in sets of a range of colours and some can also be bought in skin tones or tones from white through greys to black.

Wax crayons

Most classrooms have wax crayons and these can be used in art, especially for making rubbings and using with Brusho or ink washes to make wax resist. When using wax crayons for rubbing you need thick chunky crayons with the paper wrapper taken off, so they can be held comfortably and rubbed sideways. Wax crayons can be bought in a large range of colours and are relatively cheap.

Coloured pencils

You may have coloured pencils that are used in day-to-day classroom activities. For art you might use these or you might have sets that have a larger range of colours, are softer or have other qualities. Coloured pencils are now available in water soluble, pastel and charcoal form. These types could be considered to support children who are more comfortable with gripping and manipulating pencils than pastels or charcoal. Charcoal in particular can be quite fragile and may break when gripped hard.

Drawing surfaces

It is important to have a range of surfaces available to draw on. Cartridge paper in large sheets that you can cut to the size you want is most useful. Paper in pastel tones such as buff and grey is also useful, as you can use white, a range of tones and black on these. Paper that has been donated to schools is often too shiny and slippery to use with many drawing tools, although it can be a satisfactory surface for drawing on with some types of pens.

Viewfinders

A viewfinder is a piece of card with a hole cut in the middle. The size and shape of the hole depends on what the viewfinder will be used for. Making your own viewfinders fit for the purpose you intend to use them for is often more flexible in terms of size and shape and cheaper than buying a standard product. A viewfinder can be used to help children identify areas to concentrate on before they begin to draw. It can prevent them from becoming overwhelmed about where to start and how much to draw.

Rubbers

Your school may have a policy about the use of rubbers. In art you may discourage the use of rubbers in order to preserve the children's work. If this is your approach you should have some suggestions at the ready for when children feel that they have made a mistake. This will be discussed more fully in Chapter 7, Drawing. Soft putty rubbers can be useful for blending softer drawing materials.

Fixative

If you are using chalk, charcoal and soft pastels with children these can be easily smudged and rubbed. When the work is finished it should be 'fixed' using a spray fixative or hairspray. In terms of health and safety an adult should spray the drawings and this should take place in a well-ventilated area or outside.

Chapter 8 – Resources used in painting

Look for	Location	Notes / questions to follow up
Types of paint		
Powder paint		
Powder paint with other material added to change the texture / consistency		
Ready-mix paint		
Cromar paint / metallic / pearlescent		
Tempera blocks		
Watercolours		
Acrylics		
Brusho (washable)		
Drawing inks (waterproof)		
Tools for painting with		
Paint shapers		
Sponge paddles		
Plastic tools / palette knives		
Bristle brushes (short / long-handled)		
Hair brushes		

Look for	Location	Notes / questions to follow up
Toothbrushes		
Sticks / found and junk items		
Other useful equipment		
Drying rack		
Pegs on a line		
Easels		
Drawing boards		
Pots with lids and stoppers		
Palettes (flat / six dips)		
Spoons		
Pipettes		
Disposable pots / trays, etc.		

Guidance notes

Types of paint

There are many types of paint available to use in the classroom. Schools tend to rely on some for general use and others for special projects. The qualities and properties of these are explored more fully in chapter 8.

Paintbrushes

There are two main types of paintbrushes: those with stiff, coarse bristles and those with softer natural or synthetic hair.

Stiff bristle brushes	**Soft hair brushes**
Made from bristle, hog's hair or synthetic materials	Made from softer hair or synthetic materials
Come in different sizes and round and flat shapes	Come in different sizes
Used for thicker paint, may leave brush strokes	Used for thinner paint, applying washes, can be shaped into a point for finer marks and more detail

Paintbrushes are expensive tools and must be cared for in order to make them last. They should be cleaned after each use and never left to soak or stood with the hairs / bristles facing downwards in a pot. It is important that we teach children to choose and use the right type of paintbrush for the type of paint and the sort of marks required in their art work. It is therefore important that teachers and teaching assistants can choose the appropriate brush for the art they are planning and build in opportunities to investigate the brushes and the effects that can be achieved with them. Paintbrushes can be bought with either short or long handles and some consideration should be given to which will suit the manipulative skills of the children using them.

Other painting tools

There are other tools that can be used for painting. Recently 'colour shapers' or 'paint shapers' have begun to be used in schools. These are short-handled tools with shaped rubber ends that can be used to apply paint and make marks in it. Sponge paddles of varying widths are also available and are useful for applying large areas of colour or washes. Plastic palette knives allow children to experiment with applying thick paint in a different way – strips of very thick card can also be used for this. Found and collected items such as toothbrushes and sticks can add variety to the range of possible marks that children can make.

Drying racks / line and pegs

It is essential to plan ahead to find where finished or incomplete paintings can be left to dry safely. Some schools may have drying racks bought for the purpose. These can be a series of plastic mesh leaves with or without springs. A good habit to get into is to teach children to fill the drying rack from the bottom upwards. Drying racks without springs to keep the leaves up can be made more effective by taking out every other leaf. Drying racks with large gaps in the mesh can be covered with card or paper so that smaller pieces of work do not fall through and stick together. Lines and pegs can be useful if the paint is not thin and prone to running. Alternatively, you may need to use the floor or flat surfaces and be ready to move the paintings as soon as they are dry and can be stacked.

Pots / lids / stoppers / pipettes / spoons

Items to support painting can be bought from catalogues. If children have mixed colours that they want to use again, or if you have diluted ink or Brusho for washes, these can be stored and reused if used in a pot with a lid and a stopper or decanted into a plastic bottle. Similar items can be collected and stored so they are available and the advantage of 'junk' items such as plastic pots and trays is that they can be thrown away after use, which can save time when cleaning up after activities.

Chapter 9 – Resources used for making prints

Look for	Location	Notes / questions to follow up
Flat trays		
Hard rollers (63mm, 101mm, 152mm, 200mm)		
Sponge rollers (various sizes / textures)		
Plastic ink spreaders / spatulas		
Stamps (bought / made)		
Found natural and manmade objects / materials		
Sponge shapes / numbers / letters		
Polystyrene tiles (often called pressprint / polyprint / easyprint)		
Thin card / found surfaces		
Printing ink (tubs / tubes)		
Plastic / Perspex tiles		
Lino cutting tools / lino tiles		
Screen printing equipment		
Marbling ink / pipettes, tray		
Plasticine		
Textured wallpapers		

Guidance notes

Flat trays

It is essential that the surfaces of the trays that you use for rolling out ink are kept flat and smooth. If, for example, glue or paint are allowed to make the surface bumpy this will impede the roller and cause an uneven layer of colour when printing. Always make sure trays are cleaned thoroughly and if possible keep some for printmaking only.

Printing ink

For most types of printmaking it is more successful to use printing ink rather than paint. Printing ink is thicker and stickier and will allow children to produce a clearer print. It can be bought from educational suppliers in tubs or large tubes. It is water soluble and will wash out of clothes. For some types of printmaking such as screen printing specialist ink is required.

Polystyrene tiles and other surfaces

Many primary schools use fine polystyrene tiles bought from educational suppliers or art catalogues. Common commercial names for these are press-print, polyprint and quickprint. Although this material can be expensive it is very versatile and a safe and accessible alternative to lino for primary school children. Thin card and the foil inside cartons can also be used as a printmaking surface.

Found and collected materials

A great variety of found and collected materials can be used in printmaking. These can include natural materials such as leaves, grasses, stems and pressed flowers and manmade items such as pieces of construction kit, wooden bricks, containers and items of packaging. In addition, textured wallpapers that can be obtained from DIY suppliers, fabric with a textured surface and any paper or card with a surface texture can be used in printmaking. You may find it useful to keep a collection of these materials to use.

Bought printmaking items

Educational catalogues and art suppliers now sell a range of items to use in print-making. These include numbers, letters and shapes formed from sponge and pre-made stamps. These can be useful to use with children in exploring, developing and improving processes and techniques, but can impede creativity if they are the only printmaking experience children encounter.

It is also important to bear in mind that the surface children print onto – colour and texture of paper – will contribute to the overall effect of the work. Trying out prints on a variety of papers and other surfaces should be considered when planning.

Chapter 10 – Resources used to make collage, mixed media and textiles

1. Collage		
Look for	**Location**	**Notes / questions to follow up**
Tools		
Scissors (left / right-handed)		
Scissors (with pattern cutting blades)		
Larger, sharper scissors (for adult use)		
Pinking shears (for adult use)		
Craft knives (for later KS2 and adult use)		
Cutting mats / pads of newspaper to cut on		
Paper trimmer (for later KS2 and adult use)		
Glue spreaders		
Brushes to apply glue with		
Sticking / attaching		
PVA glue		
Wallpaper paste		
Glue sticks		
Double-sided sticky tape		
Blu-Tack		
SprayMount (for adult use)		
Laminator (for adult use)		
Materials		
Papers of different types		
Card of different types		
Magazines and catalogues		
Thread, string, wool		
Natural materials		
Pasta, rice, seeds		

1. Collage		
Look for	**Location**	**Notes / questions to follow up**
Recycled / collected materials		
Papers created by children for use in collage – printed, marbled, etc.		
Surfaces to glue onto – papers, cards, plastics, wood, etc.		
Buttons, sequins		
Labels / packets / wrapping		
Photos / text		

Guidance notes

Cutting tools

Most primary classrooms are equipped with appropriate scissors for cutting paper for both right- and left-handed children. A set of scissors that have blades designed to cut in various patterns add to the range of edges children can easily make – again these will generally only cut paper. It may be necessary for adults to cut some materials for children so it will be useful for you to have good quality adult scissors available. In later Key Stage 2 children may use craft knives in DT and art and if so these and cutting mats can be used in both subjects. If not, or with younger children, an adult may use the craft knife where necessary. The paper trimmer is also a tool that adults will use in preparation, but in some schools children in later Key Stage 2 might be taught to use it. The use of these sharper tools should follow school health and safety policies. It should also be noted that when working with paper, tearing can create unexpected edges that could be more interesting than cut edges.

Sticking and attaching

Typically, PVA (white glue) will be available for all sorts of sticking in the primary classroom. When using PVA in art it has several qualities that can add to the outcome – PVA can be used as it comes out of the tub or diluted with water to make it easier to paint onto or over surfaces. When it dries it will be both clear and shiny and this can add to the finish of the collage, both in terms of sealing small items into the surface and enhancing the overall appearance. Children often have access to glue sticks for the routine sticking of paper and these may also be useful when making paper collages. Being able to put down and lift up and replace is a useful quality of this type of glue. SprayMount can also be useful for this, but should be applied to surfaces in a ventilated area by an adult. Wallpaper paste

can be useful for some sorts of sticking, especially when covering large surfaces with paper or creating three-dimensional surfaces through papier-mâché.
Double-sided sticky tape can also be used effectively to place onto, especially
when the materials to be stuck on are unlikely to stay in the arrangement chosen
– string, for example. Glue spreaders can be used to apply glue to smaller surfaces and where control is needed. Brushes of different sizes can also be used,
perhaps to apply glue to large surfaces. Care must be taken to wash brushes
thoroughly after they have been used to apply glue, or some brushes should be
reserved for gluing only. As with cutting tools, health and safety policies should
be followed when using glues in school.

Materials to use

There are so many materials that can be used to make collage that compiling an
exhaustive list is almost impossible. One of the advantages of making collage is
the opportunity for using materials that are readily accessible in school or in the
local environment. Children and their families can be involved in collecting the
items and materials to be used. Many areas have access to scrap stores –
organisations that collect unwanted materials of all kinds that can be used by
playgroups, nurseries and schools. Usually, an annual subscription and then a
fee for each visit is required to use the facility. Your nearest scrap store can be
found with some research online. One of the challenges for this aspect of collage
is storage – primary schools will vary in how this is approached and it is important
to find out what is readily available and what you must plan in advance to collect
for your unit of work: perhaps as early as the previous term or half term.

2. Making fabrics and textiles		
Look for	**Location**	**Notes / questions to follow up**
Materials to use:		
Wools		
Threads		
Strings		
Tools to use:		
Knitting needles		
Crochet hooks		
Frameworks / cards / looms to use for weaving		
Needles / bodkins (variety of)		

Guidance notes

Wool, threads, string

When planning to weave, knit or crochet your choice of thread will be guided by what is available, what can be found or collected and the teaching and learning experience itself. Investigating what is available through joining a local scrap store and appealing to parents and the local community can be a good idea, supplemented by buying some more special materials where required. Look out for interesting textures and colours as well as a variety of thicknesses and thread made from both manmade and natural materials. Think also about found and recycled materials that can be used as thread such as ribbon, raffia, strips of plastic, etc.

Tools – knitting needles / crochet hooks

If teaching children to knit it is advisable to start them off with thick (4mm) short plastic needles, as these are easier to manipulate.

Tools – needles / bodkins

Starting with flexible plastic needles with a large hole to thread through, or plastic bodkins, can be supportive when children begin to sew. Alternatively, a piece of thick card with thread anchored to it and wrapped around can be useful to weave or thread in and out with.

Tools – weaving cards / frameworks / looms

Weaving can be structured by making or buying these. Making your own or helping children to make their own frameworks on which to weave can allow for more choice and flexibility of size and shape.

2. Surface decoration		
Look for	**Location**	**Notes / questions to follow up**
Dyes (cold water)		
Fabric paint		
Fabric crayons / pens		
Fabrics of various types and qualities		
Binca, plastic canvas		
Threads / wools / strings		

2. Surface decoration		
Look for	**Location**	**Notes / questions to follow up**
Decorative items to add – sequins, beads, buttons, feathers, etc.		
Tools		
Needles (different types)		
Scissors		
Embroidery hoops		

Guidance notes

Dyes

Fabric can be dyed using Brusho and other cold water dyes.

Fabric crayons / pens / paint

Materials familiar from drawing and painting on paper can be bought as versions that can be used on fabric. Fabric medium can be used with paints to allow them to be used on fabric more easily. Some of these can be fixed by ironing.

Textiles and fabrics

A variety of these can be decorated and changed: the choices you make will be guided by the technique or process that you are teaching. Plain, light-coloured cotton is perhaps easiest to draw, paint and print onto, whereas cloth with a more open weave or holes in it can be useful for sewing, especially with younger children. Collecting and using a very wide range of fabrics and textiles, taking in consideration not only colour and pattern but texture, allows children to explore and use the sensory as well as visual qualities in their making.

Tools – needles

Starting with flexible plastic needles with a large hole through to thread can be supportive when children begin to join fabrics and sew materials together. Later, using sharper, metal needles will be essential. Identifying the appropriate type of needle for the manipulative skills of the children is important.

Tools – scissors

Fabric can be very difficult to cut, especially with the scissors children use. It may be more practical for children to mark out lines and shapes and allow an adult to cut with sharper scissors.

Tools – embroidery hoops

When stitching with older children, using embroidery hoops to keep the fabric stretched can be helpful.

In addition to these tools and materials, specific techniques such as batik, felt-making and screen printing might form part of this aspect of art. It is likely that the tools and materials to use in these activities would be kept together in sets for use in specific projects. Learning about any of these so that you can use them in teaching would be a next step and would enhance your subject knowledge.

Chapter 11 – Resources used to make art in three dimensions

Look for	Location	Notes / questions to follow up
Materials that can be manipulated and moulded		
Clay (natural)		
Air drying clay (manmade)		
Plasticine		
Salt dough (home-made)		
Fimo		
Play dough (bought or home-made)		
Sand (damp / wet)		
Materials that can be poured and used with moulds or casts		
Plaster of Paris		
Papier-mâché		
Linear materials		
Wire		
String, thread		
Withies		
Art straws / plastic straws		

Look for	Location	Notes / questions to follow up
Sticks, twigs		
Pipe cleaners		
Sheet materials		
Boxes, cards, papers of different types including newspaper, tissue paper, cartridge paper, sugar paper, magazines, etc.		
Paper lamination		
Plastic – bags, sheets, corrugated plastic, packaging		
Modroc / plaster bandage		
Tools and equipment for:		
Cutting: scissors, craft knives, paper cutters, wire cutters (for use by older children and adults)		
Shaping: clay tools – wooden or wire, wooden roller and guides, items to press into a malleable surface, items to mould onto, garlic press		
Joining: tape, staples, glue, string and thread		

Guidance notes

Malleable materials that can be manipulated and moulded

There are a number of materials that can be squashed and shaped by hand or by using tools to make sculpture, ranging from home-made (salt dough and various recipes for play dough) to bought (clay, fimo). Many of these could be used and reused, as well as made into a finished outcome. Clay (a natural material that needs to be fired in a kiln) is different to air drying clay in that the latter has different tactile qualities. The latter is fibrous and does not require firing: to make this material hard separate 'hardeners' must be bought and applied.

Materials that can be poured and used with moulds or casts

Materials that can be pressed onto an existing mould (dish, plate, balloon, etc.) to hold their shape whilst under construction can be useful when making a shape that would be hard to create from nothing. Some malleable materials can also be used with casts.

Linear materials

Some materials are linear in nature: some come in manageable lengths when bought or collected and others require cutting to different lengths for using to make art work. Some of these can be shaped and will keep their shape, such as wire, and others, such as withies, need to be held in place by tying or using tape.

Sheet materials

Flat, sheet materials can be draped and wrapped to transform objects or frameworks into three-dimensional sculptures. Modroc can be used when wet to wrap and cover frameworks or objects and will set so that the new form created can then be added to and decorated.

Tools and equipment for cutting, shaping and joining materials

These will vary depending on which materials are being cut, shaped or joined. As with all other aspects of art, having the appropriate tools and equipment available is important and will vary according to the age of the children and the particular unit of work.

Chapter 12 – Resources used to make digital art

1. Hardware		
Look for	**Location**	**Notes / questions to follow up**
Computers (PCs, laptops)		
Tablets (iPads, other)		
Mobile devices (phones)		
Cameras (standard / panoramic / 360)		
Stands / tripods		
Robots and programmable toys		
Stylus / pen to use with screens		
Lightbox		
Visualiser		
Digital microscope		
Photocopier / scanner / printer		
Projector / mobile projector		
VR headsets and supporting kit		

1. Hardware		
Look for	**Location**	**Notes / questions to follow up**
Sound recording equipment		
Drones		

2. Apps, tools and sites		
Look for	**Location**	**Notes / questions to follow up**
Photo editing and manipulation		
Video editing		
Art making apps and tools (open)		
Art making apps and tools (closed – one purpose)		
Green screen app		
Stop motion apps		
Digital animation apps and tools (Keynote / PowerPoint)		
AR and VR apps and tools		
Sounds apps and tools		
Coding apps and tools		

Guidance notes

Hardware

There will be a range of devices available for general use that will also have potential for use in the art curriculum. Make sure that you are aware of what is available to you for day-to-day use and what is perhaps more specialist and needs to be booked or collected. Some of these devices might be nominally part of other curriculum areas such as science or computing.

Apps, tools and sites

The challenges for using apps and tools are that there are so many available and there can be practical challenges in terms of having them added to devices. It can be more productive in the long term to consider some key functions (listed above) and choose apps, tools and sites that allow you work in these ways, rather than collect many that each only work in one way.

Index

Lightning Source UK Ltd.
Milton Keynes UK
UKHW050010190722
406047UK00001B/1